T0298285

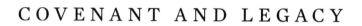

COVENANT AND LEGACY

COVENANT AND LEGACY

The Story of

THE AVI CHAI FOUNDATION

1984–2019

Volume Two

TONY PROSCIO

WICKED SON

2023

A WICKED SON BOOK
An Imprint of Post Hill Press
ISBN: 978-1-63758-873-4

Covenant and Legacy:
The Story of the Avi Chai Foundation, 1984–2019
© 2023 by Tony Proscio
All Rights Reserved

Cover and interior design by Richard Ljoenes Design LLC
Photograph in volume two by Alen MacWeeney
All other photographs/portraits courtesy of the Avi Chai Foundation

Post Hill Press
New York • Nashville
posthillpress.com

Published in the United States of America
10 9 8 7 6 5 4 3 2 1

CONTENTS

THE YEARS OF PLENTY, 1999–2008

THE FORMER SOVIET UNION

A Time of Awakening

Jewish life in the vast former Soviet empire—an expanse of 20 million square kilometers in which all ethnic and religious identity had been forcibly suppressed for close to seventy years—was much less developed in the early twenty-first century than in North America or Israel. Far fewer organizations and institutions were available to satisfy the desire of Jewish families to rediscover and explore their heritage and to provide their children with a Jewish education. Those organizations that did exist to help them—including the international outreach organization Chabad and the Israeli government's educational program Lishkat Hakesher—were stretched to their limits to meet even a portion of the demand.

In 2002, in his inaugural presentation to the AVI CHAI board about the prospects for a program in the former Soviet Union (FSU), David Rozenson started with the massive challenge of trying to carve out a manageable set of issues and places on which to focus. Summarizing recommendations he had formulated with program officer Miriam Warshaviak and consultant Marvin Schick, he began by zeroing in on four cities with sizable Jewish populations: Moscow and St. Petersburg in Russia and Kiev and Dnipropetrovsk in Ukraine. He then laid out an expansive menu of nine possible areas of activity. But most of those clustered into just three general fields: Jewish day schools, university programs, and informal education for youth and adults.

In the first category were initiatives that, in broad strokes, mirrored the North American "mosaic"—training and mentoring for teachers and principals, new curricula for Jewish subjects, marketing assistance, and better school facilities—plus a few elements unique to the region's needs and opportunities—salary subsidies for teachers, transportation, improvements in the general academic program. Rozenson's suggestions for university campuses and informal education likewise included many elements that echoed AVI CHAI programs in North America and in Israel, such as Hillel programs at universities, overnight camps, Shabbatonim, activities in Jewish community centers, and public programs featuring Jewish culture and tradition. But the unique social and economic landscape meant that all these lines of work would have to take on a distinctively Russian and Ukrainian character and, in most cases, would need the help of partner organizations that were already experienced and knowledgeable. AVI CHAI would not be able, as it had often done elsewhere, to design whole new programs on its own or to go it alone in search of unexplored philanthropic terrain.

Its most eligible partners included Chabad, whose Or Avner program had become Russia's largest and most influential force in Jewish day schooling. Or Avner's network comprised forty-two schools with more than 5,000 students. Rozenson and his colleagues were encouraged by the program's big-tent approach to serving Jewish students and families, including those who are only marginally observant or not observant at all. It also provided a relatively high quality of Jewish instruction, compared with the norm elsewhere. Meanwhile, Lishkat Hakesher was providing both curricular materials and Israeli teachers in a large number of Jewish schools, offering four hours of Hebrew language and two to three hours of Jewish history and tradition per week, along with in-service training and mentoring for local teachers. These two organizations represented a strong foundation on which AVI CHAI could help build an expanded education program, with improved curricula, more support for teachers, and new or expanded facilities.

In many cases, individual schools would themselves prove to be valuable partners for the foundation, given that some of them had struggled against long odds (and within strict government limits on school activities that might be deemed religious) to provide a rich Jewish education. Several seemed keen to go further, improve teaching and extracurricular activities, and enroll more Jewish students, lacking only the resources to fill out their aspirations.

At the university level, among Jewish studies scholars, the umbrella organization Sefer, housed in Russia's prestigious Academy of Sciences, was eager for recognition and support to help it reinforce the place of Jewish disciplines on college campuses. In the informal realm, several prominent organizations sponsored camping programs, including the Jewish Agency for Israel, the Joint Distribution Committee, Chabad, Yeshiva University, and the Orthodox Union, among others—all of which would benefit from enriched Jewish content and trained personnel. Other informal education programs were more local or independently sponsored, although, as with camping, several offered opportunities for enriched Jewish content and expanded reach.

Encouraged by the focus and ambition of Rozenson's report, the board started by setting aside nearly half a million dollars to make Jewish schools more competitive. The money would mainly be used for various means to improve general studies, in the hope of attracting more and better students to those that had room for them. Rozenson, Warshaviak, and Schick had identified nineteen schools that met a standard of "religious purposefulness"—another concept borrowed from the North America program—sufficient to ensure that students who were drawn to the enriched general program would also get a high-quality, well-rounded Jewish education. Another million dollars was set aside for Jewish after-school and extracurricular activities in these same schools, including Jewish study programs, Shabbatonim, and bar/bat mitzvah preparation.

At the same time, the board authorized Rozenson and company to begin exploring other areas of work, including new or improved Jewish studies curricula, teacher training, and the creation of "model schools"— academically superior Jewish schools that could compete with the most elite state schools for Jewish students. In 2005, again borrowing from AVI CHAI's earlier work in North America, the foundation brought the Hebrew language curriculum NETA to four Russian high schools, guided by a Russian-speaking emissary from NETA's North American program. The program expanded to more than a dozen schools the following year, with teacher training seminars in the summer and an opportunity for the best teachers to take NETA's Master Teacher's course in Boston.

The foundation's first grant in the FSU to reach beyond day schools was a 2003 award to Sefer, aimed at building a strong interdisciplinary cadre of advanced scholars with Jewish expertise. The post-Soviet field of academic Jewish studies and research was at that point barely a dozen years old in Russia and Ukraine, and, as Rozenson pointed out, "its growth has been hindered by the lack of scholars capable of teaching at the university level, insufficient educational materials, and the absence of an institutional mechanism that enabled the growing number of people interested in the field to meet and share their knowledge and ideas." These appeared to be gaps that AVI CHAI could help Sefer fill.

Sefer was already coordinating a mentoring network for academics and providing lecturers to various universities throughout the FSU. Its annual Interdisciplinary Conference on Judaica drew some 500 people in 2003. With the new grant, AVI CHAI was about to dedicate significant additional resources for expanding these activities, alongside the financial and in-kind support already coming from the Joint Distribution

Committee and the Jewish Agency. The foundation would also add money for training and mentoring programs for young scholars to help populate the field and raise its profile among the recognized disciplines of Russian and Ukrainian universities. Beyond that, the board authorized further research into ways of directly expanding Jewish studies courses at universities in Moscow, St. Petersburg, and Kiev.

With three initiatives for formal Jewish education underway—two in day schools, one at universities—the FSU team was now ready to turn its attention to informal education, first with camping, then with literature.

"Probably the best mode of informal education in the FSU is summer camping," Rozenson, Warshaviak, and Schick reported in their initial survey of the post-Soviet Jewish landscape. "Practically all of the Jewish schools in the FSU operate independent camps, which typically serve as powerful recruitment tools for the schools. Most of the school educators with whom we met spoke of the tremendous impact the camp experience has on the Jewish identity and commitment of the campers. Additionally, summer camps are sponsored by almost every Jewish organization."[1] Not only was the number of Jewish camps large enough to form the basis of a significant program for AVI CHAI, but interest among their leaders and counselors in creating meaningful Jewish experiences was unmistakable. The informal experiences they offered were not especially deep, to be sure, nor were their staffs well trained in how to create effective Jewish programs. But for families looking to understand their roots, the intimate setting of a summer camp (some others also ran during the winter break) could provide a warm, nurturing environment for learning and practicing Judaism more intently. And that is a service the camp operators seemed eager to offer and perhaps, with help, to improve.

Rozenson and Warshaviak spent most of the summer of 2002 visiting camps and talking to directors and counselors, testing whether a

foundation initiative would be welcome and likely to make a real difference. What they found was a large, energetic community operating on
meager resources. Just the three largest sponsors—the Joint Distribution
Committee, Chabad, and the Jewish Agency—accounted for 128 camps
serving 28,000 people a year, many of whom were encountering Judaism
for the first time during their one- or two-week stay. Nonetheless, the
meagerness of the resources was obvious everywhere. "The camps were
financially unable to accommodate additional campers," Rozenson and
Warshaviak reported, "the physical conditions were, at times, poor, and
the educational programming was often not well designed." They continued their explorations the following summer, this time accompanied
by trustee Avital Darmon, who spent weeks in the FSU visiting and
researching grantmaking opportunities for the foundation.

The AVI CHAI team concluded that the camps presented a prime
target, not only because many of their managers seemed to share the foundation's vision for enriched Jewish education, but also because the campers represented a population acutely in need of the kinds of programs
the foundation could fund. Rozenson and his colleagues concluded that
"50 to 60 percent of campers at most of the camps . . . have minimal
connection with Jewish life outside of the camp experience." And yet the
camps' educational programming and staff training were plainly in-
adequate to make a major difference in participants' understanding of
Judaism.

Unfortunately, the needs and gaps varied widely across the field, as
did the types of programs run by the different sponsoring organizations.
Some camps were for families, some only for children; some were primarily for recreation, others were built around planned activities and
learning opportunities. No single, wholesale initiative—say, a counselors
academy or a building-loan program or a grant for equipment or learning
materials—would solve all or even a large percentage of the problems.
Even camps run by the same organization had markedly different budgets, program offerings, levels of staffing, and needs. Consequently,

whatever improvements AVI CHAI chose to fund would have to leave plenty of room for variations between and within the sponsoring organizations.

To find a solution that would be both substantive enough to satisfy the foundation trustees and flexible enough to meet the assorted needs of the different camps and their sponsors, Rozenson and Warshaviak spent months deliberating with FSU representatives of the Joint Distribution Committee, the Jewish Agency, and Or Avner, Chabad's education affiliate. Each of those organizations then submitted proposed packages of educational programming and curricula, staff training, camp libraries, Shabbatonim, improved facilities, and, in the JDC's case, the creation of a website to establish communication channels and shared resource libraries to link all the camps in its network. The various improvements would be piloted in roughly twenty camps in total, and evaluations would track all the proposed improvements to determine which ones should be replicated more broadly. [2] The board allocated more than $1 million for the three proposals and awaited the evaluators' findings.

The first year's experience turned out to be bumpy but promising. Staff training wasn't always sufficient or well absorbed, some camp personnel were more effective than others in implementing new programs and procedures, and some managers showed less than enthusiastic commitment to the goals. Finding local, Russian-speaking counselors with enough Jewish knowledge to lead effective programs was also a challenge (although one that had been clear from the outset), so foreign personnel had to be recruited, despite limited fluency in Russian. Yet in spite of all that, the response of campers was overwhelmingly favorable, and the demand for further improvements was widespread. All three initiatives proceeded to a second round, and evaluators found varying levels of progress on both the scope and quality of the new Judaic programming. Annual rounds of grant renewals followed for several years, though some of the pilot projects failed to jell sufficiently well to justify an expansion.

By far, the most successful initial effort was that of Or Avner, which

demonstrated particular zeal for creating top-quality programs. It returned to AVI CHAI in 2005 with a proposal that put less emphasis on expanding the pilot (just two camps were added) and more on getting the
model right—preparing staff and counselors more effectively, recruiting
and training more native Russian speakers as counselors, polishing the
educational enhancements, and integrating the various components into
a more coherent whole. It added follow-up programs for counselors and
campers, held throughout the year, to extend their Jewish experience
beyond the two weeks of camp. Or Avner also added new workshops for
camp counselors on how to run engaging programs, and instituted a
four-day team-building period before the opening of camp, in which
counselors planned and organized their activities for the coming session.

Rozenson particularly admired Or Avner's project for training local
young people as counselors, equipping them with both Jewish knowledge and pedagogic techniques, which he described as "revolutionary"
in the Russian camping world. Like all the other camping initiatives, Or
Avner continued to struggle with many operational complications, like
the need to involve counselors more fully in the development of programs, adapt programs to specific local conditions and needs, and ease
the burden on the sponsoring agencies as they struggled to manage such
a major change process in so many places. But Or Avner's plans for dealing with each of these challenges were deliberate and well managed, with
measurable improvements year by year. The program expanded further
in 2007 and '08, with still more enrichment to the counselor-training
component. It was by then preparing more than 200 young people a year
to work in Jewish camps and to lead other Jewish educational programs
and holiday celebrations during the year.

In 2006, another major sponsor of Jewish camps in the FSU joined
the roster of grantees, this time with an exclusive focus on training camp
personnel. Because the shortage of local, skilled counselors was among
the chief constraints on the foundation's push for Judaic learning at
camps, AVI CHAI allocated $100,000 to create a series of monthly four-

day educational training seminars for 160 counselors in Moscow, Siberia, Ukraine, and Belarus. The grantee was Netzer Olami, the youth movement of the World Union for Progressive Judaism. Its program, conducted on Shabbat and over long weekends, aimed at strengthening Jewish identity; deepening knowledge of Jewish history, tradition, literature, and Hebrew; and encouraging traditional observance. The program was an almost instant success, and the foundation renewed and slightly increased its annual support steadily over the next few years.

The greatest difficulty for AVI CHAI in assembling a camping program in the FSU— a problem that was never solved—was that the field was essentially Balkanized among the different sponsoring organizations, with their particular missions, personalities, and styles of operation. Each of them had interests and priorities that, while they rarely conflicted with AVI CHAI's outright, were not always a perfect match either. Although the field of camping in North America is likewise fractious and competitive, the foundation had a formidable ally there—the Foundation for Jewish Camp. It had proven to be a crucial mediating force for AVI CHAI in its relations with a wide variety of sponsors and managers. In the former Soviet Union, by contrast, the tiny AVI CHAI staff had to negotiate with each sponsoring organization separately, often in fine detail, over protracted periods, and had to monitor progress across an enormous landscape. That often turned out to be prohibitively difficult. However, at least in the cases of Or Avner and Netzer Olami, where agreement on goals was the closest, the result of AVI CHAI's support was overwhelmingly positive: an assortment of widespread and lasting changes to the way camps contribute to Jewish life in the FSU, with resulting benefits for many thousands of young people and their families.

––––––

In a 2018 conversation about AVI CHAI's work in the FSU, Rozenson mentioned one of the first aspects of everyday Russian life that had struck him, upon his arrival there, as remarkable: Books were everywhere.

From classic Russian literature to contemporary writing, both fiction and nonfiction, he said, "Books are a big part of the culture, especially in the big cities like Moscow and St. Petersburg. Everybody reads. And especially before the internet and social networks and Facebook really took hold, people took reading very seriously. You don't tend to meet kids who haven't read the classics, or at least been exposed to them in school." Although much Jewish writing had been suppressed in Soviet times, the few Jewish writers who were tolerated, such as Sholem Aleichem, were widely circulated. After the fall of the Soviet empire, popular appetite for newly available titles soared. So it seemed to Rozenson that some kind of program to promote Jewish writing would suit both public demand and AVI CHAI's particular strengths and mission.

Mem Bernstein thought so, too. Under another of the charities endowed by her husband's estate, she and Arthur Fried had launched an American program called Nextbook, which held literary programs around the country, published new work, supported Jewish collections in public libraries, and curated a sophisticated literary website, all focused on promoting the best Jewish writers and texts. AVI CHAI had meanwhile sponsored publishing projects of its own, including Avigdor Shinan's book projects in Israel, with considerable success. Although Mem and her colleagues on the board still knew relatively little about the post-Soviet market, Rozenson's observations about the importance of books in Russian culture persuaded her that literature could become a fertile part of AVI CHAI's FSU program.

After visiting Nextbook and other U.S. literary outlets, and concluding that they would not quite fit the Russian and Ukrainian context, Rozenson decided to start with what he considered a relatively sure route into the Jewish literary market there: children's books. Families wanted their children reading from an early age, he observed, and Jewish families still had few opportunities to introduce their children to Jewish authors and subjects.

"While it is universally true," he wrote to the board in late 2003, "that books serve as a child's gateway to understanding the history, culture, and society of the world in which they live, this is especially the case in Russia, a country that prides itself on its fluency with text. This appreciation of literacy is heightened within Jewish circles, which makes it all the more surprising, as well as disconcerting, that virtually no children's books on Jewish themes are currently available in Russian. A small number of books have been translated into Russian from Hebrew and English, but most are poor translations and adaptations largely ignored by the Jewish market." This in turn, he wrote, "prevents the functioning of a powerful educational mechanism of informal Jewish study for a large number of children and their families."[3]

The idea was an instant hit with the board, which set aside $300,000 to get started. Besides the creation and publication of the books themselves, the grant also supported some marketing and overhead costs. Rozenson, convinced that no FSU program should be solely a creature of AVI CHAI, made it a point to find other donors willing to contribute as well. The initial project would roll out five series of titles over two years, with colorful illustrations, on subjects related to Israel and to Jewish history and tradition. Original works would be divided between those focused on younger (age 7–9) and older (10–13) children. A separate series would provide high-quality translations of twentieth-century writing from the original Hebrew, Yiddish, or English.

A few months later, the focus broadened to books for adults, with a grant to develop a Jewish Book Festival as part of Moscow's International Book Fair, beginning in autumn 2004. The remarkable success of that event, which surprised even Rozenson, led to a still more adventurous idea: programs in popular intellectual clubs and urban cafés focused on Israeli and Jewish literature and culture.

The popularity of these sophisticated cultural hotspots is a distinctive feature of post-Soviet life in Russia, directly linked to the elevated place of literature in the wider society. Yet, as with children's books, Rozenson pointed out that these literary events hardly ever featured Jewish and

Israeli literature, which remained "practically unknown to even the avid Russian reader."[4] While a few small organizations did sponsor Jewish literary events, these tended to appeal mainly to small, already devoted Jewish audiences. The opportunity to reach a young, well-educated, largely unaffiliated market—people who had not yet had the opportunity to connect their Jewish identity to their literary and cultural enthusiasms— struck Rozenson as a ready opportunity practically begging to be seized.

Beginning in Moscow and later expanding to St. Petersburg, the resulting long-running series of programs came to be known as Eshkol. Led by two prominent members of Russia's young literary community whom Rozenson recruited personally, and with whom he worked side by side, Eshkol had grown by 2008 to encompass a wide variety of cultural venues and audiences, averaging as many as six programs a month drawing a total audience of more than 6,000 a year. Programs included roundtable discussions on Jewish and Israeli literature, literary contests on Jewish themes for young authors, Jewish/Israeli art and photography exhibitions, pre-holiday celebrations, bi-monthly screenings of Israeli films, and later, special programs geared for Jewish children and their families. The appeal to families was so strong that Eshkol's leaders spun off a separate project, called Eshkolit, just for kids and their parents.

Best of all, the audience was a strategic bull's-eye for AVI CHAI. The intellectual clubs and cafés, Rozenson wrote in mid-2008, had proven to be "an ideal setting to reach an audience that rarely participates in any organized Jewish activity."[5] Annual foundation support ran to nearly $400,000 a year, with a trickle of other contributors beginning to be drawn in. An enthusiastic board in 2008 added funding for an accompanying media campaign advertising the programs and promoting the books and authors they featured.

Still, despite their strength and popularity, the impact of the literary events remained geographically limited to Moscow and St. Petersburg. Physical expansion was possible, of course, but it was unlikely to be as cost-effective as the early venture had been. Too few other cities offered the combination of population density (especially Jewish population density) and major intellectual hubs where literary clubs and events could draw big crowds. Fortunately, by the early twenty-first century, geography was quickly becoming a technicality. The internet could now conjure intimate "communities" of enthusiasts out of widely dispersed populations. And AVI CHAI was becoming more at home with online tools for pursuing its mission. It was time for the energies of Eshkol to go virtual.

As Rozenson searched for routes into the Russian internet, he was introduced to Sergei Kuznetsov, a successful author and founder of a digital marketing agency who happened to be a devotee of Eshkol. Kuznetsov was convinced that a Russian website on Jewish literature and culture could attract the young, literate, but marginally affiliated Jewish audiences that had thronged Eshkol, and he agreed to summon a group of other Russian intellectuals to think through how such a site might work. The result, in early 2006, was a proposal to create Booknik.ru, a virtual gathering place for Jewish Russians ranging from the intellectual elite to the casual reader, offering "book reviews, interviews with Jewish and Israeli writers, essays, a section on the latest publications in the Jewish world, and a forum for discussion."[6] Other features, including new topical sections, interactive forums, podcasts, a children's section, compatibility with mobile devices, and publication of a hard-copy *Booknik Reader*, would be added over time. AVI CHAI provided half the cost of developing and launching the site, just under $250,000, with the remaining half paid by an American philanthropist who would become a regular collaborator in the FSU with AVI CHAI for several years.

Booknik's opening was timed to coincide with the inaugural Russian Open Book Fair in July 2006, an event covered widely across the Russian media. The website almost instantly drew more than 6,000 users, a number that increased to around 30,000 before the year was out. A core group of between 4,000 and 6,000 people visited the site regularly and spent considerable time there. Increasingly impressed by both the quality of the content and the growth in visits and user participation across Russia and even in Israel, the board steadily increased funding and added periodic grants for marketing and site development. By the end of 2008, nearly 50,000 people were visiting the site at least twice a month. Here, it seemed, was a project that could actually span the eleven time zones of the former Soviet Union and build a virtual community center with the potential to reach a growing share of its Jewish population.

Unlike North America and Israel, where the study of Judaism held a respected place in any number of distinguished universities, the former Soviet Union had only a relatively small and recent cadre of scholars who considered Judaic studies their discipline. There were, to be sure, Biblical scholars, historians who specialized in Israel, professors of Semitic languages, and experts in the politics, economics, and international relations of the Middle East. But in many cases, these scholars adhered to and identified with their underlying disciplines. They were professors of history or literature or religion, not professors of Judaism. That was beginning to change, as evidenced by the emergence of Sefer, the group dedicated to creating a coherent field of Jewish scholarship. But the change was still embryonic and uncertain. Funding for dedicated departments of Judaic studies was scarce, and the few existing departments found it hard to assemble a well-rounded faculty and retain top talent.

This, Rozenson thought, was something that could and needed to accelerate, and AVI CHAI could play a role. The foundation's early grants to Sefer, which continued for several years, were plainly helping to raise consciousness and stimulate strategic thinking among people dedicated to promoting Judaic studies. But they did not, by themselves, do anything to build actual departments in any particular universities. Increasingly, Fried and Darmon, among other trustees, were urging more direct action to fortify Jewish scholarship at the front lines, by helping to build distinguished, well-funded departments able to satisfy a growing demand from Jewish students and prospective scholars.

Rozenson's search for answers led first to Moscow State University, whose five-year-old Center for Jewish Studies and Jewish Civilization, known by its Russian acronym Tzietz, was then the leading program of its kind in the FSU. On visiting the program, Rozenson was immediately struck by its "impressive leadership and significant growth potential," but also by its "serious financial challenges." Moscow State University was the logical place for AVI CHAI to start, not just because of the quality of the program there, but because the university was an eminent institution—"Russia's equivalent of Harvard or Oxford," in Rozenson's estimation. Tzietz's academic pedigree (it had been founded jointly with the Hebrew University of Jerusalem), combined with Moscow State's prestige, made it the kind of potentially "first-rate" endeavor that suited AVI CHAI's normal predilections. Thus far, however, the "financial challenges" had held back that potential.

In mid-2004, the foundation provided a starting grant of $250,000 to Tzietz to begin building up its academic and organizational heft. The grant would be a down payment on a bundle of full four-year scholarships and stipends for five top entering students, plus stipends for three additional students who have already won competitive full scholarships of their own. It would pay for leading scholars to spend time teaching and counseling at Tzietz, and would furnish new textbooks for students. Marketing and some administrative costs would be covered as well. A much larger two-year award of nearly $700,000 followed less than a year later, after a quick, preliminary evaluation showed that the starting grant had been put to good use. This made it possible to add new laptops to the package of support provided to top students, and also to start a small program to cultivate outstanding high school students interested in pursuing advanced Judaic study.[7] Less than a year into the second grant, following another stellar evaluation, Rozenson felt confident in reporting that Tzietz had "raised the bar for academic Jewish studies" and "served as a precedent for the establishment of other Jewish studies programs in universities across the FSU."[8]

The progress of the Tzietz initiative—both its academic gravitas and its efficient use of resources—impressed both Rozenson and the board. But paradoxically, the prospect of a major success in this area was also starting to raise some alarms. It seemed clear that demand for Judaic studies credentials was real and growing, and that it would grow even faster as the discipline gained stature and took root at more universities. But at this point, as Fried pointed out, AVI CHAI's grants for Sefer and Tzietz had overwhelmed all other sources of support in this field. The foundation was, by 2006, by far the prime philanthropic funder of advanced Judaic studies in the FSU, followed at some distance by the Chais Family Foundation, a frequent funding partner and close collaborator of AVI CHAI. But the bill for these university activities was only going to increase, probably steeply, as the field grew, and AVI CHAI could not afford to keep up with all of it. Nor, in Fried's view, should it attempt to do so. The field needed not just more money, but more champions and sponsors. The emphasis, henceforth, should be not just on funding top-notch activity, but on drawing in new, dedicated backers.

That search began in earnest in 2006, and although it didn't develop as quickly as some trustees hoped, the quality of the Tzietz initiative, plus Sefer's increasing membership and growing range of programs for rising Judaic scholars, did draw the attention of additional funders. Meanwhile, as Fried had predicted, the ranks of rising young scholars were swelling. By the 2007–08 academic year, Tzietz had 103 students, including eighty-six undergraduates, nine graduate students, and eight doctoral candidates. The number of participants in Sefer's weeklong summer and winter programs, led by prominent professors from the FSU and Israel, had nearly doubled, to 650 students in 2007. The oldest and most advanced of these students were now taking teaching positions in the Judaic studies programs and departments beginning to appear on more and more campuses across the region.

Most important, from the perspective of AVI CHAI's mission, these burgeoning academic programs were laying down a marker in the former

Soviet Union, establishing a place for Jewish learning among the recognized, accredited, and celebrated fields of advanced study. The beneficiaries of this achievement would run well beyond the academics themselves. Jewish young people, whose prospects for knowledge about their heritage had previously been limited to Sunday school or synagogue or, for some, Jewish day schools, now had avenues of further learning at university. Even for those not destined for university degrees in Judaic studies, any interest in future reading and exploration would now be fed by a growing academy of authors and experts.

The target for AVI CHAI, in other words, was not solely those whose passion was Jewish knowledge, or whose professional interests included some form of Jewish writing or art or scholarship. It was, as Darmon put it in an early presentation to the board, "the students of physics"—gifted Jewish young people pursuing all sorts of careers and interests, for whom *all* knowledge is precious, but for whom Jewish knowledge remained scarce. The challenge, she believed, was to reach those with hearty intellectual appetites, for whom the banquet of Jewish study would be a new —but potentially lifelong—discovery.

"In the course of the past five years," Rozenson wrote in 2007, the central focus of AVI CHAI's work in the FSU has turned to reaching out to the widest and most diverse Jewish audience, which represents the overwhelming majority of post-Soviet Jewry." The foundation's initial programs in the FSU—in informal education, day schools, literary circles, and universities—had by now extended beyond what Rozenson called "conventional Jewish establishment activities." It had begun to answer a more fundamental, widespread, and only recently recognized longing: for a way to be Jewish in what had once been a homogenizing and repressive Soviet Union, but was now an increasingly pluralistic, creative, and reflective region offering multiple ways to live a committed and inspired life.

XII

THE RECKONING

On September 15, 2008, Lehman Brothers filed for bankruptcy. The news ignited a financial chain reaction that erased trillions of dollars of global wealth in a matter of weeks. In the process, philanthropic endowments collapsed, and charitable contributions dried up around the world. The Standard & Poor's 500 index sank by more than 50 percent. The assets of many American foundations, despite maintaining well-balanced portfolios, took losses of 30 percent and more. At AVI CHAI, the harm eventually proved to be milder than that, but in the feverish weeks after the Lehman debacle, the extent of the coming losses was still unknowable. The sense of dread in the foundation's boardroom was little different from that at nearly every other philanthropy watching its assets shrink day by day, with no clear end in sight, and with virtually all of its spending plans now obsolete.

The cause for alarm hadn't started with the Lehman bankruptcy. The cataclysm had been at least a year in the making, dating back to early 2007, when the U.S. market for mortgage-backed securities began to implode. AVI CHAI's endowment had been losing value steadily throughout 2008.

"What should we do," Arthur Fried asked his fellow trustees in late October, "in light of the difficult financial markets we've been in for the last year and the horrible financial markets of the last two months?" After a precipitous drop toward the end of the year, the endowment would end 2008 down 15 percent from the previous year's peak.

Plenty of foundations, reeling from far steeper losses, would consider that figure enviable. But unlike most foundations, AVI CHAI would not have much time to recover what it had lost, especially if matters were to grow any worse. Its planned sundown was little more than a decade away. A substantial erosion of value would mean, as Fried put it to the board, that "we should reassess where we are and decide either to shorten our sunset duration, or to spend less." And if the fallout from the crisis were to last several more years (as, in fact, it did for many institutions), then "you could have a combination of the two."

The market meltdown was so severe in the autumn of 2008 that it had exceeded even the worst-case projections of the foundation's financial planners at Bernstein & Co. "If this continues even at one-tenth of the last two months' evaporation of capital values," Fried warned, "even taking down our spending by two-thirds will make it difficult for us to get to even 2017" before running out of cash. Until that week, AVI CHAI's plan had been to continue operating, more or less at its current level of spending, until 2020, and then leave a substantial sum as an endowment for Beit AVI CHAI. Now the expected end date was just one more variable, along with annual outlays and the level of support for each of the foundation's grantees, that would soon have to be recalculated.

"We are not only looking at planning," Fried noted. "We also have commitments for the next two or three years that add up to about $95 million." He was referring to grants already promised but not yet paid, on which grantees would, in most cases, have been relying to meet payroll and fund other obligations. Although foundations can renege on these promises—and many had to do so in the aftermath of the crash— they generally consider that a last resort, to be contemplated only under the gravest conditions. The consequence of such a pullback is almost always disastrous for grantees: the cancellation of programs, projects abruptly shuttered, employees suddenly made jobless, and sometimes whole organizations wiped out. Fried was adamant that AVI CHAI would not take that route short of outright catastrophe.

"Although our capital has not eroded anywhere near as much as the overall market," he concluded, "there still has been significant erosion. When it comes together with spending at a rate of about $55 million, which is what it will be for this year, it's a double whammy: The market takes it, *and* you spend it. The two together have a compound and significant effect."

Heeding the caution of members with financial expertise, the trustees decided to make no firm decisions in the panic atmosphere of autumn 2008. But within a few months, as the debris began to settle and the extent of losses became clear, the board would have to start reviewing and revising its budgets. For starters, total program outlays were trimmed by roughly 20 percent beginning in 2009. With cuts of that magnitude, it would be reckless simply to impose automatic, across-the-board decreases proportionally on all grantees. Some projects and programs simply couldn't continue at so steep a reduction. Some were too valuable to suffer any substantial cut at all. And thanks to AVI CHAI's long-standing practice of sheltering some grantees from the burden of fundraising, some of them had almost no other funders to whom they could turn. Rather than starve every grantee equally, the foundation would have to make a much more painful set of decisions, akin to triage: determining which projects should be sustained at near-current levels, which ones could survive by other means with steep reductions, and which ones would no longer measure up to a straitened and more demanding set of funding criteria.

"The financial crisis was a turning point in the history of AVI CHAI," trustee Leif Rosenblatt observed a decade later. "But it wasn't just a financial turning point. It was a rethinking of a lot of things, including a rethinking of how to budget. Before 2008, it was as if we weren't budgeting, as if funds were unlimited for almost any projects we liked. Bring on the new projects. Spend more on the old projects. Suddenly, there had to be a more disciplined view."

To a degree, Rosenblatt was speaking with intentional hyperbole. The three geographic programs had, in reality, been subjected to at least notional caps on their spending—although Fried, Mem Bernstein, and others admitted that they regarded those caps more as guidelines than as hard ceilings. Staff members, reluctant to push their budget limits too hard, had routinely filtered out patently unaffordable or overpriced proposals before they ever reached the board. Nonetheless, trustees and staff members almost unanimously confirmed Rosenblatt's underlying point: decisions about grants had tended to be based not on the amount of money available, but on the quality of the proposal, the likely significance of what it might achieve, and the consistency of that achievement with AVI CHAI's mission. "We felt almost as if we had infinite capacity" is the way Yossi Prager had put it. "Decisions were based on, 'Is this worth doing, or not worth doing?' . . . We could do this *and* that, not this *or* that."

Beyond budgeting, Rosenblatt cited another way the crash of 2008 permanently altered how the foundation worked. He said, "The old view that AVI CHAI goes its own way and doesn't look for partners suddenly changed. We explored partnering. And in time, we actively sought out partners." This was a far more consequential change than the introduction of hard budgeting. AVI CHAI's pioneer mentality in its grantmaking, its willingness to walk untrodden paths and forgo any worries about whether other funders might come along, had been a hallmark of its institutional character since its earliest days. Along the way, the foundation had acquired a reputation, as one of its fellow funders put it, of not "playing ball with others," with the result that other foundations "either didn't know what AVI CHAI was doing, or they didn't see any stake for themselves" in those endeavors. To change course on such a fundamental matter—after twenty-five years of going it alone, and with barely a decade left in its intended grantmaking—would take a Herculean effort of both management and salesmanship. Suddenly, with little experience in wooing other donors, AVI CHAI would attempt to start marketing its projects and helping them to market themselves.

"I don't think that would have happened," Rosenblatt concluded, "without 2008."

For AVI CHAI's finances, the immediate aftermath of the crash was better than expected. The endowment rebounded by 7 percent in 2009, making back around two-fifths of what had been lost the year before. But Fried's "double whammy" nonetheless took its toll. The lost value of 2008, combined with outstanding spending commitments, produced a shrinkage in total assets over the next few years that made a hard reckoning unavoidable.

By year's end, in an extraordinary meeting held by conference call, the trustees asked for a process by which they could sort among current grants and determine, project by project, which ones should continue to be funded and which should not. Only those that represented what Fried called the "highest and best" use of foundation resources would remain. Those that were less critical to AVI CHAI's mission—even if they were, as most assumed, worthwhile activities—would go. The process they requested would begin early in the new year and set in motion months of painful choices.

Henceforth, to adapt Prager's earlier formulation, every grant would now be a weighing of alternatives within a strictly limited capacity: "We cannot do this *and* that; we can do this *only if we do not do* that."

And thus, in the dark months at the close of 2008, AVI CHAI's Years of Plenty came to an end.

PART III

FACING THE END

XIII

WINNOWING AND SOWING

At the start of 2009, as the dust was beginning to settle from the global financial implosion, AVI CHAI's assets were likewise showing signs of stabilizing. True, the foundation could no longer continue making grants at its accustomed rate of $40 million to $50 million a year, if it hoped to survive all the way to its planned sunset and provide lasting support for Beit AVI CHAI. But the board's worst fears hadn't materialized. After plunging by a little over 30 percent at the end of 2008, the endowment's recovery in the first quarter of the new year was healthy, and it would stay that way. Even after above-average expenditures on new grants and prior commitments, the endowment would ultimately end 2009 with about $40 million more than it had a year earlier.

Of course, that decent outcome was far from assured in the early months, and Arthur Fried, Alan Feld, and Lief Rosenblatt, the foundation's primary asset-watchers, were determined to play it safe. It was important, Fried later said, to pare budgets to a level that would be sustainable even under the harshest projections, so as to guarantee that current commitments would be met, the most essential work would continue, and at least $135 million would be left at the end as an endowment fund for Beit AVI CHAI. Having reached that safely reduced spending level, it would then be necessary to stick to it for at least a few years. More trouble could still lie ahead.

But just as important, at least to Fried, was the opportunity the present crisis provided to train a bright light on the foundation's spending habits and to shed projects that he sometimes described as merely "OK" or "not bad." The grant portfolio, he believed, had become "bloated" with decent but not outstanding projects that had been tolerated when money was plentiful, but that did not warrant the same level of support in leaner times. In short, even if the market crash had not ultimately cost AVI CHAI one-third of its wealth—or had done so only for a few bad months—the shock of a sharp financial loss was an excellent reason to put the spending on a diet.

"The year 2008 came, in a way, as a real blessing to our foundation," Fried told consultant Joel Fleishman soon after the crash. "We used to do almost everything. We tried almost everything. . . . We spent liberally across a broad portfolio." The year 2008, he said, gave the foundation's three governing members (Fried, Mem Bernstein, and Lauren Merkin) "an ability to put forward a proposal to draw back. It couldn't be a guillotine, but we would change our targets."[9]

He had accordingly sent a letter to the full board in November 2008—well before the scope and duration of the crash were clear—asserting that the three members had determined that "excruciatingly painful decisions will have to be made; yet nevertheless they may be unavoidable." He continued:

We propose a process that will enable us to determine what the Trustees think are the highest and lowest priorities for AVI CHAI, in terms of existing projects. We propose to ask our three executives—David, Eli, and Yossi—to create, perhaps with the assistance of their colleagues, a short, less-than-one-page, summary of each of our

programs, disclosing our previous spending and future commitments, and an evaluation grid that will enable the Trustees to pri-
oritize our activities in three buckets along geographic lines. That
will enable us to determine what we think is most important, down
to what we think is least important. It goes without saying that the
least important will, in the course of the next few years, have to be
eliminated.[10]

What the governing trio had in mind, Fried explained later, was a
kind of triage. The foundation would preserve or increase support for
projects that were strategic "bull's-eyes," perfectly aimed at AVI CHAI's
core mission, and achieving their objectives. It would reduce, but not
eliminate, grants to projects that contributed significantly to the mission
but were overvalued or could be sustained with less money. And for
projects that were mediocre—or that were peripheral to the mission,
even if of high quality—it would withdraw support altogether. In a foundation where every project was personally attached to at least one trustee,
where that trustee had worked side by side with staff members to formulate a rationale, set goals, and recommend grant amounts, this process
required, as one board member put it, "deciding which of your children
to disinherit."

In setting this course, the authority of the three governing members
was crucial. The procedure did not enjoy universal support among trustees, and some later objected to either the severity of the process—one
called it "Darwinian," another complained of a "tyranny of the majority"—or to the particular outcomes it produced. At least one trustee
argued instead for trimming every grant by the same percentage, to avoid
invidious cuts and the abandonment of some long-standing projects.
(Most other board members disliked that idea on the reasonable grounds
that, despite its seeming fairness, it would inflict more damage on fragile or heavily dependent grantees than on stronger ones, and the difference would have nothing to do with the relative importance of those

grantees to the foundation's goals.) Others suggested continuing to spend at current levels or even higher, recognizing what one trustee called a time of "deep crisis" in the Jewish world—even if that meant draining the endowment much faster than planned.

The "deep crisis" was real, not just in the Jewish world but throughout the nonprofit sector. The financial cataclysm had not only depleted the assets of foundations and donors, thus shrinking total grantmaking worldwide, it had also struck at the heart of many operating nonprofits' fundamental business model: earned revenue from sources like student tuition, membership fees, and government contracts. With families, governments, and businesses all reeling from huge losses (in Israel, for example, tax revenue dropped 12.9 percent between 2009 and 2010, and the government budget deficit rose to 5.15 percent from 2.1 percent the previous year[11]), spending on charities of all kinds was plummeting.

For many of AVI CHAI's grantees, however, the damage was arguably even more acute. For example, the loss of operating revenue struck at the heart of the day school economy. Day school parents in North America, suffering from market losses or lost employment, could trim their family budgets substantially simply by transferring children to public schools. Marvin Schick warned the board in early 2009 about "schools around the country that are hemorrhaging students." Declining enrollments were especially severe in the Conservative, Reform, and Community schools where AVI CHAI had focused much of its effort. In Israel, where attendance at batei midrash, community programs, or Beit AVI CHAI events was purely voluntary, the prospect of dwindling revenues was frightening. Add to this a sudden diminution of philanthropic support—including, as seemed likely, from AVI CHAI—and the question for some grant recipients became not only about managing austerity, but about survival.

To prevent what looked like a massive constriction in the nonprofit sector, some prominent foundations chose to boost their spending in the immediate aftermath of the crisis, despite depleted assets. In 2009, when overall grantmaking fell by more than 2 percent across the United States, more than 20 percent of American foundations sought to compensate for that loss by raising the percentage of their assets paid out in grants, and in 2010, almost a quarter did so.[12] In many cases, however, the foundations that boosted spending in these lean years were very large and secure, like the Bill and Melinda Gates Foundation, or else were operating in perpetuity, so that their budgets could always be tightened in future years, when markets were stronger and the foundations could gradually recover their lost wealth. AVI CHAI, falling in neither of those privileged categories, faced much more limited options.

So, the governing members' choice ultimately made sense to most trustees, however much they found it unsettling, and a few of them saw real virtue in the discipline and focus it would impose. In his book *The Foundation: A Great American Secret,* Joel Fleishman of Duke University took a similar view of the virtues of this approach. He lamented that few foundations ever perform such a thoroughgoing dissection of their grant portfolios—mostly for the same reasons that some AVI CHAI trustees chafed at the idea. It entails an analytically difficult comparison of disparate kinds of work, and a partly subjective assessment of how relevant that work is to the foundation's mission. One likely outcome of these kinds of comparative assessments is that, in the winnowing process, some very good organizations and worthy causes will lose support. More to the point, some favorite projects of individual board and staff members are sure to be sacrificed to a majority judgment that they are not worthy enough. Nonetheless, Fleishman pointed out, a comparative review of this kind is practically the only way for an institution to decide the relative merits of its various lines of work and to refocus its resources periodically on the things it does best.

To make the process as fair and deliberate as possible, Fried directed the staff in each of the three geographic programs to summarize every project and grantee, then assess and rank them from 1 to 5, according to staff members' collective judgment about cost and benefit, risk, and pertinence to the mission. The staff summaries and rankings wouldn't determine any grantee's fate; that decision was reserved for the board alone. Instead, the staff's work supplied trustees with a baseline of information and the judgment of the people closest to the frontlines. After that, each trustee scored projects on his or her own, using the same 1-to-5 scale, with 5 reserved for the very strongest. The trustee scores were submitted anonymously and combined into an overall average. Projects were then ranked from lowest to highest, and the lowest-scoring areas of work were set to be wound down. In the mid-level ranks, staff were told to look for ways to trim the budget, until the aggregate savings brought total spending down by 25 percent.

In thinking about costs and benefits, a project's centrality to AVI CHAI's mission was the most important element in the definition of "benefit." But another key factor was how far the results of a project would reverberate or multiply over time. For example, a new curriculum, once produced, would benefit thousands of students both now and for years to come. A scholarship for an aspiring teacher or principal would touch the lives of many students year after year, over the course of that professional's career. A scholarship for one student, however, would benefit only that student, and perhaps his or her family. Grants that had little or no ripple effect—the student scholarship, say, or a one-off program with no follow-up—were known disapprovingly at AVI CHAI as "retail philanthropy." In scoring and ranking grants, trustees tended to assign the lowest scores to anything that looked like retail.

Yet that approach to the cost-benefit calculation troubled at least a few participants, both on the staff and the board. For a foundation dedicated not mainly to providing services but to altering attitudes and lives—to deepening Jewish identity and knowledge of Judaism, and promoting harmony and unity among Jews worldwide—surely the *depth* of an experience mattered as much as the number of people it touched. A decade later, looking back on the rating-and-ranking exercise, Yossi Prager cited two examples to illustrate the problem.

One was a program called Alot, in which American public school students were welcomed into two Orthodox summer camps, where they had a thoroughly immersive Jewish experience, with the goal of persuading them to enroll in Jewish day schools. Roughly 40 percent of the participants did ultimately enroll, and, as Prager put it, "their life's trajectory changed." Even among those students who didn't change schools, an evaluation suggested that the summer experiences seemed to have an awakening effect on their emotional and intellectual attachment to Judaism, creating an appetite for further discovery. Still, as Prager remembered the calculations at the time, "It was a retail program. There was just no leverage in it. It was a beautiful program, but you were recruiting something like thirty or forty kids a year to day schools, and you can't change a whole field at that scale."

By contrast, he cited TaL AM, the highly regarded Jewish studies and Hebrew language curriculum, which at that point was in use in some 400 schools, involving 30,000 students a year. Although TaL AM's annual grant was nearly three times the size of Alot's, it was reaching 1,000 times as many people. It was still spreading to more and more schools (Alot was intended to spread to more camps, but it never did), and later years would see an online version of the curriculum extending its market even farther across the world. On the retail-wholesale spectrum, TaL AM was a wholesale home run.

But, Prager cautioned, "You could also argue that Alot has the greatest return on investment, because every one of those kids went from being a non-day school student to being in day school. TaL AM had a small influence on the school day of many, many kids—but it did not amount to a profound change in their day. Which one has the better return? It turns out, how you measure return on investment is not just a matter of numbers; it depends on a whole set of values."

Here, it seemed, was a perennial debate, dating back more than fifteen years. Did the mission of bringing Jews to greater commitment, understanding, and practice call more for a deep, personal transformation, one

soul at a time, or for what Schick had long ago called "great numbers"?
Was the premium on quantity or quality? As Avraham HaCohen had
argued in the 1980s, each person's relationship to Jewish heritage is
unique and personal. The journey of discovery and devotion takes place
in "the context of one person's life." As Schick added some years later,
"Jewish religious outreach is the most retail experience one can imagine."
When AVI CHAI shifted from an emphasis on outreach to one of education and study, it seemed to be seeking a way of balancing these two
approaches to personal awakening: reaching larger numbers of people
with resources that might, in time, bring each person to a deeper engagement with Judaism. Providing people with Jewish knowledge and experiences might not, by itself, produce profound transformation, but it
would equip them with the prerequisites for seeking that transformation
in their own lives. And an intervention at that level, the foundation
reasoned, might perhaps reach "great numbers."

Still, the hope for deep spiritual awakening on the individual level—
of the kind that Zalman Bernstein had experienced, and that had
inspired him to create AVI CHAI—had never disappeared from the foundation's ambitions. The quest for experiential learning in schools and
camps, and for imparting "religious purposefulness"; the cultivation of
batei midrash that would inspire a lifelong desire for textual discovery
and understanding; the effort to reach young people on American and
Russian campuses and in Israel's pre-military gap year, during an in-
tensely formative point in their lives—all these efforts strove at least as
much to penetrate "the context of one person's life" as to rack up "great
numbers."

Throughout the Years of Plenty, when it seemed possible to pursue
all opportunities no matter where they lay on the horizon, those two
views of the mission could coexist without tension. Now that it was time
to choose and scale back, however, pressure was building to demonstrate
the "highest and best" use of every dollar, shekel, or ruble. And that, to
the AVI CHAI trustees, tended to mean widespread change. "'Retail,'"

Prager recalled, "became a bad word here. 'Retail philanthropy' meant things with insufficient leverage." By that reckoning, TaL AM scored near the top of the survival list, slated not only for preservation but expansion. Alot scored low and was canceled.

In Israel, the provision of sabbaticals for heads of grantee organizations was likewise brought to an end, despite creating what most agreed was a valuable, rejuvenating opportunity for gifted leaders. On balance, trustees considered them too small to make much of a difference, with just a few beneficiaries at a time and only an indirect impact on the field. Even some projects with a long history of AVI CHAI support were now viewed more skeptically if they appeared too "retail" in nature. Several batei midrash—venerable projects that dated to Bernstein's years—drew harsh questions from trustees about whether they were "niche" products with "often small audiences." Most survived, but some suffered budget cuts, including the early beit midrash Kolot, which took a 30 percent cut; MiMizrach Shemesh, 32 percent; and Alma, 22 percent. By contrast, film and media projects and efforts in the state school system, all of which reached large numbers and seemed to generate significant ripple effects, scored high and were held harmless or only slightly reduced.

Not all the difficult choices were matters of quality versus quantity. Some had at least as much to do with fidelity to mission. Birthright Israel, for example, brought large numbers of young people from North America to Israel but, lacking a longer-term engagement with its alumni, it seemed too brief an engagement to satisfy the mission's demand for deepening "commitment to Jewish observance and lifestyle." It also struck AVI CHAI trustees as "not our main business," as one board member put it, given that there was no connection to day schools or summer camping. Beyond that, at its most fundamental level, even Birthright was essentially a retail project, despite its size, touching students one at a time with no assurance of any ripple effect in their later lives. AVI CHAI support for Birthright ended in 2010.

In Israel, the travel-and-research program Journey to Jewish Heritage, which took young people to Diaspora communities to learn their history, had long drawn questions about its relevance to AVI CHAI's mission, given that its work took place outside Israel and did not emphasize religious–secular understanding. Those questions now prevailed, and the project was cut by 50 percent in 2010, then zeroed out. The Bible Study curriculum developed by Yad Ben Zvi, which was not sponsored by the Ministry of Education and thus penetrated only 10 percent of state elementary schools, felt to most trustees like a mainly boutique project not integral to promoting either stronger Jewish identity or mutual understanding between more- and less-religious Israelis. Its grant for 2010 would be its last.

In several cases, trustees' ranking of projects diverged sharply from that of the staff. The program at Israel's Hartman Institute, which trained educators in Jewish thought and oral law, was popular with staff members but less so with trustees. While the staff focused on the high quality of the program itself, some board members considered it peripheral to the foundation's mission and others believed Rabbi David Hartman could be raising substantial support from other sources (as in fact it did). The Yahalom program, which promoted Jewish learning by parents and children together, had been shown in a 2007 evaluation to have a significant positive effect on students' learning and attitudes toward Judaism, and staff consequently ranked it highly. Trustees, on the other hand, saw it as limited in scope and unable to expand beyond the twenty-five schools that had piloted it. Both Hartman and Yahalom ended up with a period of reduced support that ended in zero.

In North America, trustees were considerably more enthusiastic about some projects than was the staff. This was particularly true of two Israel advocacy projects, The David Project and the on-campus advocacy programs led by Hillel and the Israel on Campus Coalition. In both cases, staff members were concerned that the programs were hit or miss—more successful in some places than others—and too dependent on AVI CHAI funding to have a meaningful future after the foundation's sunset. Trustees, on the other hand, saw them as crucial means of defending Israel at a time of growing adversity, and thus central to AVI CHAI's mission. Both projects survived, though their support was curtailed in later years. Another such program, called Write On for Israel, trained high school students in writing about Israel, but it had a small enrollment and few of its participants were from day schools, so both the staff and board considered it a weak competitor. It did not survive the cuts, though it managed to survive at a smaller scale on its own, without AVI CHAI support.

In the end, the painful threshing of the grant portfolio brought the budget for North America down from $25 million a year to $20 million, and Israel's budget down from close to $20 million to $16 million. It was a significant shrinkage, and some grantees continued to speak of it ruefully as much as ten years later. As an exercise in fiscal and strategic discipline, it was remarkable in the philanthropic world. But it made for a long period of stress and turmoil that took more than a year to subside.

Over time, many trustees and staff members would come to have second thoughts about some of the decisions in the great triage of 2009. Several people mentioned projects they wished had survived, and others regretted prolonging some efforts that later failed to meet expectations. But these regrets were relatively mild and tended to be more speculative ("What might we have accomplished if we'd continued with Project X?") than solid. In fact, several people who initially found the winnowing process unsettling later came to think of it more favorably. A prime reason for that change of heart was that reductions made in 2009–11 freed resources to undertake new work. As markets strengthened in the ensuing years, the foundation was able to start new initiatives, try variations on established themes, and even create whole new organizations— a process of creation more intense than any the foundation had experienced since the late 1990s. There would be no more Years of Plenty, but at least the time of crisis had been brief, and a new normality—with opportunities for fresh thinking and experimentation—was about to begin.

The months of reflection on mission, priorities, and return on investment had focused the minds of both staff and board on questions of impact and scale: how to make the greatest possible difference in the time remaining. In North America, working groups of staff and trustees began to explore options for new lines of work that might extend the appeal of day school education further—including an intensified push for public funding of religious schools and other efforts to strengthen day school finances. Another working group examined ways the foundation might exert greater "thought leadership," through more aggressive communications, participation in communal and philanthropic conferences, and outreach to allies in the field. In Israel, the focus of the program began to shift from nurturing individual seekers and learners (in schools, in informal study, in pre-army mechinot) to influencing movements and communities, where larger numbers of people could be drawn into activities of Jewish discovery. The early focus on cultivating "leaders"— people likely to acquire influence in society by virtue of intellect and personality—was shifting subtly toward "change agents," whose leadership abilities were more specifically trained on altering social and cultural dynamics.

And in all three of AVI CHAI's geographic regions, the prospect of using the internet to reach wider audiences and deliver new kinds of content had climbed to top-priority status. "I feel we are very far behind the mark in terms of the internet," Mem Bernstein said at the opening board meeting of 2009. "That's not on a project-by-project basis; it's the entire concept: everything from fundraising to getting out the message to hearing what the communities say." Chief educational technology officer Eli Kannai spent the first half of 2009 developing an analysis of where his field was heading in the coming decade and how AVI CHAI could use this progress both to promote Jewish education and to create more effective educational tools. Strategy director Sarah Kass organized a working group of staff and trustees dedicated to analyzing trends in online learning and social networking. "We had a library of books we insisted everybody read," Mem said, "and everybody devoured them. It was a great education for all of us." Within a year, new initiatives began to take shape from the working group's research.

In the early months of 2009, of course, discussion of new directions and opportunities remained largely theoretical. They stood in sharp contrast to the immediate reality of budget cuts and trimmed grant portfolios, and their prospects depended at least partly on how well the foundation's finances would recover in the next few years. Nearly all board discussions dealt with reaching a sustainable level of spending on current priorities and preserving the most valuable lines of work, not on new adventures. Yet even in the midst of the budget constriction, the North American working groups and the staff in Israel were beginning to hint at fresh endeavors reflecting new priorities in the post-crisis era. As early as 2009, Fried was assuring the board that he would "keep some powder dry," in the form of unbudgeted funds that could be used to seize opportunities, provided the markets didn't impose further big losses.

This was, in many ways, predictable. If AVI CHAI had merely tightened its belt in 2009 and continued to fund its remaining grantees (or similar ones) to do essentially the same work (or perhaps slightly more of it), the result would have been an institution running in neutral. Monitoring and managing existing projects and programs would have been important work, surely, but not especially demanding intellectually, nor emotionally invigorating, for either the board or staff. AVI CHAI trustees and employees had been recruited for their creativity, savvy, and strategic judgment. Little of that would be called for in an institution that was not undertaking anything significantly new, challenging, or innovative for its last ten years.

This principle is hardly unique to AVI CHAI. New grantmaking is the oxygen foundations breathe. Their motto might as well be "Change or Die." A funder that simply maps out a plan, chooses a cluster of key grantees, and stays on course year after year would fail to attract the most creative employees or, arguably worse, risk micromanaging its grantees. (If the foundation isn't exploring new frontiers of its own, then creative staff members have little to do but involve themselves in their grantees' deliberations and decision-making.)

So there was virtually no chance that AVI CHAI was about to settle into a quiet, ten-year decline as it spent down its endowment and prepared to exit the stage. Even in the midst of its financial constriction, thoughts were already trending toward new technologies and new ways of conceiving and pursuing the mission. Fleishman, in a 2015 report to the foundation, took note of the burst of new activity that began a year or so after the 2009 belt-tightening, and he saw three advantages in it:

> First, exiting from existing programs is inherently depressing, or at least discouraging, because it constantly reminds staff and trustees that their foundation is inexorably coming to the end of its life. Second, as the end approaches and the full picture of what the foundation has accomplished comes increasingly into focus, some gaps or unfinished challenges are likely to clarify as well.
>
> There is another reason to build in some new programming opportunities, alongside the conclusion of past work, toward the end of the foundation's life: Ending with a bang rather than a whimper is a way of taking full advantage of program officers' talents, experience, and knowledge of the field just when those are at their peak. By encouraging program officers to take on time-limited new initiatives simultaneously with the foundation's exit from old initiatives, and by reserving financial resources with which to support those new initiatives, a spend-down foundation can avoid wasting its cumulative investment in its most precious resource. That resource is not money; it is the talent of its human resources, its program officers, at the very point in time when they know more than they ever did before.[13]

On the other hand, new initiatives take time to mature. Their flaws and vulnerabilities often appear only after a few years of piloting and testing; surprises inevitably pop up along the way, and dealing with them can then take a few years more. With less than a decade remaining in AVI CHAI's working life, the launch of complex new lines of work—not just a new grant here or there, but broad efforts to tackle whole new objectives—posed a considerable risk. In some cases, the new work undertaken in 2010 and beyond stirred up major new activity, often with very promising new grantees and methods of operating. But even as this nascent work was unfolding, several people on the staff and board confessed anxiety about the "short runway" the new endeavors faced, with little time for incubation and adjustment before their final grants left them to fend for themselves.

In 2008, as the foundation was approaching its final decade, Fried and Mem began searching for precedents or guidelines that might help the board manage its concluding years and ensure an orderly sunset. Ending a foundation demands a complex set of interconnected plans—for managing finances, for preserving staff loyalty and morale, for weaning grantees off of their longtime support, and for preserving documents and records that may be useful to future researchers. To help them think through all these requirements, they called on Fleishman, a Duke University professor and one of the country's preeminent thinkers about philanthropy. What does the historical record tell us, they asked, about the best way to spend down? Are there some known pitfalls to avoid? Who has done this best, and what did they do? Intrigued, Fleishman started a literature search, and then searched some more.

What he came up with, after weeks of digging, was a thin manila folder containing a few articles from foundation trade publications. Scholarly research and management case studies were effectively nonexistent. A few months later, in early 2009, Fleishman was able to add to the folder one newly published report chronicling the ten-year spend-out of the Beldon Fund, a $100 million environmental foundation in the western United States.[14] The Beldon report, while thorough and helpfully focused on practical choices and lessons, was of only partial relevance to AVI CHAI, a much larger institution with international programs and a completely different grantee profile. Still, it was a start. "OK," Fried and Mem responded, "what else have you found?" The answer: Nothing.

In that case, Fried suggested, why not fill the gap by using *us* as a real-time case study? Whatever we do, for better or worse, will surely be informative for the next funder that decides to go out of business. Fleishman pointed out that this would entail an outsider's close observation of the foundation's internal deliberations, choices, and struggles. The observer would be inquiring into sensitive decisions while they were being made, and the scrutiny might become uncomfortable. That's fine, Fried responded; AVI CHAI has a record of transparency, and no one here is shy. He signed Fleishman on for what would become a decade of research and a series of eight nearly annual reports on how the foundation managed its finale. On occasion, Fleishman also broadened his scope to reflect on the likely survival of some major grantees, the ways the foundation defined success, and the importance of its mission in the face of social headwinds that undermined Jewish identity, tradition, and continuity.

Fleishman submitted his first draft report at the beginning of 2010, and it created a stir almost immediately. Rather than merely describing AVI CHAI's planning for its conclusion ("I never just describe anything," he told a colleague), his report trained a critical eye on what Fleishman saw as the foundation's three main shortcomings: the board's preoccupation with individual grants, its aversion to working with other funders, and its relatively meager support for grantees' organizational development and management. While the trustees' initial reaction to these criticisms was skeptical (and a few took real umbrage at them), the board soon came to take each point seriously and to make substantial changes to the way the foundation functioned.

On the first point, Fleishman argued that the board had spent too much of its time "on the making, renewal, and/or dynamics of individual grants."[15] Long stretches of many board meetings had been routinely devoted to parsing and critiquing grantees' activities, materials, communications, and operating style. It was not unusual for several board members to weigh in on the merits of a particular study aid in a beit midrash, or a module of some Jewish studies curriculum, or a grantee's method of recruiting participants to one of its programs. While these discussions drew from the diverse expertise around the table and furnished valuable guidance to staff members, they were not, in Fleishman's view, the best way to exercise a board's responsibilities.

Instead, he wrote, "The Trustees need to think about what the goal for the remaining life of AVI CHAI is to be," and then to steer the foundation's work in its final years toward that goal or set of goals. To some extent, this reflected an already prominent view in philanthropy, particularly among foundations that had limited their lifespans or were considering that option. Gara LaMarche, who at the time was CEO of the Atlantic Philanthropies, another foundation spending itself down within the decade, had recently written that the central governance challenge for a limited-life foundation is to "imagine the end . . . and work back from there."[16] While that may have seemed like merely a logical starting point for Atlantic and some other foundations, Fleishman's exhortation to the AVI CHAI trustees represented a marked change from how they had operated for the past quarter-century: Spend less time on the direction of individual projects and more on the world as you hope it will be when AVI CHAI's final check is cashed. Your attention for the next ten years should then be focused on the big goals, the combination of ideas and resources needed to achieve them, and the choices to be made when surprises erupt or circumstances change.

Although this advice would demand a profound change in the board's work life, it got the warmest reception of Fleishman's three recommendations. The challenge of bringing the foundation to a close was increasingly drawing trustees' attention to the prospect of leaving an enduring legacy—a preoccupation that Fried had long discouraged, on the grounds that legacies are decided in the retrospective gaze of history, not in plans and forecasts. Now, though, with the end in sight, both the board and staff were finding it nearly impossible *not* to think about what would be left when the foundation was gone. That question, and the need to "imagine the end and work back," persuaded several trustees that a new way of thinking and working was essential.

Already, in mid-2009, a few months before Fleishman's first report would be submitted, Prager wrote to the board that "spend-down calls for more focused, more ambitious, more measurable goals," and that these goals need to aim at the field's systemic needs, rather than at tacking on discrete programmatic enhancements here and there.[17] At least one trustee had concluded by mid-2009 that the grant-by-grant approach to decision-making had led to "a process whereby every person, whether he/she is staff or trustee, is looking at particular trees and not at the forest. . . . This period of spend-down, with its defined scarcity of time, is all about looking at the forest."

So, by the time the final draft of Fleishman's report reached the board, staff and trustees were already starting to define a range of broad issues and fields that seemed ripe for final-stage concentration. These included the day school finances, leadership, and educational innovation in North America; leadership and community mobilization in Israel; and the role of technology in Jewish education worldwide—some of the main pillars on which the foundation's ultimate goals would eventually rest. In the coming year, the board would start organizing its docket and decision-making under broad thematic headings of this kind, voting to allocate large blocks of money for each category of work and then leaving decisions about individual grants to the staff, under close supervision and review by Fried and Mem. The board would review these decisions ret-roactively, but a detailed discussion of strategy for each broad subject area would occur just once a year.

For trustees long accustomed to a close, personal relationship with individual projects and grantees, this was a dramatic change in role. No longer required to be personal advocates for grantees or close collabora-tors with staff, some board members found the new, less-frequent pro-gram reviews less fulfilling (and, in some cases, less informative) than in the past. But they appreciated how the new approach freed up time to spend on setting general direction and reviewing overall progress, so on balance and over time, it became popular. Still, the transition was jarring at first. Moving from a "trustee-driven" foundation to what Fried called "trustee-managed" entailed a subtle change in vocabulary that masked a dramatic, briefly disorienting, shift in reality.

Another of Fleishman's recommendations likewise found general ap-proval, at least among the staff and some trustees, despite representing a sharp departure from the past. He argued that AVI CHAI had too long starved its grantees of the administrative and general operating support with which organizations form competent management teams and carry out essential business functions. After years of limiting "overhead" sup-port to 7 percent of the total grant—nowhere near enough to cover the many peripheral costs grantees have to bear, like financial controls, rent, communications, fundraising, and other core activities—some trustees were beginning to have second thoughts. When AVI CHAI was no longer keeping these organizations on financial life support, how were they supposed to survive on their own?

Running an organization on a shoestring was noble, some people had come to believe, but only so long as the foundation was around to pay for the shoestring. Raising *new* money, post-AVI CHAI, would require skilled development staff, people and systems to manage and account for funds from multiple donors, and enough executive talent to guide their orga-nizations and to build and maintain a network of outside alliances. AVI

CHAI had rarely provided those kinds of resources, much to the quiet dismay of its staff, who saw firsthand the difficulties grantees faced in keeping their organizations afloat. Now, however, Fleishman concluded that, "For the goals of the Foundation's philanthropic vision to survive and endure by means of the seeds which it has planted and nourished, it will need to spend a significant part of its remaining years in building the organizational strength of key grantees . . . [and] in developing, with them, plans for their long-term sustainability."[18]

This approach disturbed a few members of the board, at least two of whom felt that AVI CHAI should devote itself to measurable, near-term accomplishments and to the promotion of important ideas and principles, not to creating permanent institutions. However, much to the relief of Prager, Silver, and the rest of the AVI CHAI staff, Fleishman's recommendation took root with a majority of the trustees, and the following years would be devoted, in significant part, to the kind of "capacity building" by which grantees would be helped to become better fundraisers, more accountable, and more durable.

The third of Fleishman's critiques met the strongest resistance. It provoked an enduring skepticism (alive and well even after ten years) among a handful of trustees who considered his prescription naïve at best, and at worst a waste of the foundation's remaining time and resources. In brief, Fleishman urged that AVI CHAI stop funding projects mostly on its own, and instead seek out alliances with other funders to support causes of common interest. To this, two or three board members responded that AVI CHAI's view of Jewish education and continuity is, if not unique, then extremely rare. Finding others who share it, as one trustee put it, "probably leads nowhere—unless, of course, we redefine what we're trying to do, so that it appeals more to other [donors]. But then, if we do that, that's the end of what made AVI CHAI: a relentless focus, persistence, dedication to mission." It didn't help that earlier efforts to entice more

philanthropists to support Jewish education, which had flared and sputtered around the turn of the century, had ended in frustration. Revisiting
that experience struck a few board members as a kind of institutional
masochism.

"Market information is out there," another trustee said to Fleishman
at a board meeting in late 2009, referring to a broad awareness among
Jewish communal institutions about where AVI CHAI was putting its
money. "Eventually, if there's a market for what you're doing, [other
funders] will come to you. We've been doing this a long time. We're out
there. People know about us. If they haven't come forth by now, there's
probably a reason for that." Others at the meeting agreed. We've "marketed our message" for years, they said, and we still have few other
funders willing to join us on major initiatives. There aren't many Jewish
funders out there to begin with, and their attention is all focused elsewhere. Why waste time chasing shadows?

"I think you're wrong," Fleishman replied. "You have *not* marketed
what you're doing. You may have published it, but you haven't marketed
it. Everyone in the nonprofit or foundation world knows if you want to
get anything done, you have to market it. You are speaking silently.
Nobody knows what you are doing to the point that they've been *touched*
by what you've done and might be inspired to do something with you. . . .
When I talk to wealthy individuals or foundation people in New York
and elsewhere, their perception is that the AVI CHAI Foundation wants
to do its own thing and isn't interested in having anybody else work with
them, full stop."

A few trustees agreed—particularly Mem, Rosenblatt, and George
Rohr, who were accustomed to raising money for other organizations
and believed that AVI CHAI hadn't yet put the full tool kit of marketing
techniques to use for its chosen causes. Rohr and David Rozenson, the
executive director in the former Soviet Union, had been successfully
pursuing other funders in that region since the day the foundation started
working there, and they had built a program in which AVI CHAI was

almost never the sole funder of anything. Still, much of the board remained doubtful—either because they believed the search for co-funders would lead nowhere, or because they considered the odds of success too iffy to justify the requisite time and money. After much discussion, enough were willing to suspend disbelief so that a push to seek funding partners was formally launched. It began in North America, where the vast majority of Jewish philanthropy (including philanthropy dedicated to Israel) is headquartered. The foundation tapped the nonprofit consultancy Bridgespan, a highly regarded specialist in philanthropic strategy and management, to come up with an approach.

After more than four months of research and consultation, Bridgespan recommended a process that depended heavily on forming "co-creative relationships." Its core principle was that although AVI CHAI was seeking other funders to contribute to projects it had started, and to carry on funding those projects after AVI CHAI's departure, it could not ask these funders just to sign on to the foundation's agenda as if they were merely supporting players or recipients of a torch being passed. Instead, it would have to "define broader strategic problems or opportunities surrounding the success of camps and day schools," and invite other funders to join in devising projects to pursue parts of those broad aims, rather than approaching them with specific requests to fund Organization X or Program Y or Objective Z.

This was exactly the kind of change Fleishman had been urging—in fact, the introduction to Bridgespan's initial report closely mirrored Fleishman's language in his original recommendations—but it was still a foreign language to AVI CHAI. "It's on paper," Fried told the Bridgespan consultants at a meeting where they presented their findings, "and we have sort of ingested it mentally if not emotionally. But . . . the very process of beginning to openly engage with others is hard to imagine after a quarter of a century doing it our way and going it alone."

One or two trustees still remained unconvinced. For example, one viewed the Bridgespan approach suspiciously as putting AVI CHAI in a

"defensive posture"—meaning that it would essentially cast the foundation in a supplicant's role, pleading with other people to see the world
AVI CHAI's way, but then having to surrender to an alternate worldview
if that plea failed. Another trustee thought the whole idea would give a
false impression, in the context of the foundation's plan to spend down—
that it "confuses the outside world into thinking there's a sale of our
assets going on, and we're looking to rid ourselves of this money as
quickly as possible."

Still, the voices of dissent were becoming fewer and quieter, and signs
of new behavior were already beginning to sprout. In North America,
communications director Deena Fuchs was reassigned to work full time
on outreach to other funders, a move that quickly started to pay off. Just
as the Bridgespan report was being finalized in early 2011, the Jim Joseph
Foundation, a then-five-year-old institution dedicated to Jewish education, had reached out to AVI CHAI for an exploratory conversation, as a
way of learning more about the field. Prager quickly responded with an
offer to exchange views on the needs of Jewish education and "set up
some common areas where we could co-create." As Fried pointed out,
this was a radical change in foundation behavior. Only two years earlier,
he said, "asking someone else to suggest a field for AVI CHAI was blas-
phemy!" Within a year, the partnership with Jim Joseph would begin to
blossom, and it later became a significant factor in the continued funding
of North American grantees as AVI CHAI's grantmaking was drawing to
a close.

In Israel, where foundations are scarcer and few philanthropists invest
in the formal or informal education systems, the opportunities for large-
scale funding partnerships were slim. To get started, at least, staff members suggested creating a matching-grant program for pluralistic Jewish
education similar to the AVI CHAI MATCH program that had been
running in North America, with varying degrees of success, since 2004.
The new program, called *Pseifas* ("Mosaic" in Hebrew), launched with
an inaugural conference of prospective contributors at the end of 2009,

which drew more than one hundred Israeli donors and foundations. Three pledges were in hand within a month; by the April deadline for proposals, offers of grants eligible for matching amounted to more than double the $500,000 that AVI CHAI had made available to match them. Nearly 90 percent of the donors who sought matches had never contributed to educational causes before. The foundation promptly provided more matching money and got additional contributions from the New York Federation and the Jewish Funders Network to help match the flood of contributors. Pseifas continued through two more rounds, each lasting about three years, before ending in 2018 as the foundation was preparing to close.

Meanwhile, beyond Pseifas, staff and trustees in Israel also sought funding partners for each of their new initiatives, hoping to build the "co-creation" into each project as it developed.

For most of AVI CHAI's history, through all the years in which it resisted any suggestion of seeking other funders to share support of its projects, the most consistent dissenting voice on the board had been that of Henry Taub, the business software entrepreneur who believed adamantly in co-funding. Time after time, in his early years as a trustee, Taub would ask how a project funded 100 percent by AVI CHAI, with no other backers, could survive in the long run. He argued that it would be prohibitively difficult for such a grantee to replace foundation support, or to raise additional money for future growth. These organizations, he believed, would be perceived as purely creatures of AVI CHAI, in which no other funder would ever have a stake. Joining forces with other foundations and donors, by contrast, would show that the foundation's projects had broad appeal. It would help other funders understand what was important and powerful about them, and it might create buzz even beyond those who joined AVI CHAI in funding them. In later years, it would leave grantees with alternate resources and allies when the time came for AVI CHAI to step aside. But Zalman Bernstein had always disagreed, and

Taub soon accepted defeat on this issue, though he would raise it every so often anyway, just to test the waters.

In 2011, as the Bridgespan report was being finalized and AVI CHAI was at last moving to embrace a strategy of recruiting and working with other funders, Taub died of leukemia at age eighty-three. His death was a body blow to the board, on which both his business judgment and his philanthropic spirit had long been revered. It was fitting, perhaps, that the one issue on which Taub had never prevailed at AVI CHAI—the question of whether to market grantees to other funders—was the one that, at the end of his life, was finally resolved in his favor. On this, the board ultimately decided, as on many other things, Henry Taub had been right all along.

One other organizational change at AVI CHAI took place slightly later, and although it marked a milestone of sorts, its effect on the foundation's routines was only subtle. After fourteen years as chairman, Arthur Fried passed the gavel to Mem Bernstein at the end of 2012. The foundation's bylaws had called for a leadership transition in 2014 in any case, so the handoff merely came a year early. But, in stepping aside, Fried explained that he wanted Mem to have seven full years at the helm, rather than six (seven is the Biblical number for completion), and that her long apprenticeship at his side had already made her more than ready to step into the job.

In reality, the two had been a team since Mem joined the board in 1999. They shared offices in both New York and Jerusalem; they conferred with one another on every important decision and spoke with a single voice both internally and externally. Although they often disagreed on small matters, they were careful to resolve more substantive disagreements privately, so that they could publicly present a single point of view when they spoke for the foundation. By the time she took the reins, Mem had effectively been a part of AVI CHAI's top leadership for more than a decade. And even afterward, her collaboration with Fried—the shared offices, the consultations, the consistent public positions—continued exactly as before.

Still, her style in the job differed in some ways from Fried's, and the change in style nicely suited the board's new ways of doing business. Most notably, Mem preferred to walk through the main issues on the board's docket with each trustee in advance. In these preparatory conversations, she would seek an early consensus or, failing that, at least spotlight possible disagreements early enough so that she and the staff would be prepared to answer questions and the agenda would provide enough time to reach resolution. "People understand things differently," she told a consultant during her first year in the job. "Their mode of imbibing information is different. If you can speak with trustees one-on-one, by the time they come to the table, they've been able to absorb what you want to accomplish, and then they can listen to what other people say."

Her approach was hardly a radical departure from the past, but it fit the kind of meeting the AVI CHAI board would be conducting from now on: focused on a strategic horizon just a few years away and preoccupied not with operating details but with big ideas, major goals, and the setting of priorities—all matters on which early thought, frequent consultation, and a careful search for consensus would be essential.

Collectively, the decisions that followed the 2008–09 crisis changed AVI CHAI in profound ways—both internally, in its governance and structure, and externally in the way it related to grantees, other funders, and the wider Jewish world. But although the changes were diverse and wide-ranging, they all had one common origin: the impending sunset. The need to "imagine the end and work back from there" provoked hard thinking about what the world should look like when AVI CHAI departed—with better-equipped leaders and stronger organizations populating a better-funded field, where the forces of Jewish knowledge, identity, solidarity, and continuity are stronger, more plentiful, and longer-lasting. To be confident of reaching that goal, or at least to give it their best shot, trustees needed to devote their time and skills not to tactical preoccupations, debating and tweaking each individual project, but to ensuring that the foundation's resources were strategically arrayed to provide the best possible chance of achieving the vision.

Along with that shift came a change in how the board thought about new grants and lines of work. As Prager described it in a 2019 interview, "Before, it was: 'What opportunities are out there for very good new programs?' A great person or a great idea would come along, and our response would be, 'How can we help turn this into something big and great?' It was more opportunistic. That doesn't mean it wasn't coming from a strategic place—we were still testing things to see if they advanced our goals, and trying to help them go further if they did. We were always reasonably strategic that way. But now, we became more oriented toward a Theory of Change." In other words, instead of looking for intriguing projects and programs and fitting those into a strategic framework, the board would start with the framework—defining what was needed and why, setting a course for a particular outcome within ten years or so, and then try to find or build whatever was missing, to complete the vision in the time remaining. In North America, this even led to the creation of a new staff position, director of strategy and planning, to lead the process of strategic reconnaissance and construction.

Part of that process focused on a desire to spark *movements*, to inspire the efforts of other people—funders, operating organizations, influential writers and thinkers, and even the government—to rally behind Jewish identity, knowledge, and culture in new and more vigorous ways. In North America, this effort included a burst of writing, speaking, and publishing by AVI CHAI staff members, elaborating on the foundation's view of Jewish learning, tradition, and peoplehood, and suggesting paths toward a more secure Jewish future. And AVI CHAI's push for U.S. government support of religious schools continued and grew, with goals that sometimes seemed tantalizingly close and at other times quixotic. Even after the foundation's backing for those efforts had ended, the cause remained very much alive, with significant cases reaching the Supreme Court in 2020.

In Israel, the quest to fuel movements took more direct aim at grassroots organizations in municipalities, in kibbutzim and moshavim, and in youth and adult communities around the country, explicitly seeking to bolster and amplify the strongest and most promising agents of change. In the former Soviet Union, the various projects to promote Jewish literature, culture, and scholarship were nearly all aimed, at least indirectly, at connecting Jews into networks of creativity and leadership.

As time went on, this interest in fomenting movements led AVI CHAI to a much broader and more ambitious program of communication and advocacy within the world of Jewish philanthropy. As Prager put it, "It got more and more specific as it became clear, with spend-down approaching, that this was, in a way, all we had left." The stakes were high. If the foundation's ideas didn't find a receptive audience of people in philanthropy who might absorb and carry them forward, chances were good that they would eventually fade into obscurity. But disseminating ideas is a smaller and more manageable challenge than creating real movements—especially in the ten years the foundation had left. Movements, complete with leaders and visionaries and legions of foot soldiers, usually form slowly and fitfully, often taking decades to solidify, if they form at all. Along the way, factions tend to form and break away, leaders come and go, charisma fades, and passions don't happily coexist with organizational discipline. Even when all goes reasonably well, a durable movement normally takes decades, not a few years, to solidify.

Some twenty years elapsed between the earliest proposals to create charter schools in the United States and the first state law recognizing a charter school movement.[19] At least half a century passed between the early formation of American conservation campaigns and the consolidation of a broad-based environmental movement. Foundation backing for community development in low-income American neighborhoods evolved for nearly a quarter-century before national community development institutions and umbrella groups started to form. AVI CHAI would not have the luxury of that kind of patience and perseverance, even assuming that technology could accelerate the process in some ways. The foundation would have to try to set things on course—supplying information, forums, and networks; making persuasive arguments; meeting in person and communicating on social media; devoting as much talent and energy as could be marshalled for the cause—and then turn its strongest projects and advocates loose to soldier on.

Nonetheless, even if the prospect of creating whole movements was out of reach, it was surely true that, at the dawn of AVI CHAI's last decade, cultivating leaders and disseminating ideas was "all we had left." In North America, the 1990s' boom in day school formation and enrollment had faded; the forces of secularism and multiculturalism had continued their corrosive drag on Jewish identity and tradition (indeed, all cultural identity and tradition). In Israel, the idea of Jewish heritage had been weaponized in national politics, where vocal minorities for and against religion threatened to drown out the moderate aspirations of most Israelis for a diverse but richly Jewish modern society. In the former Soviet Union, the seedlings of Jewish learning and cultural discovery remained fragile, at constant peril of being overwhelmed by broader societal forces. Against all these threats and pressures, a midsize foundation with only ten years left would have to stake at least part of its legacy on the hope that others, passionate and determined as Zalman Bernstein and his successor trustees had been, would find ways to rally their peers and charge forward.

That is a common conclusion of foundations that choose a limited life over a permanent endowment: the best hope of a lasting impact comes not only from concrete things the foundation may accomplish—institutions and buildings established, reforms enacted, products created and distributed — but even more from the people and ideas the foundation helps to raise up. This was a conclusion increasingly emphasized by Mem as the years of AVI CHAI grantmaking drew to a close: "The legacy," she said, "is the people"—the inspired, the energized, the influential, the informed, the educated, and the driven, and, over time, the communities and trends and movements that they stir to action.

XIV

NORTH AMERICA

An 'Energizing Nucleus'

S tepping into a new era of grantmaking, AVI CHAI's program in North
America still had plenty of lingering challenges from the old era left
to confront. Chief among these was the drive to raise the quality of
teaching and learning in day schools, and of their leadership and management, in ways that would promote Jewish literacy, religious purposefulness, and a dedication to Jewish peoplehood—the formula known in
brief as LRP. Though the terminology had changed a bit over time, this
had been the core objective of the program since the foundation first
anointed day schools as the cornerstone of its North American mission.
And now, although its strategic window on education was about to open
much wider, the main question of the past fifteen years was still para-
mount: how to create schools whose Jewish experience was so rich, and
whose leadership and educational quality so strong, that more and more
parents of every denomination would want to send their children there
in search of a more committed, more knowledgeable Jewish life.

Many of the foundation's long-standing grants for teaching and
school leadership were notching tangible results, confirmed by detailed

evaluations. The three largest school-leadership programs   one at Har vard, one at the Jewish Theological Seminary, and one housed at RAV-SAK, the organization for community day schools—all ranked highly in the board's scoring and winnowing exercise of 2009. All continued with strong AVI CHAI support well into the foundation's final years.

Among programs to promote better teaching, one was especially highly regarded: the Jewish New Teacher Project. The in-service mentoring program had led to unquestioned, widespread improvements in teaching quality and was creating a growing cadre of experienced mentors who were now able to bring the program to more and more schools. Other funders were beginning to contribute to parts of it, though the project still remained highly dependent on AVI CHAI.

Similarly, the Pardes Educators Program, the two-year degree-granting program based in Israel, now had scores of alumni setting a standard of excellence in classrooms across North America. It, too, relied on AVI CHAI funding for survival, and at upwards of $100,000 per graduate, it was a Cadillac program that was hard to sell to other donors. In the 2009 triage of grants, Pardes survived, but with reservations from several trustees concerned about how it would continue beyond the foundation's sunset. One described it as a "poor financial model for a great program." Its quality, at least, was widely admired, and there seemed to be time left to remedy weaknesses in the financial model.

Specialized programs aimed at Bible instruction, Hebrew language, and Israel-related studies all likewise remained strong, though most (not all) were similarly reliant on AVI CHAI's largesse. TaL AM and NETA (later *Bishvil Ha'Ivrit*, "For Hebrew") stood out as possible exceptions, given that they were designed to be self-sustaining, in the long run, on fees from participating schools. But in nearly all other cases, as the first decade of the twenty-first century was drawing to a close, the foundation's grants still represented 80, 90, and sometimes 100 percent of grantees' budgets—a factor that made the search for outside funding sources by 2020 a life-or-death matter for many of them.

A few other teaching programs had not fared so well. A project to improve the teaching of Jewish history, run jointly by New York University and RAVSAK, brought teachers and administrators to a summer workshop and then made NYU graduate students available as consultants in beefing up schools' Jewish history offerings. But AVI CHAI balked at the relatively high cost, offering to cover only 50 percent of the budget after year one. NYU and RAVSAK tried to make up the remaining 50 percent but could sustain the program only for two more cohorts. A master's program in Jewish education at Hebrew Union College struggled to get off the ground and was discontinued. Programs to bolster the quality of teaching in schools that primarily serve immigrant students lasted half a dozen years and showed some success, but again, the foundation resisted bearing the full, high cost of the program and ultimately withdrew.

But as the foundation began reassessing its strategy for its final decade, the quality of this or that project was no longer the central question confronting the board and staff. As Sarah Kass, AVI CHAI's director of strategy and evaluation, put it in a 2011 memo, "We have moved from an abundance mindset . . . to a scarcity mindset—trying to make a difference with scarce financial resources and scarce time." The consequence of that shift, Kass wrote, was to elevate the foundation's attention from influencing one or more aspects of schools' operations and instead looking for ways to buttress the whole field—to create engines of improvement for Jewish education, including both the quality and the financial health of day schools, that would continue to build momentum after AVI CHAI had left the scene. Kass continued:

[S]carcity shifts our attention from pushing products to strengthening markets—of consumers and producers. Specifically and practically, this new scarcity mindset is leading us away from exclusively planting trees and toward fertilizing soil—away from providing LRP *programs* to day schools and camps and their personnel, and

toward attending to the *conditions and contexts* that will enable those
settings and people to thrive. Whereas we once focused exclusively
and successfully on curricula, personnel enrichment programs, and
other LRP enhancements for camps and schools, we now also consider how to ensure that day schools are affordable for the foreseeable future (strengthening the viability of the day school market for
its consumers), and that core institutions that serve day schools are
strong (strengthening the viability of the day school market for its
producers).[20]

From this shift in perspective, three new guiding concepts were born.
The first was a desire to draw educators and leaders into tighter and wider
networks of communication, creativity, and collaboration. Extensive
reading on twenty-first century techniques of organizing and marketing
had led several trustees and staff members to focus on the creation of
"tribes," groups of people who identify with one another and with a common cause, and who feel inspired to promote the cause and to exchange
ideas and experiences in a continual drive to improve their field and
popularize their message.

The idea of tribes was closely related to the desire to support "movements," but in this case, the goal had more to do with forging supportive,
nurturing relationships among people who participated in AVI CHAI programs, to create a sense of common, tribal identity that would make
them—rather than any particular foundation project or grantee—a lasting legacy and wellspring of future progress.

So, for example, new grants to projects such as the Pardes Educators
or the various principal training programs would now include a component for linking alumni across schools and communities to encourage
them to become what program officer Michael Berger called "a cadre of
LRP ambassadors" and an inspiring, close-knit society that others would
seek to join.

A second broad idea to emerge from the new "scarcity mindset" was a focus on the core business model of day schools—an attempt to help them make more efficient use of slender resources, raise money (especially endowments), and seize innovative opportunities for boosting educational quality at reduced cost. This was a direct application of the principle of "capacity building" that Joel Fleishman had urged on the trustees in 2009. It meant, among other things, helping schools gather and understand financial data from across the day school industry and to aim for higher, field-wide standards of financial management, fundraising, and operational efficiency.

As a first step in this direction, the foundation supported a new project at Yeshiva University with the imposing, business-school name of Comparative Financial Analysis and Reengineering (producing the optimistic abbreviation CFAR, or see-far.) It would facilitate the collection of industry-wide data and help individual schools apply those data to their own operations, identifying areas where each school lags or outperforms the rest of the field. Schools would produce three-year plans for making improvements suggested by the data, with a goal of increasing revenue by 4 percent and shrinking expenses by 6 percent. Other efforts to sharpen the day school business model included initiatives sponsored by PEJE, the Project for Excellence in Jewish Education, and several local federations to help schools raise and manage endowment grants. The pursuit of government funding for religious schools was another way of trying to shore up the industry's bottom line.

The third new strand of strategic thinking involved technology, and it undergirded all the other new ideas—movements, tribes, better teaching and learning, thought leadership, peer-to-peer communication, and educational efficiency. Following Mem Bernstein's urgent appeal for more use of online tools and web-based communication in Jewish education, the foundation was now determined to introduce a raft of technological innovations. It would promote greater use of social media in day schools' communications, recruitment, and fundraising; introduce online learning as a tool for personalizing education; and encourage grantees to use technology for networking their participants, faculty, and alumni into virtual tribes of change-makers.

––––––––

Of all these initiatives, the push for what became known as "Online and Blended Learning" (later, "Online and Personalized Learning") proved to be one of the most ambitious and original. The idea started with an observation in 2010, in a memo by chief technology officer Eli Kannai and senior program officer Rachel Abrahams, that "[d]ay schools have barely begun to take advantage of the world of online learning, which could yield both educational and 'game-changing' financial benefits." Noting the rapid growth in the online learning market—then expanding by around 30 percent a year—Kannai and Abrahams pointed to the obvious benefits for day schools, especially small ones and those in remote areas: "The panoply of courses available online allows students access to almost any subject they wish to study, without needing faculty on site." The Orthodox Union, they reported, had estimated that a day school could save nearly one-third of its budget by using online courses in general studies. For a field strapped for money and struggling to pay competitive salaries to skilled teachers, the prospect of offering state-of-the-art courses with sharply reduced personnel costs could be revolutionary.

AVI CHAI had already experimented with remote or distance learning, having supported courses in American day schools through web-conferencing with teachers based in Israel. Although the model had its difficulties, it was providing very high-quality courses for schools that might otherwise have struggled to offer any courses at all on some Jewish subjects. But the proposed new online model would be both more technologically sophisticated and, if done right, educationally far richer—because it would personalize instruction, allowing students to use the online courses at their own pace, in and outside of the classroom. Teachers, meanwhile, would get real-time data on students' progress from their computerized exercises and would be able to tailor their support for each student accordingly.

The vision became more expansive and ambitious over time. The idea, Yossi Prager explained in 2020, was not simply to transfer ordinary teaching (or even first-rate teaching) from a classroom to a computer screen. It was to create "a different way of thinking about pedagogy. The full realization of this would be about personalizing instruction. The computer allows you to assess individual students' needs as they're learning, then provide a personalized instruction for each student, one by one, that is impossible to do en masse in a classroom. So, for us, the concept went from using tech as a tool to creating a whole different role for the teacher, and then ultimately to real personalization based on real-time assessment of each student's progress."

Schools would probably start simply, by adopting the most elementary version of the idea ("using tech as a tool"), and gradually progress further and further toward a fully personalized kind of instruction. At that final stage, the greatest change would not be on the screen, but in the relationship between student and teacher.

The risk here, as in many of the new directions on which the foundation was embarking, was that online learning was not a desire that had percolated up from the day school field. It was mostly AVI CHAI's idea. A few other visionaries, and at least one other funder, had embraced the concept and begun experimenting with it, including a family foundation that was starting a new high school in New Jersey with an online learning component. But unlike teacher training, enriched curricula, or leadership development—which schools broadly clamored for, even if many were slow to grasp their full potential—online learning would be a cause for which the foundation would have to "seize the attention of the field," as Kannai and Abrahams put it, and try to stir up demand where it currently didn't exist. So, the initial plan was simply to "test the waters and see if interest in this type of schooling can be generated."

That meant that the challenge for AVI CHAI, in the first months after

scizing the online banner, would be double: devise a credible, economi
cal approach to using computer-based learning in day schools, plus stoke
enough demand among enough schools to make the technology infectious—that is, lift it from niche status to the spreading momentum of a
movement. With an initial budget of $1 million, the staff began by plant-
ing seeds in three garden beds.

The first was a handful of established schools that began pioneering
online courses. Efforts in this area started by working through JESNA
(the Jewish Education Service of North America, the educational arm
of the Jewish Federation system) and the Jewish Education Project, a
New York-based nonprofit. Torah Umesorah joined ranks soon afterward, adding some of its network of Orthodox schools to the demonstration. Two years later, the foundation released a Request for Proposals,
together with the nonprofit Affordable Jewish Education Project, that
helped it identify five schools to receive extensive technical help in incorporating online courses into their teaching. These early experiments
gained further steam when the Kohelet Foundation joined in funding
that project, now branded BOLD Schools (Blended and Online Learning in Day Schools).

A second seed bed was smaller but even more intriguing: a few brand-
new schools that wanted to make the most of advanced educational technology and online learning. These schools could, if successful, be national
models of innovation in both teaching and cost-saving. In 2010 and 2011,
the foundation started with grants to two new schools that were still
under development and one existing school that was completely over-
hauling its educational model to become what staff members described
as "a twenty-first-century skills-based program." Staff members had also
been making connections with other funders and educators interested in
forming new schools, and in 2001 they started a "school incubator program so that each interaction with a new venture can be guided by similar principles and funding guidelines."

A third area for cultivation was Jewish content. Given the relatively

good supply of general courses like math and literature, AVI CHAI considered the lack of online Jewish studies courses an obvious, specific need
for day schools that it could help fill. So program officer Galli Aizenman
was dispatched to find course developers who could marshal the right
combination of technical, educational, and Jewish expertise. She started
with Tel Aviv University, which was hoping to develop middle school
courses in Jewish archeology and history, and she opened discussions
with several universities interested in creating courses at the high school
level. Other staff sought to engage Bar-Ilan University in an exploration
of ways to adapt its current distance learning program, which AVI CHAI
had helped launch, to become an online course that students could use
at their own pace.

Meanwhile, the foundation commissioned research on the field and
unveiled it before a gathering of Jewish educators and education funders
in hopes of whetting their appetites for the online model. The gathering
featured booths for educational vendors, among whom AVI CHAI set up
a stand and a separate room for hands-on experience. More than one
hundred participants, including schools and lay leaders as well as funders,
attended programs and presentations, and even more stopped by to visit
the booths. "One of the things everyone commented on," Abrahams
reported, "is the change from two years ago, when we first presented our
new interest [in online learning]. . . . There was a feeling now that this
is the beginning of a movement."

By the end of 2011, the staff had burned through the first $1 million
set aside for this pioneering work and were promptly granted another
$1.5 million. Another $1.4 million followed, and then, in response to a
full five-year plan for all three tracks, plus evaluation and communications, the board approved a stunning $11.5 million roughly a year later.
That plan called for the creation of 200 new Judaic studies courses, a
move toward online and blended learning at 150 established schools, and
the creation of ten new schools built at least partly on an online approach.
It also described the formation of an Online Judaic Studies Consortium,

in which experienced, innovative Jewish studies teachers would create courses and make them available across a network of participating schools. The plan forecast an average 15 percent reduction in operating cost and a measurable boost in instructional quality, with students spending, on average, 35 percent of their time in blended/online sessions. "Within the next four years," Abrahams, Kannai, and Aizenman wrote, "we hope that 150 schools (half of the 300 schools or so in our ambit) will have reached, or will be on their way to reaching, that goal."

Among the staff, enthusiasm for the idea surged in their first few years of seeding the field. "The question," Abrahams told the board in late 2012, "isn't whether or not we should be working in this area." In her view, the only significant question by that point was how to weave the technology, pedagogy, and economics together to create a band-wagon across the day school industry. "We do believe we need a game changer," she concluded, "and this has the potential to be that." Early reports from the research AVI CHAI had been funding showed significant potential for better learning through online and online-plus-classroom study.

Although board discussions on the topic were subdued in the first year or two—more a willingness to listen and see what developed than any sort of confident embrace—a growing receptivity from the field, plus the staff's increasingly buoyant reports, began raising the temperature of board discussions. For example, Mem, who acknowledged being "nervous" at first, grew more enthusiastic about a path that might lead, in a single stroke, not only to a superior education for students—both in Jewish subjects and in everything else—but to marked cost savings for schools. "There will be people who say, 'But you don't know what the outcome of the learning will be—will it be better or not?'" she acknowledged at a board meeting. "I think we should address that right up front. 'We're uncertain, but that doesn't matter. This is the way education will go, and we have to figure out how to make it better.'" Her main worry, at that point, was that the staff may not have been asking for enough money, especially for promoting the idea to schools and funders.

"I was exhilarated by this," Lauren Merkin declared. "I think this is what philanthropy is for, and to see it happen in the Jewish world is an unusually beautiful thing. The pieces are coming together in this rapidly evolving field of online education. Two years ago, we didn't know this would happen." In fact, by 2014, not only was the change happening, but some members of the board and staff believed that the foundation was driving it. "AVI CHAI is now the leading actor in the promotion of BOL [blended and online learning] in Jewish day schools," Prager reported that year. "It seems to our staff unlikely that many day schools would be experimenting with BOL but for AVI CHAI's encouragement, programming, and funding."

Still, a couple of board members remained skeptical. If "this is the way education will go," they asked, why does AVI CHAI need to pour so much money into it? "I want to learn that we aren't doing things that others would have done without our money," said Avital Darmon, a specialist in education. She wondered whether the most advanced and enthusiastic schools and course developers might all have traveled down this path on their own, even without grants. And in that case, might AVI CHAI end up being "left to deal with those who would not have done it themselves"—that is, the less-committed and less tech-savvy players?

Even more grimly (and, as it later turned out, with a dispiriting accuracy) Darmon concluded: "There is no truth to the idea that tech-based whatever could lower the tuition or cost of education. I would not make that promise." Sure enough, within a few years it was becoming clear that the best educational results were coming not from purely online learning, but from the "blended" alternative, where an in-person teacher and a real classroom were an essential part of the student's experience. That model, as Darmon noted, erased much of the savings from computer-based teaching because of the schools' continued need to supply technologically trained educators and maintain physical classrooms and equipment. Barring a giant increase in student-teacher ratios—with uncertain but probably not positive effects on learning and discipline—the hoped-for economic breakthrough could be mostly a chimera.

These views became more prevalent—or at least they raised more and more questions—as time went on. With AVI CHAI's lifespan ticking away, even the more enthusiastic board members worried that the project was too big, demanding too many cultural changes, to end up in secure, durable shape when the foundation's door closed in 2020. Several, including Arthur Fried, frankly doubted that the foundation's contributions would have the desired effects within four to five years, as Prager and his staff had been forecasting. And indeed, by 2017, when the program was supposed to have wrapped up, updated plans were still calling for two more years of foundation effort, plus the need to create a "continuing operating organization" to carry that effort beyond 2020—"since it is increasingly clear that promoting BOL [blended and online learning] will need to be a longer-term activity."[21]

Both the enthusiasts and the skeptics, it seemed, had gotten it right in some respects. Schools had, as hoped, responded avidly to the opportunity to weave online learning into their instruction. Teachers, principals, and parents reported mounting satisfaction to AVI CHAI's evaluators, despite some lingering concerns over the difficulty of mastering the technology and the distance that online tools can sometimes place between students and teachers. The use of the technology in classrooms was climbing sharply year by year—but that trend, and the expressions of satisfaction that evaluators were hearing, were just the first halting steps toward real personalized learning. The change, in most instances, still consisted of what Prager called "using tech as a tool." By 2016, after five years of steady effort, the project was on track to meet its most basic goal of having 150 schools spend one-third of their instruction time in online and blended activities. The Online Judaic Studies Consortium, which launched in 2015, was beginning to show its potential as a source of new courses, with nine schools signed up as members and eleven new courses created in its first two years.

Apart from that, the pedagogic revolution the foundation ultimately hoped for—with real personalized learning in a large number of class-rooms—was still far off. As some skeptics had feared, the culture change that online learning demanded from teachers and schools was taking longer than expected, with more obstacles on the path and a slower rate of adoption, even by the more enthusiastic teachers. Moreover, different online classes and tools worked in different ways, so teachers using different products could not easily learn from one another, and data on student performance were typically not comparable from one online course to another.

As a result, although the use of online tools was spreading, it was uneven and not yet deeply embedded. "In most schools," staff reported in late 2016, "the current use of BOL has not shifted the core instructional model to personalized learning based on ongoing analysis of student performance data." Teachers were using online resources, but many were not fully personalizing instruction, properly using real-time data on student progress, or changing the way they interact with students to make the best use of the new technology. "With all of these challenges," a memo to the board ruefully concluded, "most day schools will not be deeply implementing personalized learning by the time AVI CHAI closes."

Nor would they be saving much money. As Darmon had warned, principals were overwhelmingly concluding that the technology could achieve real improvements in educational quality, or it could help squeeze out meaningful cost savings (mostly by increasing student–teacher ratios), but not both. The idea of imposing revolutionary new teaching methods while also piling significantly larger class sizes onto teachers' shoulders struck most principals as a nonstarter. Some saw a possibility for cost savings later on, once personalized online learning had become standard and teachers were all fully at home with it. But others still suspected that once class sizes swelled enough to make a big difference

In the budget, teaching, learning, and enrollment would all suffer. "When this first came out, it was supposed to be a cost-saver," Merkin acknowledged in 2017, some two years after the program's launch. "This is not a cost-saver. This is a cost."

Nonetheless, these disappointments were not so much signs of failure as of the natural growing pains of an infant industry. The education expert Tom Vander Ark, a former Gates Foundation executive, noted in a September 2016 blog post that the promise of online learning was slow in being realized throughout the country, in schools of every kind, even though adoption was accelerating and the benefits were becoming clearer. "We've made a great deal of progress in the last five years," he wrote, "but we're still very early in the personalized learning revolution."[22] If public and secular schools were struggling to find the best use of this kind of technology, it was no wonder that Jewish day schools, with their leaner budgets and narrower room for error, were likewise still finding their footing. "It might not be a cost-saver today," Mem predicted, "but it ultimately will have to be."

In all, AVI CHAI spent close to $20 million in a decade-long effort to instill personalized online learning across the North American day school landscape. Repeated evaluations had confirmed that "schools participating in our programs see themselves on the path to a new pedagogical approach that they expect will improve learning and increase student enthusiasm," staff reported at the end of 2017. Although most schools had traveled only part of the way down that path, the trend was encouraging. Concerns about teachers' difficulties in using the full pedagogic potential of the new technology were partly eased beginning in 2016, when AVI CHAI piloted a new teacher training and mentoring program run by BetterLesson, a for-profit professional development company. A year later, the Jewish New Teacher Project, already a highly regarded grantee, agreed to expand its mentoring program to cover online and personalized instruction. Both of these steps were aimed at helping teachers adopt a more personalized approach to their work

and embrace what Prager called "a different way of thinking about pedagogy."

But foundation support for these two late-stage efforts could extend
only till the lights went out at the end of 2019, leaving both of them still
in an embryonic stage when AVI CHAI funding ceased. In truth, the whole
body of work in this area remained a grand experiment, promising but
unproven and in many respects still inchoate, when the foundation made
its last grant. By that time, Prager and most of the staff had come to
regret the program's late start and were anxious about its prospects for
future gains. Even so, trustees mostly expressed satisfaction with the
effort and a reasonable level of comfort with the uncertainties that lay
ahead.

Then, when the coronavirus pandemic reached North America in the
spring of 2020, the initiative suddenly acquired a new and more urgent
significance. With schools closing from coast to coast, struggling to hold
classes remotely and uncertain about when or how they could reopen
safely, day schools that had started to incorporate online courses found
themselves with a slight head start. Online and personalized learning
was never meant to be a substitute for brick-and-mortar classrooms, of
course. But an ability to guide students through virtual learning was
plainly an advantage for teachers trying to navigate the difficult new
world conjured by the pandemic. Writing in the online journal *Mosaic*,*
Jason Bedrick, an expert in educational policy, suggested that the spread
of virtual learning in Jewish day schools might well be "opening up new
potential to deliver high-quality instruction that is also affordable," and
that the pressures of school closures and partial reopenings would likely
increase interest in the new technology.[23]

"It was a leap of faith to go into this," Ruth Wisse said as the foundation's support for online learning was drawing to a close, "but I think it

---

* *Mosaic* is published by an affiliate of the Tikvah Fund, a nonprofit that, like AVI CHAI, was
created and funded by Zalman Bernstein.

was a necessary one. This was an experiment we had to begin to work
with. As far as evaluating it is concerned, the only way to test it is to see
what happens once it becomes routinized. Will the routinization of this
kind of learning work better than the routinization of the teacher stand-
ing in front of the room? You won't know that [before the program ends],
so you won't be able to use that as a selling point" in pitching the idea to
other funders. "The selling point," she concluded, "will have to be your
faith in this as an experiment."

————

Although the push for personalized, online education was among AVI
CHAI's most ambitious attempts at pedagogic change in day schools, its
earlier efforts in curriculum development were also intended to make a
lasting change in the way certain subjects were taught. Chief among
these were the high school Hebrew language curriculum called NETA
and the combined Jewish studies and Hebrew program known as TaL
AM, both of which had sailed through the 2009 winnowing exercise
with high scores. But from that point on, the question for AVI CHAI was
how to ensure that the market for both programs would ultimately keep
them alive beyond AVI CHAI's approaching sunset.

NETA offered an elegant but demanding study regimen for high
schoolers, intended to produce functional fluency in modern Hebrew by
the time students graduate. It consisted of written, audio, and video
teaching materials, plus intensive professional development, mentoring,
and certificate courses for teachers. Its exceptional quality and high
(some said unyielding) standards won praise from language-learning
experts, but it demanded a level of commitment from both schools and
students that wasn't always attainable. It also demanded exceptionally
skilled Hebrew teachers, who were not exactly abundant in the work-
force. In schools that shared NETA's passionate dedication to full Hebrew fluency (of which there were nearly ninety in North America and
thirty in other countries as of 2012), the program tended to be popular

with educators, if not always with students. But raising those numbers was going to be a challenge. Market penetration was leveling off, and when AVI CHAI's subsidies for schools using the program ended in 2011, a few started dropping out.

In the struggle between maintaining excellence and widening the market, NETA's creator and leader, Hilla Kobliner, had rated excellence above all. Privately, many at AVI CHAI worried that the result, once the foundation was no longer supporting NETA, could be just a gorgeous failure—a beautiful feat of pedagogy that was too perfect to survive in the real marketplace.

As in so many other areas, a good part of the solution seemed to lie in technology—making the program more interactive and flexible, "more intuitive and easier for students to use with less teacher mediation," as program officer Leah Meir summed it up in a 2012 memo. The foundation approached the Center for Educational Technology in Jerusalem, a frequent grantee and collaborator, to see if a partnership between NETA and CET might help more schools adopt the program, expand its appeal to students, ease its demands on teachers, and harness technology to make it what Meir called "a 21st century program for Hebrew language teaching." CET welcomed the challenge, though the idea of altering the program in significant ways was likely to demand careful deliberation with Kobliner and her team.

The eventual plan called for CET to acquire NETA in full, with the gradual merger completed by the end of the 2015–16 school year. It would require roughly $250,000 a year more than AVI CHAI was already contributing to NETA, but the end goal seemed to be worth the expense: the program was projected to be self-supporting, primarily from fees from participating schools, by the time the merger was a year old. Kobliner would oversee the content of all the new material, both digital and in print, ensuring that it would preserve what was best about the original curriculum. Given all the complexities of the merger—organizational, financial, pedagogic, technological, and personal—the best Meir could say about it in 2012 was that it "has at least a reasonable prospect for success." But of all the risky paths forward, it seemed the brightest.

By late 2016, when financial independence was supposed to be in sight, big questions remained. Although revenues from school fees were roughly on track, the expected cost reductions hadn't yet fully materialized. Along the way, AVI CHAI had contributed another $2 million, mostly to develop a more affordable teacher mentoring program. With additional effort, however, the gaps seemed fillable, and the prospect of a sustainable program, renamed Bishvil Ha-Ivrit, was well within reach. Some aspects of the merger had been bumpy, and as many observers feared, relations between Kobliner and CET were often strained. By 2016, nearing retirement age, she had agreed to step aside as director and assume a consultant role, but the transition was difficult both for her and for some members of her staff. Nonetheless, even acknowledging all the difficulties, Prager concluded that AVI CHAI's $20 million investment had produced something of tremendous value—both as a practical means of instruction for close to 20,000 students a year worldwide and as a standard of superior teaching of Hebrew that has garnered respect and widespread use even in Israel.

AVI CHAI's other major investment in Hebrew language instruction, TaL AM, likewise involved both a technological makeover and a corporate merger, as well as an eventual transition from visionary founders to a new generation of leaders. In the case of TaL AM, however, the market dynamics had been consistently positive. The product, aimed at the early elementary grades, was popular with both schools and students, and the project's financial management had been astute and steady enough so that it could clearly have carried on, at least to some degree, well beyond AVI CHAI's last grant. It had also become, like NETA, a centerpiece of the foundation's program for Jewish and Hebrew education in the former Soviet Union, where TaL AM was taught in more than two dozen schools by 2012. Its proliferation there, reaching thousands of students, had the backing of the Jewish Agency for Israel and a major Russian–Jewish philanthropist.

For TaL AM, the main question was not about financial sustainability, at least in the near term. It was about the riptides of twenty-first-century education: unpredictable, crosscutting currents of technological change, a trend toward personalized learning, and a frantic search for efficiencies in school costs. At the dawn of the tech era, this was still a program anchored in print publications, with all the expense of production, distribution, and updating that entailed, and where teacher training was still done in person, through costly seminars and one-on-one mentoring. At this point, a portion of those costs was still being subsidized by AVI CHAI grants, but those would not last more than a few more years. For TaL AM, therefore, conditions on the horizon could well be hazardous even if the present seemed calm.[24]

And AVI CHAI's investment in TaL AM had been formidable: close to $13 million as of 2010. Rather than cast such a successful program, and such a huge investment, to the unforeseeable winds of educational change, the foundation chose in 2011 to start a whole new conversation with TaL AM. It asked Tova and Shlomo Shimon, who had created the program fifteen years earlier and had led it admirably ever since, to draw up a vision of what a fully digital TaL AM would look like—in essence, to tailor AVI CHAI's vision of blended and online learning specifically for this program.

Their first response struck the foundation as too modest, essentially just a digitized version of the print curricula. The problem was that a more thorough reimagination of the program was beyond the Shimons' technical acumen, however fully they might conjure it in their imagination. It would need real experts in command of the full arsenal of interactive tools and methods. But to be really useful—to help make the digital TaL AM as popular and effective as the analog version had been—those tech experts would also need to be at home both in Hebrew and in the practical world of teaching and managing in real-world schools. But after scouring the landscape, the Shimons and AVI CHAI's chief technology officer, Kannai, came to the dispiriting conclusion that no organization in the nonprofit world could meet that set of requirements.

When Kannai reported their disappointment to the AVI CHAI board, he got a question that changed the conversation. "Why does it have to be a nonprofit?" trustee Alan Feld asked. "Why don't we look for a for-profit company?" Merkin, another trustee at the table, remembered thinking, "Hey, right! Why not?" From that point on, she said, "It created a curiosity in Tova [Shimon] and everybody else. It was one of those 'Aha!' moments where something completely un-thought-of becomes something obvious." And, as it happened, at least one for-profit firm came reasonably close to fitting the whole bill.

Feld's idea would have posed no special challenge, if all that was needed was for a team of consultants to work with TaL AM under contract, produce a digital product, collect a fee, and leave. But Fried and Prager, among others, had long felt that that wouldn't be enough. In their view, a real twenty-first-century educational product would have to be owned and maintained not only by great educators, but also by the same kind of tech specialists who helped create it. It would need continual updating, an ability to adapt to technological and educational change, and a means of absorbing data from schools and students to guide future versions of the program. In short, the relationship between TaL AM and its technical experts needed to be not contractual but co-equal. This needed to be a partnership, and that would mean marrying a nonprofit to a profit-making firm.

It would be unconventional, for sure, and in some circumstances it might be a recipe for conflict. But this case seemed different. Under Shlomo Shimon's organizational and financial management, TaL AM already operated in many ways like a business—funding its operations largely with revenue from products sold, reinvesting excess revenue in the maintenance and improvement of its curricula. A for-profit firm dedicated to education, with sufficient respect for TaL AM's mission and strengths, might well be able to form a productive relationship. The firm in question, the Israel-based company Compedia, had carved a significant market niche in educational gaming—a good fit with the all-enveloping, fun-but-serious approach that the original TaL AM had perfected. And although the relationship between the company and the nonprofit had been "strongly encouraged" by AVI CHAI, the resulting interaction seemed to function relatively well. ("Strongly encouraged" was Prager's phrase; at least one staff member privately noted that a nearly $6 million grant, conditioned on a full partnership, made it "an offer TaL AM couldn't refuse.") Most importantly, the brains behind the pedagogy—in this case, Tova Shimon—would retain considerable influence over the content.

Admittedly, that was not always an easy proposition. Much like Kobliner, Tova was a perfectionist, accustomed to overseeing every element of the curriculum and how it was used. In creating the original program, she had scrutinized and revised the placement of every graphic element, the vocabulary in every line of text, the exact shade of every color, often in multiple iterations. The result had been a crushing workload and a pace of development far below what most fast-paced tech firms would tolerate. But it ensured that the quality of the end product was unparalleled.

Digital products aren't made that way. They aren't refined and polished and refined again to achieve perfection before anyone ever uses them. Unlike books and printed materials, which are prohibitively expensive to reprint and redistribute after they're sold, software can be revised, corrected, and enriched continually, including long after a product has been released into the market. Besides, the new vision for what would now be known as iTaLAM would have many times the number of elements that went into the analog version—hundreds of activities and games, animations, songs, and spoken and written texts, including nearly one hundred e-books, making up a whole learning environment online, specifically tailored to each student's needs. The complexity was far more than anyone could manage at the level of precision Tova preferred. She recognized the complexities and learned to accommodate the faster pace of development, at least to some extent, but the adjustment was never easy. AVI CHAI program officer Joel Einleger, an admirer of hers who eventually joined the iTaLAM board, described the adjustment as "painful" but ultimately productive. She maintained as much control as she could—with beneficial effects that no one else would likely have produced—and yielded where she had to. "She's a perfectionist," Einleger said, "but not an obstructionist."

With AVI CHAI's new multimillion-dollar investment, the digital re-engineering of TaL AM began in 2013 and proceeded—much as the creation of the original product had—grade by grade, year by year, with the curriculum for each new grade developed in year X, field-tested in year X+1, and released in year X+2. As each grade was launched, the next one was in development. Meanwhile, melding a nonprofit organization into a for-profit one proved at least as complicated as the software development. After five grinding years of negotiation, the new organization, housed at Compedia's headquarters in Tel Aviv, was essentially finalized with a "Founders Agreement"—a governing document that some compared to a constitution. Even then, some aspects of the partnership remained open for review. By the time the document was completed and signed in 2018, much of the new iTaLAM had already been designed, piloted, and in use in more than 150 schools.

One other factor in iTalAM's leadership had been part of the original idea of restructuring, though it was an especially difficult one to conceive. Tova and Shlomo Shimon were nearing retirement age, and they had always been the living embodiment of their program. "They were the soul of TaL AM," as Einleger put it. "It was almost impossible to think of TaL AM without the Shimons." Yet they could not run it forever. The organization had no succession plan and no obvious successor—at precisely the moment when it would be making a yearslong market transition from print to digital production that would demand an array of new technical and business skills from its managers. For AVI CHAI, arranging a smart leadership succession—acceptable to the Shimons, consistent with the spirit and exacting standards of the program, but also ready to excel in the digital marketplace—was as crucial as launching the new technology.

Despite all the obvious emotional difficulties, Tova accepted this challenge as well as all the others. After a long search, she recommended Shoshi Becker, a leader in education and language instruction with experience in both North America and Israel. The iTaLAM board, which included representatives of the program's founders, funders, and Compedia, approved the selection in 2014, and Becker took over in July of that year. Tova remained a consultant in the completion of the curriculum and a resource to both Becker and the board.

The blended learning product that Tova, Compedia, and eventually Becker were developing was unlike anything in Jewish education (and so was the scale of its development, with as many as forty-five people working on the program, most of them full time). Organized around a few core domains of content—Shabbat, Torah, holidays, daily Jewish life, and Hebrew—iTaLAM covers a panoply of academic, language, and life skills relevant to Jewish text and practice. Any given task, such as a game or exercise, can be presented to a student at his or her own level of proficiency, with the degree of difficulty escalating or declining as students make their way through the material. Students can experiment, make mistakes, and try out newfound skills without fear of embarrassment or awkwardness in front of their classmates—because their "classmates," for any given exercise, are a group of virtual peers on the computer screen, whose abilities match the students' own. The digital environment in which all this takes place is all-encompassing, engrossing, and often fun.

By 2016, the product was passing its most important initial tests. In that year, as the Grade 2 curriculum came onto the market, demand from schools proved to be at least as strong as expected. Subsequent releases have likewise sold well. AVI CHAI made a final $3.2 million grant in 2017 to allow for the completion of Grade 4—bringing the foundation's total investment in iTaLAM and its predecessor to around $22 million. Soon thereafter, in 2018, the Azrieli Foundation, based in Canada and Israel, committed $5 million to produce material for Grade 5, expand the assessment tools by which teachers measure student progress, and broaden online training opportunities for teachers. The combination of the Azrieli investment; contributions from the Gruss Life Monument Funds, a Jewish educational foundation; the remainder of AVI CHAI's final grant; and strong sales performance now appeared sufficient to carry iTaLAM to the end of its product development, and to let it begin thinking about ways of expanding to more markets.

Looking ahead in 2019, as AVI CHAI was preparing to close its grant-making window, Merkin—who had been serving as chair of iTaLAM's board—pointed out that plenty of challenges still loomed on the horizon. The demands on schools' time were multiplying, she said, and the number of hours devoted to Jewish study was shrinking. Parents' anxieties about studying Hebrew, compared with other languages, had not gone away. And products competing with iTaLAM, even lower-quality ones, could put it at a price disadvantage.

"The whole transition to being a company that has to compete to sell things isn't something that the old TaL AM had to face," she noted. "Back then, there was nothing comparable on the market. A lot of things have happened at the same time: technological change, market change, educational change, and Tova's personal transition. There was a lot going on, but in the end, everybody played to their strengths." That included the foundation, as she saw it: AVI CHAI's funding had been generous and flexible, and she considered its investment of time and energy in the merger close to heroic. "We saw this as an opportunity and a responsibility," Merkin concluded, "so we never did it on a shoestring. It's a gift to a foundation to find something like this to support."

Even in the midst of widespread changes in education and technology, some challenges for Jewish education remained familiar and perennial, including finding top talent to lead schools and pursue excellence. This was a subject AVI CHAI had been laboring on since its earliest commitment to day schools, but in the final decades of its grantmaking, the topic didn't seem ripe with new possibilities. Principals and heads of schools needed training in leadership, management, administration, and pedagogy. Many of them had relevant expertise and experience, but also some big gaps—especially in the specific skills needed for running a school steeped in Jewish culture and learning. Programs like the summer institute for principals at Harvard and the Day School Leadership Training Institute at Jewish Theological Seminary had been supplying a portion of those needs year after year, and they would continue to do so. A newer program at Yeshiva University, called YU Lead (later renamed YOU Lead), nurtured teachers and junior administrators for eventual promotion to become heads of Orthodox day schools, and that program was likewise carrying on and meeting its targets.

But as AVI CHAI's attention zeroed in more specifically on cultivating Jewish literacy, religious purposefulness, and an attachment to the Jewish people worldwide—the LRP formula—the question increasingly arose: Are these training programs recruiting and nurturing school leaders with a *specific passion for these three values*, and the skills necessary to inculcate them in their students? Even assuming, as evaluations had routinely found, that the programs produced markedly more effective principals, and thus better-run, higher-quality day schools, was that enough? Or was there a deeper Jewish challenge for schools and their leaders that AVI CHAI might still be able to tackle before its last check was signed?

In 2013, even as the foundation was starting to plan a gradual diminution in its support for these programs—to encourage them to start raising money from other sources—it also sought to layer on some additional content in Jewish literacy, religion, and peoplehood. In response, JTS added these components to its leadership training curriculum, and AVI CHAI created a pre- and post-summer component for participants in the Harvard program, where they would master ways of "raising the bar on the level, quality, and depth of Jewish studies and Jewish life" in their schools. This extra component was costly, and the odds of its continuing beyond AVI CHAI's lifespan weren't great. But together, JTS, Harvard, and YU trained more than 700 people between 2013 and 2019. The additional layer of effort meant that those programs would now be seeding the field with leaders who spoke the language of LRP, saw it as a core part of their job description, and were better equipped to translate that language into educational reality.

Still, as the foundation faced its concluding years, its hope for these programs went beyond just training a few hundred principals with more attention to L, R, and P. The bigger question was how to spread the message *beyond* those programs and give it momentum that would outlast the foundation. What could be done to help those newly trained and inspired principals promote these core concepts among their peers—broadcasting the message that to offer a quality Jewish education, schools needed L, R, and P at the heart of their leadership, teaching, and student life?

As in other matters, the answer seemed to lie in building networks and fomenting tribes and movements. And for that, the tool of choice was the internet. To "intertwine a network of day school leaders,"[25] a staff memo suggested—to help them learn from one another, share their achievements and difficulties, work together on common projects, and generally reinforce the centrality of L, R, and P—the foundation set out in 2013 to create the LRP Collaborative, "a central nondenominational clearinghouse" for day school principals everywhere. Starting with a $1 million budget, the foundation designated a coordinator to recruit participants for an online community of day school leaders and help them get started working on common challenges.

The participants would focus on projects developed jointly with peers in other schools, aimed at advancing the LRP agenda. Some early examples included adapting Jewish studies or Hebrew curricula to suit particular groups of students, or helping teachers devise new methods or activities to deepen students' Jewish experience. Perhaps, the foundation reasoned, with enough encouragement and support in the next few years, the network would become so valuable to its members that they would sustain it beyond AVI CHAI's lifetime. But even if not, the channels of communication and collaboration that it would create might help to galvanize a sense of common purpose among the more dedicated principals, and help galvanize the network into a sort of tribe, or even the vanguard of a movement.

It was far from a typical AVI CHAI project—it was decentralized, bottom-up, somewhat free-form in content, driven by the participants themselves rather than by the foundation or a designated grantee. But it was inexpensive, and it followed Mem's determination to make maximum use of technology before the foundation ended its run. That was enough to make it worth a try. Beginning with just eight participants in 2014, the LRP Collaborative had grown within two years to some three dozen schools, with nearly twenty peer-to-peer projects under development.

But the number of participating schools and projects mostly plateaued after that point, and too few principals, who were supposed to be the network's prime users, were able to devote much time to it. Evaluators found that the information members were exchanging and the projects they were developing together had demonstrable, positive consequences, at least for the schools where they were applied. But neither the number of schools nor the enthusiasm of participants had risen to the level that AVI CHAI had hoped for, or that the power of the internet seemed to promise.

It was also becoming clearer that the small field of day school principals was an especially difficult place to build momentum and movements. For one thing, the demands on day school principals were onerous. They had to be accomplished educators, managers, financial planners, fundraisers, marketers, and communicators. All of those skills were covered, one way or another, in the AVI CHAI-sponsored training programs, but none of them can be mastered in a matter of months, much less weeks. Under all these pressures, principals often burned out in a few years, and the most accomplished ones could often be lured to bigger, better-paying schools. Lay boards at day schools could also be demanding, sometimes unwisely so, which only added to the stress. The result of all these factors was a short average tenure for principals, which made the expense of training them a risky proposition both for the foundation and for the schools that were paying part of their tuition.

Nor was LRP always an easy proposition for principals, their boards, and their teachers to rally around. In a darkly frank assessment in 2015, a staff team acknowledged that "increasing percentages of American Jews find AVI CHAI's LRP aspirations—serious text study and literacy, a life of committed practice, and allegiance to Israel and one's people— irrelevant and uncompelling." In twenty-first-century society—even among Orthodox Jews, and more so among other denominations— religion was increasingly being seen as a personal, private matter, not a call to a larger, communal responsibility. Regular attendance at non-Orthodox synagogues was down, and the search for individual spiritual meaning, rather than inherited precepts and traditions, was increasingly common. Because LRP bucks all those trends, the staff memo concluded, it is inherently "countercultural"—a fact that "makes it harder and harder for leaders infused with AVI CHAI's ideals to find allies and supporters to changes they want to implement back in their schools."[26]

Still, the board chose to persevere, even against the "serious headwinds" the memo had described. School leadership made so great a difference in the quality of a school—and particularly in its Jewish quality—that even incremental progress was worth the struggle. If the foundation was unable to have a transformative effect on the whole field, it could nudge the bar upward, introduce aspirations, demonstrate ways of meeting them, and hope that the freshly trained and motivated corps of principals graduating from AVI CHAI programs would, little by little, spread the news outward.

Evaluations could not measure the odds of that happening, of course. But they could, and did, show that the training had a profound effect on the principals who took part in it. Toward the end of AVI CHAI's grant-making, in 2018, the principal of the lower school at Hebrew Academy of Long Beach, New York, Rabbi Richard Altabe, wrote a spontaneous note to Prager to thank the foundation for training opportunities that had left him permanently "enriched, revitalized, and burning with a passion to implement new ideas."

"Most programs give participants that feeling for a brief period of time," he continued. But his experience in the Harvard summer program "changed the way I view education" in ways that "serve me to this very day." Later, he attended the AVI CHAI-sponsored program at the Look-stein Center of Bar-Ilan University in Israel, where he delved more deeply into methods of curriculum development, particularly in Judaic studies, and management planning—techniques and skills that he has not only used but has passed on as a mentor to other principals.

"I am not sure every dollar the AVI CHAI Foundation has invested in Jewish education was used to the fullest," he concluded, "but I can tell you that every dollar invested in me helped hundreds if not thousands of children in the New York area. If not for the professional development I had, I would have left the field years ago. If there is an argument to be made for the value of top-level professional development for school lead-ers, consider me your poster child."

———————

Another perennial challenge for day schools—and in some ways the most fundamental of them all—was their chronically skeletal financial structure. This was a concern that AVI CHAI's board had agonized over

almost since the beginning of its involvement in Jewish education, and
the picture had grown no sunnier in the intervening years. Not only did
schools tend to function with barely balanced books and little to no
operating cushion, but their budgets often required them to charge tuition at levels that excluded many otherwise interested families. Now,
with the foundation set to close its doors in less than a decade, the time
seemed ripe for one final push for ways to make day schools—at least a
decent number of them—financially stronger, more stable, and more
affordable.

The theory was that schools not only needed more donors—which
pointed to a separate line of AVI CHAI effort, in its search for funding
partners and successors—but that they might also be able to achieve
some efficiencies that could bring costs down. Those efficiencies might
involve sharing some administrative and training functions or reducing
educational expenses, such as through online learning. Best of all would
be some form of reliable government funding to ease the tuition burden.

For all those hopes, Prager recalled, the decade began at "a point of
optimism, where we thought some combination of blended learning,
government funding, and greater efficiencies of some kind would offer a
way of making day school dramatically more affordable." In 2012, the
foundation hired Dan Perla, a new program officer with a background
at investment firms and hedge funds, to guide the push for a stronger
day school business model.

As a direct effort to boost fundraising and stabilize budgets, the foundation first backed a program called Generations, based at the funding
alliance known as PEJE, the Project for Excellence in Jewish Education.
The aim was to help schools build endowments by giving their lay leaders and on-staff fundraisers high-level training and then following up
with further coaching as they began seeking endowment grants. As an
incentive, schools that met their targets would win a $25,000 bonus. The
program plainly wasn't suited to all day schools—many didn't have professional fundraisers, and not all boards had the kinds of connections

that made large-scale fundraising feasible. But where it worked, Generations racked up remarkable results. By 2018, forty-four schools had completed the program and had fed a total of $80 million into their endowments, an average of $5,300 per student. That amount was more than 25 percent above the most optimistic initial estimates of what the program could achieve.

Encouraged by the success of Generations, AVI CHAI next supported two new "revenue academies" at PEJE, beginning in 2015. The first helped day schools' boards become more effective at general fundraising and financial oversight; the other sought to improve student recruitment and retention to boost income from tuition. Both academies followed the Generations model of skills training followed by eighteen months of effort guided by coaches. And although they didn't match the breakout performance of Generations, both academies exceeded their performance targets.

Perla meanwhile spun out a host of other experiments, including soliciting proposals from groups of schools willing to work together on issues like energy savings, back-office integrations, and joint fundraising. Two of these were aimed at community-wide fundraising, through Jewish congregations and community organizations, to offer tuition assistance for needy children attending any day school in a designated area. The idea was not only to raise money, but to encourage whole communities to see day school education as a communal responsibility, to which everyone felt called to contribute. Another experiment involved working with a few schools to try a means-tested approach to tuition, in which the full tuition would be raised for better-off families, but those with lower incomes or more children could get a break.

Another initiative was meant to build on the success of the ongoing MATCH program, which doubled the contributions of first-time donors to Jewish education or those who made much bigger donations than they had in the past. MATCH had poured almost $60 million into day schools nationally by the end of 2015, and people who joined the program overwhelmingly continued donating to day schools even after they no longer qualified for a match. From that record of success, the foundation concluded that a new, more locally focused version of the program might achieve even more. The theory was that wealthy day school donors might be persuaded to create mini-MATCH programs in their own localities, where they could appeal to new contributors with a locally focused message. The program started in Chicago and Montreal in 2015, but the amounts raised were well below expectations, and outreach to three other communities went nowhere. Another matching program was focused on the New York area and concentrated on endowment building. It was funded jointly with the New York Federation and the Jim Joseph Foundation, but it likewise ended up benefiting only about half as many schools as had been hoped.

By far the most ambitious of AVI CHAI's efforts to shore up the economics of day schools was its support for campaigns to win government funding. Under U.S. tax law, a private foundation may not pay for lobbying, so AVI CHAI could not, and did not, directly support attempts to push legislation. But foundations can make general operating grants to underwrite research and public information projects undertaken by organizations that also, separately, promote legislation. Although foundation money could not be spent on attempts at persuading lawmakers to back a particular bill, it could fund other aspects of the campaign, including public advocacy for the general idea of public tuition assistance and research to determine the costs, benefits, and other policy implications of any given approach.

The foundation backed two such campaigns. One was by an interreligious coalition seeking a new tax credit in New York State, under which donors who provide scholarships for private school tuition would receive a state tax credit in return. The idea made surprising progress for a while but ultimately hit a roadblock in the State Assembly. The outreach to legislators did help in winning a one-time state grant to private schools, including day schools, but not an ongoing subsidy. After that, the sponsors turned their attention to Washington, seeking a similar scholarship tax credit in the 2017 tax reform bill, which was then making its way through Congress. But that, too, ultimately fell short. A separate effort by Yeshiva University sought a more modest federal tax deduction for a portion of day school tuition. It didn't succeed either.

These were always going to be uphill battles, given the long history of political and legal obstacles to public funding for religious schools. AVI CHAI spent only $1.5 million on the two campaigns, so trustees generally considered them a reasonable, small bet on something that might, if successful, have paid huge returns. And the momentum they built still continues to some extent, even if immediate success has been elusive.

The deeper problem was that the whole panoply of projects to shore up day school economics ended up making far less of a difference than anyone on the board or staff had hoped. Several of these projects made measurable improvements, particularly the "revenue academies," which raised the standard of practice for many schools and strengthened their finances. The local grant-matching programs, despite the disappointing level of participation, certainly benefited the schools that did participate.

But these were incremental improvements, not a fundamental change in the brittle economy of day schools. The search for efficiencies was probably the most disappointing. Day school budgets are generally too lean for cost-cutting measures to have much effect. The suggestion that schools ought to share some of their administrative functions or otherwise shake up their basic operations for just a morsel of savings proved to be a blind alley.

Even so, incremental improvement is still improvement, and most trustees considered these efforts worth the time and money that went into them. Many schools had benefited, even if the underlying business model remained unsteady. But, as Prager put it in the last months of the foundation's grantmaking life, "I feel like we never really solved the

problem. I don't know what we should have done that we didn't do—
maybe if we'd started earlier. But in the time we had to spend on this;
I don't think we licked it."

Although she encouraged all these efforts, Mem confessed some
years later that she had never really believed the goal was achievable.
"There is no way that we were going to make schools affordable without
government support," she said in an interview in 2020. She pointed out
that Jewish education survives in the rest of North America, in Canada
and Mexico, with national subsidies, not primarily from philanthropy.
"We gave government support our best shot. We tried. But it just wasn't
going to happen in America at that time. And without that, nothing else
was going to bring day school tuition to a level that would be affordable
to most families. It was a good dream, but it was a dream."

For most of its history of supporting Jewish education, AVI CHAI had
backed institutions that provided field-wide services and support to large
numbers of day schools. This was in keeping with the foundation's determination to deal with the field not just as a collection of separate,
struggling enterprises, but as an educational and cultural system—not
just individual stars, but constellations. The larger institutions AVI CHAI
supported were mostly associated with particular religious denominations—the Schechter Day School Network for the Conservative Movement, RAVSAK for Community schools, Yeshiva University's School
Partnership for the Orthodox. PEJE was also a broad-based support
institution like these, though it was nondenominational.

The value of these umbrella organizations was primarily that they
provided things to schools that would be too expensive or too complicated for schools to provide for themselves. "So much of schools' outcomes depend on local factors such as funding and faculty," Prager wrote
to the board in early 2015, "but strong schools also depend on central-
ized, national efforts to develop curricula, train principals, strengthen

fundraising, generate communal advocacy, and circulate best practices," among other things. The broad-based intermediary institutions had come to specialize in these field-wide services, and schools had come to rely on them.

But as AVI CHAI prepared to close its grant windows in 2020, the future for this roster of intermediary institutions looked murky. Each performed valuable functions that would be hard, maybe impossible, to replace. Yet all of them were on shaky fiscal ground, and it seemed clear that at least a few of them would not outlast AVI CHAI for very long. It's not that the foundation had been the sole source of all or most of their support—though in some cases it was the largest single source of grants. Rather, AVI CHAI had for several years been their most consistent cheerleader and funder, especially of their core administrative expenses. Without that kind of backing, they would be on thin ice—as, indeed, they already were, even with foundation support.

In 2012, the Jim Joseph Foundation told AVI CHAI that it was interested in supporting the kind of work these institutions were doing. But it had concluded that their prospects for survival were dire, and that it would be foolish to just write checks to them until, one by one, they failed and disappeared. Instead, Jim Joseph said it would support them only if the four would merge into a more efficient single entity, pooling their expertise to serve the entire day school field across all denominations. The suggestion took AVI CHAI by surprise. Not only was the foundation not expecting the sudden ultimatum, but it was not convinced that a merger among these four disparate groups—each representing its own unique form of Judaism—was even possible.

But after well over a year of observation, consultation, and thought, AVI CHAI changed its mind. "We now view a consolidation as possible," Prager wrote to the board, "because the organizations' fundraising challenges have led us (and them) to believe that only a single group serving schools across the spectrum has the potential to draw more philanthropists into national funding." Besides, he noted, each of the four organizations had specialties and forms of expertise that would be useful to all schools but were currently available only to schools in that organization's network. Several of them also offered similar services that were inefficiently duplicative—each, for example, had a leadership development and mentoring program—and consolidating those seemed like an obvious choice. Most encouraging of all was a slow drumbeat of calls from prominent Jewish donors, including some current and former donors to PEJE, for a consolidated national day school intermediary. Several people privately told Prager that they weren't inclined to donate to several fractious groups but would welcome an opportunity to build and support a unified structure.

Admittedly, there were sensitive personal and denominational tensions that would have to be overcome. These organizations were competitive and proud of their distinctive ways of doing things; their leaders did not see the world in the same way and were not close colleagues. None of them were inclined to surrender their mission and organizational culture to the others. Would RAVSAK, for example, representing pluralistic schools with families at many levels of observance, be at home working with an organization dedicated to solidly religious Orthodox education? Would either of them be able to provide services to the other's constituents without seeming alien or discordant? The lack of familiarity among the heads of the four organizations surely made the differences in their missions seem all the more formidable and may have contributed to a level of distrust—all factors that made it hard to get a conversation started among them.

The good news was that the four had no illusions about the difficulties ahead. For several years, they had worked together on an annual joint conference, a project that was always fraught with tensions and disagreements. Yet they also agreed that some kind of collaborative union would be needed if all of them—or perhaps even any of them—were going to survive. A fifth organization soon joined the group: a cluster of roughly a dozen Reform schools, called PARDeS (for Progressive Association of

Reform Day Schools, no relation to the Pardes Institute in Jerusalem). Although this organization was smaller and more narrowly focused than the others, its inclusion meant that the prospective merger would encompass every branch of Jewish education except for the fervently Orthodox network of Torah Umesorah, which had always worked separately and was economically independent.

At first, AVI CHAI took the organizations' recognition of the need for cooperation as a promising sign. It seemed that they might work out a merger on their own, if given some planning resources, a little time, and what Prager described as "a light touch" of encouragement from the foundation. That didn't happen—the level of trust among the participants simply wasn't great enough to drive them together without an external force. So, with some reluctance—"If we keep going down this path," Merkin worried in early 2015, "it will be our project," and AVI CHAI would have to sink serious money into the resulting merger—the foundation took up the cause and applied more serious pressure. In essence, AVI CHAI told the participating groups, there would be no more support for their organizational management and capacity building unless it were part of a merger process.

If they agreed—which they ultimately did, though warily—the foundation would fund the planning and negotiations, retain top-level consultants to design a structure acceptable to all of them, provide program and operating support to each organization during the negotiations, and make a final grant to carry the new union through its first few years. That would include temporarily paying for the salary and benefits for a new CEO. (None of the heads of the constituent organizations wanted the job, which AVI CHAI regarded as fortunate.) But, for any of that to happen, the participating organizations would have to agree to be "all in," meaning that they would set the merger as their top priority, speak and behave supportively toward one another at all times, publicly and privately and at every level of their organizations, and halt all new programs and solicitation of new members until the merger was consummated.

The phrase "all in" was AVI CHAI's coinage. It was meant to define a standard of unreserved cooperation that would preclude mere lip service, hedging, or, worst of all, stirring up enmity. The price for not being all in, Prager and his colleagues explained to the prospective collaborators, was being all out. That is, organizations that were not prepared to commit heart and mind to the merger would find themselves on their own financially—a prospect that, for most of them, would mean either a slow death or a fast one. In the end, many people found that they were uncomfortable staying all in, and stepped away. A few staff or board members of some participating organizations wanted to try surviving on their own and objected to the whole effort. Eventually, most of the staff members, including all of the executive directors, made quiet exits, either during the negotiations or soon thereafter. But that left a cadre of believers and new recruits who were willing to follow the funder's lead, hope for the best, and at least try to avoid the worst.

It was, Prager later admitted, "a tremendous exercise of power" by a foundation that had long prided itself on a respectful, arms-length relationship with its grantees. This was an abrupt departure from that tradition, an unprecedented use of muscle for AVI CHAI, even compared with the Zalman Bernstein years, when exacting demands on some grantees had led to occasional hard feelings. To temper what Prager called (ruefully, and with some exaggeration) the "brute force" of this ultimatum, he and the other foundation representatives who worked on the merger were at constant pains to deal sympathetically, confidentially, and candidly with each participant and to try to build genuine harmony and trust among them.

Over the course of about eighteen months, foundation staff members, prominently Deena Fuchs and Susan Kardos as well as Prager, served as negotiators, counselors, mediators, brainstorming partners—and, most of all, provident funders whenever circumstances required an extraordinary expenditure. For the duration of the negotiations, thanks to AVI CHAI, the participating organizations were spared any need to fundraise (though, admittedly, fundraising for a cluster of not-yet-merged but no-longer-fully-independent organizations would surely have been fruitless in any case). Operating expenses and all the costs of planning and negotiating the merger, including the retention of top-ranked merger consultants, were covered by foundation grants.

The deliberations involved two sometimes intersecting forums. One body represented the organizations' professional staff and another one their lay leaders (mostly board members); the two sometimes met separately and sometimes together. One reason for the two-track structure was that professional rivalries among staff leaders—inevitable for nonprofits doing similar work and drawing donations from the same wells—could easily derail negotiations unless they were tempered by the less-immersed lay leaders. Technical matters concerning how the new organization would be structured and run, and who would do what, reporting to whom, had to be settled mainly by the professionals; governance and fundraising questions were usually the province of the lay members. Prager sat as a member/adviser on the lay panel; Kardos did the same among the professionals. The process demanded many hours a week from everyone; Prager remembered still taking calls some nights at 11 p.m., to the dismay of his family. "Everybody was incredibly anxious all the time," he said. "It was all-consuming."

Privately, he considered the odds of success less than even, and he told the board as much. Given those odds, especially near the beginning of the process, several trustees questioned the point of all the dollars and effort. "It seems like a huge amount of money," one board member said in mid-2014, "and it's full of heartache." Others agreed—particularly those with professional knowledge of mergers and acquisitions, who knew firsthand how difficult a successful union of competitors could be. But even in the face of an uphill struggle, a persuasive core on the board backed Prager's inclination to press ahead. Mem, Fried, Merkin, and Darmon in particular considered the upside potential worth the risk and argued vigorously for trying to achieve it. Prager added that the price of doing nothing, and thus losing the engines of creative programming for day schools that had brought so many AVI CHAI initiatives to the day school world, would be to miss a chance to cement a lasting capacity for excellence and innovation in day schools across North America.

"Most of the programs we fund are coming out of these intermediaries," he said, in a successful plea for patience as the merger talks were ramping up. "These are the people we've funded to do the work, and they are the most likely people to set up the next stage of work. If it's not these organizations, but something totally new and restructured, that will be fine, too. But if there isn't anyone thinking about providing service to the field, and every school is left to itself, it will be a weaker field."

In the end, working with a final foundation infusion of $3.5 million to get the deal done, the constituent organizations, the consultants, and AVI CHAI beat the odds—at least for the near term. On January 15, 2016, they finalized an agreement to create a unified service organization for some 275 day schools spanning nearly every denomination, other than the large number of Haredi schools affiliated with Torah Umesorah. Schools working with the new organization would get tailored advice and consulting on core issues of school improvement, besides access to nearly all of the programs and services the member organizations had previously offered only to their own affiliates.

Better still, several initiatives that AVI CHAI had been carrying out directly would now take up residence in the merged organization, including a few of the foundation's newer projects. This could provide a safe landing pad for these still-evolving efforts, with the hope of sheltering them for at least a while beyond the foundation's sunset date. Prominent among the foundation projects that would migrate to the new organization would be the push for online and blended learning and the peer-to-peer leadership network called the LRP Collaborative. Perla himself would become part of the new organization at the end of 2016, taking responsibility for the revenue academies and other programs to strengthen day school finances.

The new organization was named Prizmah, "Prism" in Hebrew, a reflection of the diversity of the organizations that formed it and the denominations they represent. It formally opened its doors in July 2016 with a $9 million annual budget—a full $1 million less than the combined cost of running all the organizations separately. Even so, after a four-year grant from AVI CHAI of $1.5 million a year, plus a new two-year grant of $1 million per year from the Jim Joseph Foundation, the Prizmah Center for Jewish Day Schools would still need to raise more than $1 million a year from other sources, even after accounting for expected revenue from memberships and from service and program fees. It also still faced a raft of organizational issues to resolve, including blending all the members' human resources and membership policies and streamlining such functions as financial management and information technology. These would all demand further, sometimes sensitive negotiations. For the negotiators and facilitators, including Prager, Kardos, and Fuchs, the long months of labor weren't over.

As this is written, approaching Prizmah's fourth birthday, the results have been encouraging—well in excess of what AVI CHAI had deemed minimally acceptable, though still with plenty of room to grow and improve. The organization's CEO, Paul Bernstein, and its top managers and board have steered Prizmah beyond the complexities and dangers of the first years of operation and have proven they can recruit more donors than just those few that supported the member groups before the merger. Whether that will be enough—particularly when the last of AVI CHAI's final contribution has been spent—is still impossible to know. But the reasons for hope are considerably greater than they appeared when deliberations began.

The value of the merged organization was tested soon after its fourth birthday, when the coronavirus pandemic suddenly confronted day schools with a barrage of simultaneous educational and economic crises. All at once, classes had to be taught remotely; employees were unable to show up for work and some had to be furloughed; and many schools found themselves facing families for whom the abrupt economic freeze made it impossible to pay tuition. Frustrated with the limitations of virtual education, some parents demanded to withdraw their children, and others canceled plans to enroll students in the future. A federal emergency loan program offered schools some financial relief in the early months of the pandemic, but the application process was daunting.

Fortunately, by that time Prizmah had established itself as the central resource for the field and was able to step in swiftly to help struggling schools with information, technical support, technology, and connections to funders. The organization assembled a pool of emergency aid from a group of Jewish donors who then relied on Prizmah to establish criteria for distributing the money. It is doubtful whether any of the separate organizations that formed Prizmah could have responded as quickly, or achieved as much, as the consolidated organization did under such intense pressures of time and need.

As he watched these developments unfolding, Prager was able to look back on the creation of Prizmah with pride and cautious satisfaction. But he still showed some of the frayed edges from the years of diplomacy and crisis management that went into it. "This whole thing came at a great emotional cost to everyone involved," he said, "including me. But we're now at a point where the possibilities for Prizmah are good, and the upside potential remains high. I still think, as we told the board in 2016, that this is the best chance for the continuity of many of our current programs, as well as the most likely vehicle for new Jewish day school programs and services to be developed. We've set it up probably as well as we could have for success. From here, well, there's reason for hope."

The creation of Prizmah evolved from an earlier determination to focus on the internal "capacity" of key grantees—their ability to master administrative essentials like fundraising, financial management, information technology, and personnel. But in some cases, as with the organizations behind Prizmah, the challenges grantees faced weren't just internal and couldn't be solved simply by injecting some additional personnel or technology or training. Some organizations were operating in crowded or rapidly changing fields for which their current structure wasn't well suited. The difficulties they faced were bigger than their organizations.

In a few of these cases, AVI CHAI's solution of choice turned out to be some form of merger. For projects like NETA or TaL AM, where internal capacity was not well suited to long-term survival, a merger with an economically stronger, technically more robust, for-profit firm seemed to offer a solution. In the case of the YU School Partnership, the Schechter Day School Network, RAVSAK, PEJE, and PARDeS, for whom there was no already-strong institution to step in and save the day, the solution would have to be an entirely new institution, created to streamline the core management and to make the best of the component organizations' strengths.

The logic was unassailable, at least in the abstract. It would lead—or, more accurately, it might be hoped to lead—to organizations that are more efficient, more astutely run, more competitive, and more appealing to risk-averse funders. But mergers are a difficult business in any field, whether nonprofit or for-profit, and their failure rate is high. Although foundations often find the idea attractive (usually for the same reasons that AVI CHAI was drawn to it), the outcomes of nonprofit mergers offer many more cautionary tales than heroic successes. Among many other things, nonprofit organizations are created because their leaders and staff deeply believe in a specific, particular mission and way of doing business. Two organizations that may, on the surface, offer similar services to similar schools are usually, at their core, not so similar at all. They tend to be passionately different in their values, talents, techniques, and sense of purpose. Blending them amounts to asking them to suspend or dilute the very things that had made them special—the things that had summoned their founders and leaders to sacrifice and service in the expectation of building something unique and great.

Predictably, in all three of these AVI CHAI mergers, by the time the consolidation was complete, the founders and key leaders of the nonprofit partners had moved on or were preparing to do so. The staff at Prizmah barely resembles the combined staff of the five organizations that created it, although the talent mix is still broadly what the foundation had hoped to achieve. The leadership and staffing of Bishvil Ha-Ivrit (née NETA) and of iTaLAM are now markedly different from that of their predecessors. But that outcome was almost unavoidable. The point of resorting to the relatively drastic step of a merger is to save the underlying institutions and to equip them for a new generation of service—not to preserve in resin their founders' original vision and style. At the time this is being written, three or four years after the mergers were complete, the positive news is that the consolidated organizations still survive and function—with, as Prager put it, "reason for hope" that they may yet persevere.

For all the drama confronting AVI CHAI in the field of day school education, in the foundation's other main field of endeavor, overnight summer camping, the winds were blowing considerably more gently. One obvious reason is that their financial health was mostly solid. Camps are almost entirely self-sustaining, with nearly all their costs covered by tuition. Nor are they expensive to run, on a per-student basis, so even if they choose to fundraise, they usually don't need to seek large amounts of money. Day schools could not even dream of such a straightforward business model. But another reason why AVI CHAI enjoyed relatively smooth sailing in this area was that, in camping, it had a strong operating partner, an anchor organization that could provide services and programs across many denominations and types of camps. AVI CHAI's support for the Foundation for Jewish Camp, which began in 2002, had only become deeper and more extensive as time went on, and it provided a solid platform on which to expand current programs and build new ones. The foundation continued to fund some initiatives of its own outside this partnership, but the FJC relationship provided a center of gravity around which other activities tended to revolve.

Over the years, camps had proven their appeal to families and their value as seedbeds of Jewish identity. They had weathered the 2008 financial crisis and the ensuing Great Recession, including the years of slow recovery that followed, with small but steady year-on-year growth. Between 2010 and 2016, enrollment rose 17 percent. However, as families increasingly planned vacations of their own, and youngsters juggled competing activities during the summer, the length of most camping sessions was getting shorter. That reduced somewhat the opportunity to impart Jewish learning and tradition during the time available, and put a premium on offering the most engaging, focused, and memorable programs—a goal that AVI CHAI and FJC had made central to their work together.

The two organizations' partnership ballooned in the first ten years of their collaboration. What had begun as two or three projects, aimed mostly at training camp leaders and staff, including visiting counselors from Israel known as shlichim, had by 2013 grown to a roster of nearly twenty different programs aimed at every aspect of camp life that could convey a Jewish message. Several of these programs had begun independently, under other sponsorship, and then been adopted by or joined forces with the Foundation for Jewish Camp as a way of putting them on stronger footing.

The relationship between AVI CHAI and FJC had begun with the Cornerstone program to train returning camp counselors. A stream of other initiatives followed, including *Lekhu Lakhem* and *Yitro*, training and mentoring programs for camp directors and assistant directors, respectively; *Nadiv*, in which day school educators took summer jobs at camps to help bolster their Jewish content; *Chizuk*, a training program for the camps' Jewish program directors; *Daber*, a Hebrew language curriculum tailored to summertime learning; and a push for teaching modern Israeli history at camps, sponsored jointly by FJC, the Jewish Agency for Israel, and iCenter, a nonprofit that promotes education about Israel in North America. All of these programs tried to help camp personnel infuse the camp experience with ways of experiencing and learning about Jewish life and Israel that would stay with campers long after summer was over.

Most encouraging of all was that FJC, despite running many programs funded by AVI CHAI, was not overly dependent on the foundation. Its popular subsidy program for first-time campers, for example, was funded entirely by another donor. A large and highly successful incubator program for specialty Jewish camps—those that concentrate on particular disciplines or activities like sports, tech, or the arts—was funded only 20 percent by AVI CHAI, with the rest coming mainly from the Jim Joseph Foundation. That made the incubator a rare case in which AVI CHAI was a minority funding partner in a project that nevertheless fit squarely within its mission and priorities.

Other initiatives with FJC likewise were attracting additional funders. By 2018, roughly 80 percent of the Cornerstone program was coming from the Marcus, Crown, and Morningstar Foundations, and its last grant from AVI CHAI accounted for less than 8 percent of Cornerstone's budget. The program had trained nearly 4,000 camp counselors in its first fifteen years and enjoyed a sterling reputation among Jewish donors. Ramah, the camping network of the Conservative movement, had been the main locus of the Hebrew program Daber, and it was committed to continuing the initiative after AVI CHAI's support ended. The Israel education program, called Israel@Camp, was similarly drawing interest from possible sponsors, and the Jewish Agency hoped to continue funding it as well, though its commitments could be made only one year at a time.

AVI CHAI's building loan program for camps, begun in 2006, also seemed poised to carry on under new management beyond the foundation's lifetime. It had grown to $27 million in aggregate loans over six years, financing three dozen construction or renovation projects by the time the last loan was closed in 2014. The program ended then, despite continuing demand, to allow time for the full five years of repayment before the foundation's sunset in 2020. But the idea was promptly taken up by the Maimonides Fund, which started its own lending program the following year.

Other cases were not so securely provided for, and by the time the foundation was preparing to close its grants window, a few of them had folded or were about to do so. But that didn't always constitute a defeat—the training programs Lekhu Lakhem and Yitro, for example, had so thoroughly penetrated the field of camp leadership that by 2018, there were hardly any eligible leaders in FJC's network left to train. FJC assured AVI CHAI that it stood ready to revive the program and seek new backers later, when attrition would once again create a need for leadership training. Similarly, an innovation fund meant to field-test new, independent Jewish education programs for camps ran for three years and spotlighted a dozen or so high-quality activities that camps could adopt. From there on, the next steps were up to the camps, and the program itself had served its purpose. At the end of these projects' lifetimes, as Einleger, AVI CHAI's senior program officer, put it, their demise "was less a case of insufficient funding and more one of Mission Accomplished."

In any case, by the close of AVI CHAI's grantmaking, the significance of its intervention in Jewish summer camping had less to do with the fate of any one program than with the totality of the foundation's impact—the cumulative effect of such an intense, prolonged concentration on camps as incubators of Jewish identity and learning. As early as 2013, with six or seven more years of activity still to go, evaluators were already finding a profound change in the way camps saw their mission as purveyors of Judaism. The web of AVI CHAI programs, evaluators wrote, "make an extensive impact on Jewish camps, improving the Jewish environment and program for both staff and campers." The wide-ranging effects lay not just in the people who had been trained or mentored or otherwise fortified in Judaizing their summer activities; an even greater consequence was in the many more people those participants would go on to lead, train, or inspire in later years. The most fundamental and important change, evaluators believed, was not in the behavior of individual staff members, but in the general expectations among managers, staffers, counselors, campers, and their families—expectations that increasingly included a meaningful Jewish experience for a young person's entire time at camp, embedded in everything that happens, and rich in learning, practice, and appreciation.[27]

That was a vision of camp life that AVI CHAI had played a seminal role in creating and promoting. In one of its earliest forays into camping, at the turn of the millennium, the foundation had supported a three-year-long study of camps across the United States, with particular focus on their contribution to young people's Jewish learning and experience. The resulting report, titled "Limmud by the Lake," drew widespread attention from Jewish funders and helped start a decades-long discussion about the importance of camps among the drivers of Jewish continuity in North America. Alongside the Foundation for Jewish Camp, and through direct support of FJC's advocacy, AVI CHAI had been a megaphone of support and challenge to inspire Jewish education in the summertime.

As the foundation's work in summer camping was beginning to wrap up in 2017, Fried posed a final, blue-sky question to the program's primary architect, Einleger: If you had a magic wand and could do one more "big thing" for summer camping, what would it be? Einleger's response focused not on camps themselves, but on what should happen afterward, when the "magical world" of summertime was over. "Where do we take that and make it into something that doesn't reside in a bubble?" he asked. "How does the Jewish life learned in summer camps get brought back into the rest of the year?" Come the first day of autumn, he suggested, young people needed opportunities to continue their discovery, their experience of belonging and immersion and identity, or else the inspiration they experienced at camp may well fade. This, he thought, would be a fitting challenge for synagogues, families, and community centers—and for a future generation of funders: to spin out a continuing stream of experiential learning and fellowship post-camp, ongoing exercises of mind and heart that could survive the darker, colder months, and could ultimately persevere for a lifetime.

The search for other funders as partners and successors, and the desire to foment movements and bandwagons that would outlast AVI CHAI, came to be understood by most of the board and staff as a summons to thought leadership—that is, as a call to influence the Jewish communal conversation, to publish, speak, use social media, and encourage others who share the foundation's worldview to do the same. For a foundation with a thirty-year history of working demurely backstage, avoiding publicity, to suddenly seek the spotlight was a new and, at times, uncomfortable change of course. But among the principal new directions of its final decade, AVI CHAI in 2010 took on the challenge of thought leadership with vigor.

In some ways, it was a return to the days of advertising for day schools in North America and for religious/secular harmony in Israel, but this time with the foundation's own name and personnel, not just its point of view, occupying center stage. The goal was not to promote AVI CHAI itself, of course, but to light a fire under discussions of Jewish continuity, identity, and solidarity—and to infuse those discussions with a passion for Jewish literacy, religious purposefulness, and peoplehood (the foundation's trademark LRP). Most of all, the point was to emphasize the *need for philanthropy* in cultivating and promoting L, R, and P. And for that purpose, AVI CHAI would need to take a more public stand as an exemplar of how much a foundation can do, and how much remains to be done.

As a first step, in 2010, the staff in North America proposed to the board a statement of "Aspirations for Jewish Youth." The statement broke no new ground, either strategically or tactically. It represented no change to the mission or principles that had driven the foundation's work in education and camping for many years. Instead, it tried—as the best strategic communication campaigns in other context routinely do—to inject a bit of music, to paint a more panoramic vision of what AVI CHAI stood for, the kind of future it believed in, and why others should share its hopes and vision. To the formal, somber language of the foundation's twenty-five-year-old mission statement, the new aspirations added a dash of warmth and spirit, expressed in more personal, emotional language. Jews of the next generation, the statement said, should "feel a bond to and responsibility for Jews around the world," should "continue a tradition of independent study of biblical and rabbinic texts, ideally in Hebrew," and should "appreciate the sacredness of those texts and the texts' role in the Jewish People's timeless grappling with theological, spiritual, existential, and practical questions." In the future that AVI CHAI hoped to conjure, today's children would grow into adults who "take responsibility for transmitting their Jewish heritage to future generations" and "bring a Jewish voice and Jewish values into the discourse of humankind."

This was not a new vision but a new vocabulary—significant not in the meaning of the individual words, but in the way they suggested that AVI CHAI would now try to speak to the world, explain its work, and appeal to others to take part in a common endeavor, newly described. Behind this change in vocabulary and tone lay one sobering recognition that became central to the foundation's philosophy in its last decade: AVI CHAI would not be able to touch a huge number of Jews directly. The vast majority don't go to day schools, and the number of day school enrollees in North America was no longer growing at a rate that might promise a big change in the affected population. Camps reached additional young people, beyond the day school ambit, but only for a few weeks—and still, nowhere near a majority. The old hope of someday affecting what Marvin Schick had called "great numbers" had by 2010 largely faded away.

So if a commanding market penetration was not to be the goal, then, as George Rohr put it at a critical board meeting in February 2010, "What business are we in?"

The evening before that meeting, trustees had heard presentations from Mark Kramer, founder of the influential consultancy FSG Social Impact Advisors, and Jack Wertheimer, the prominent historian who ran the foundation's think tank, the Center for Research and Policy. Both had examined the extent to which AVI CHAI was influencing the next generation of Jewish youth and how it could expand its influence in the years remaining. Their observation—and, in Kramer's case, a key recommendation—was that the foundation needed to be "catalytic" in influencing people who would influence others and, in time, alter the way North American Jews viewed their surest path to continuity. It was a variation on "movement building"—but not merely as a tool or a project that might be useful for day schools and camps. In Kramer's view, and increasingly that of the staff and many trustees, "movement building" needed to be not a means but an end.

For Rohr, for example, the message was "the importance of clarifying the business you're in, and not being stuck in just day schools or camps. We believe [schools and camps are] where LRP is most likely to happen, but there are other prerequisites or additional factors that can be brought to bear." Mem instantly agreed: "*We* may just focus on the day schools and camps, but we should be energizing others to focus on other parts."

"Energizing" was becoming an AVI CHAI byword. A few months after this discussion, in a board memo on Jewish educational leadership, Prager quoted Fried as having recently rephrased the foundation's driving purpose: "producing an *energizing nucleus* of the next generation of North American Jews through LRP-centered day schools and camps."[28] From then on, "energizing nucleus" became the prevailing description of a mission in which AVI CHAI might, on its own, touch comparatively small numbers of people, but those people would radiate passion and vision in far-reaching ways. They would be both more knowledgeable and more devoted to Judaism than in the past, their devotion would be infectious, and they would exert an enduring, centripetal force. Note here the subtle change in "the business we're in": schools and camps— and even LRP itself—which had long been the "laser-like" focus of everything the foundation did in North America, were now means, and the end was an "energizing nucleus" of inspired young people who would galvanize an enduring Jewish future imbued with LRP.

In this new vision of inspiration, aspiration, energy, and catalysis, a key philanthropic coin would have to be language at least as much as money, knowledge, and institutions. One of the most direct expressions of this new emphasis on meaning and message was a project piloted in 2012 called ELI Talks, designed to create a new pulpit for LRP advocates in the tech era. Modeled on the ubiquitous TED Talks, whose sponsor posts brief monologues by cutting-edge thinkers for free distribution online, the ELI version (tagline: "Inspired Jewish Ideas") set out to produce twenty videos a year with a goal of 50,000 total views. Each video would show a talk delivered at some Jewish event or venue, sponsored by a prominent communal organization and filmed and posted by See3 Communications, a digital communications firm for the nonprofit sector. (The name "ELI Talks" is a more sonorous variation on LRP; it stands for religious engagement [E], Jewish literacy [L], and identity [I].)

The recorded monologues covered an enormous tapestry of contemporary themes, including faith, ethnicity, family, personal spiritual journeys, education, leadership, and community—all viewed through a Jewish lens. Speakers included rabbis, authors, educators, scholars, and leaders of communal and activist organizations. Some were emotional, some learned, some funny. One talk, by Prager, examined Jewish philanthropy from perspectives variously personal, philosophical, and theological. Fuchs, AVI CHAI's leading officer for strategic communication, reviewed every proposed speaker and topic—to "ensure their ELI-ness," one memo said—sometimes participating in the development of talks before they were delivered. By the end of 2017, the project had produced

150 videos that collectively had been viewed more than half a million times, vastly more than the foundation's internal projections.

ELI Talks was spun off as an independent nonprofit in 2016 and promptly began branching out into other, related lines of work, like a speaker coaching program and a podcasting initiative, often in partnership with other Jewish media outlets. With steady development of new donors and revenue sources, combined with smarter, more efficient product development, the new nonprofit operated on gradually declining amounts of subsidy from AVI CHAI. The foundation's final grant of $100,000 in 2018 was just 25 percent of ELI's budget. Even so, the project did not survive the ultimate disappearance of that crucial 25 percent. The following year its library was transferred to 70 Faces Media, the largest nonprofit Jewish media organization in North America, where it remains a living source of insights on the Jewish past, present, and future.

Prager's ELI Talk was merely the most dramatic element in a burst of public writing and speaking by foundation employees. Starting with blog posts on the foundation website, AVI CHAI's program officers later directed a stream of essays to the bigger platform of eJewishPhilanthropy .com—a global bulletin board for Jewish funders that features daily writing on nearly every aspect of communal giving. AVI CHAI's posts on the site included reflections on trends in camping by Einleger; on teacher mentoring by Berger; on managing a limited-life foundation by Prager and Fuchs; on day school economics by planning director Susan Kardos; and on network-weaving by communications director Deborah Fishman, among many other things. The blogging began episodically, in 2012, but intensified in the foundation's final year, when staff members launched a monthly series reflecting on lessons from AVI CHAI's thirty-five-year run.

A key purpose of these essays—and especially the purpose of posting them on eJewishPhilanthropy—was to pass a baton of knowledge and reflection to surviving generations of Jewish donors and foundations. For

AVI CHAI, that goal represented a triple culture change. First, it constituted a direct outreach to other donors, something that had only recently
become part of AVI CHAI's operating repertoire and had still not fully
jelled when the earliest blog posts started to appear. Second, blogs as a
medium demand a pithy, colloquial style of communication that was
altogether new for AVI CHAI. Yes, the foundation had sometimes used
punchy language to put its message across in advertisements. But apart
from ads, it had always presented its most carefully reasoned ideas strictly
in the formal language of research and scholarship—a format that, as
Fuchs later wrote, could strike some people as "dense and unwieldy." In
its final decade, seeking a more ambitious form of thought leadership,
those ideas would increasingly pour forth as quick-read highlights,
sometimes with infographics, videos, or other tools to make a point
swiftly, engagingly, and memorably.

The third culture change, in some ways the most profound, was that
the new stream of communication was intentionally interactive. Both the
blog posts and a growing number of video and in-person presentations
and talks were meant as an invitation to conversation, not just a convey-
ing of knowledge. This was new. When the idea of blogging first arose
at AVI CHAI, in the days when posts appeared solely on the foundation's
own website, Fuchs remembered being told that she could experiment
with the new form "with one caveat—comments needed to be turned
off!" The foundation might attempt to speak the new, informal language
of blogging, but it was not yet ready to be spoken to.

"Fast forward a few years," Fuchs continued in a 2019 post on eJewishPhilanthropy, and comments had become not merely welcome, but
integral to the whole undertaking. "We now have weekly meetings reviewing social media metrics, where we gauge our success or lack thereof
on how deeply we are engaging with our audiences online." Best of all,
the audience AVI CHAI was trying to reach, other Jewish funders, seemed
to be responding. "Funder colleagues," Fuchs wrote, "thank us for the

conversations we are starting online and for exposing them to new re-sources and ways of thinking."[29]

The foray into informal online society didn't mean that AVI CHAI was abandoning the more rigorous atmosphere of the academy. Another branch of thought leadership sprang from the work of two foundation-funded research centers, Wertheimer's Center for Research and Policy and CASJE, the Consortium for Applied Studies in Jewish Education, which was jointly backed by AVI CHAI and the Jim Joseph Foundation. The Center for Research and Policy undertook a number of in-depth studies of Jewish education and philanthropy over the years, including a collection of case studies on how day schools confronted and overcame barriers to a high-quality Jewish education; a critique of teaching about Israel in American day schools and recommendations for improvement; and an analysis of trends in big giving by Jewish foundations and donors. Although more academic in tone than the blog posts, these research projects were nonetheless aimed at eminently practical objectives, deal-ing with ways of raising standards for teaching and learning in real schools, and addressed mainly to an audience of frontline educators.

Similarly, CASJE was designed to supply a practical need of day schools and the institutions that serve them: building a base of evidence on which to design new programs and evaluate existing ones, with data that can plainly identify and explain the most effective educational techniques. CASJE set its agenda by consulting panels of educators, researchers, and funders, and took on fundamentals like school management, Hebrew language instruction, Israel education, and Jewish early childhood edu-cation. Both of these research projects were intended not only to guide day-to-day practice in schools, but just as important, to improve the way Jewish philanthropies evaluate and support Jewish education—directing resources to carefully defined areas of need, with expectations and cri-teria for success drawn from data and the practical wisdom of the field.

The ultimate point of thought leadership, in all these forms, was to affect the way influential people view the future of Jewish education. At the same time that the foundation had been laboring to solicit other funders as partners and successors to sustain its own projects, it was also recognizing that individual solicitations of that kind—funder by funder, project by project—could go only so far. The much bigger impact on Jewish philanthropy would come in the longer run, and in the field of big ideas and aspirations, not in appeals on behalf of this or that grantee. It would come when and if donors began to view Jewish education as a national system of organic, integrated parts, in which the strength of the whole depended on the strength and quality of critical functions like professional training or curriculum development or smarter fundraising, each of which influences the others, and all of which make a persuasive, urgent claim on philanthropy.

Whether AVI CHAI could create that collective awareness—or even play a substantial role in promoting it—would take years to determine. The early signs seemed at least encouraging, Fuchs told a researcher in AVI CHAI's final months of operation. For starters, Fuchs noted, some of the foundation's individual appeals to its peers and partners were making a difference, and several funders were getting to know AVI CHAI's world a bit better by actually collaborating with the foundation on this or that project. But these direct relationships were essentially retail sales, resulting from one-to-one cooperation between AVI CHAI and another donor or foundation.

At the same time, she said, "We started hearing of funders who have been interested in some of our projects that were *not* done in partnership." In the course of their own, independent reconnaissance of Jewish education, some foundations and donors seemed to be discovering organizations and lines of work that AVI CHAI had funded, or promoted, or spotlighted in publications and public statements. Or they may have attended forums, like the Jewish Funders Network, where AVI CHAI staff and trustees were appearing more regularly. Or they may have seen an ELI Talk, read a blog post, heard a podcast, or come across some foundation-funded research. They may not have been drawn toward an AVI CHAI agenda per se but may have found some aspect of that agenda persuasive or intriguing. It no doubt helped, Fuchs reasoned, that "the stance we took in our partnership building, even if it didn't yield a funding partnership, it grew colleagueship and thought partnership" that may have piqued some people's interests, or might do so in the future.[30]

Will that transform the funding of Jewish education? By itself, probably not. But as Prager concluded toward the end of AVI CHAI's grantmaking life, whatever happens in the field over the next decade or two will be the result of multiple factors acting simultaneously in still-unforeseeable ways. "The foundation's values and principles will survive," he told a gathering of Prizmah members and allies in 2019, "through the continuing work of our grantees, through innovations not yet imagined that will be supported by funders here now and those who will come forward later." The seeds that may have been nurtured by AVI CHAI directly—seeds of ideas, models, leaders, and partners—need not fill the garden. But they can spread and, with other seeds from other sowers, begin to fill in a landscape far larger than any one foundation could have cultivated on its own.

XV

ISRAEL

Mind, Heart, and Community

Even before the great threshing of 2009, when the grant rolls were pared back worldwide, AVI CHAI in Israel had already begun shedding older projects and thinking about how to refocus its portfolio. Long-standing projects like Beit Morasha, Tzohar, the culture and current affairs magazine *Eretz Acheret*, and the teacher training program at the Hartman Institute had already been awarded their final, multiyear parting grants. So had the Jewish Encyclopedia in Russian, a project first funded in 2003 and increasingly a valuable online reference for recent arrivals in Israel from Russia. And the piyyut website, intended as the culmination of AVI CHAI's support for the traditional liturgical poetry, amid a burgeoning popular revival for the art form, received a three-year final grant in mid-2008. All of these terminations were decided before the financial crash, and all of them provided a relatively slow decline to zero, as each project found new sponsors or prepared to shrink its operation.

Most of these decisions reflected not so much a lack of confidence in the projects (some enjoyed more trustee support than others, to be sure), but a sense that foundation underwriting had gone on long enough, and it was time for the grantees either to survive on their own or to wrap up their business. In the 2008 meeting where most of these tie-off decisions were made, Arthur Fried had asked why, "after ten years or more of support, [do] we need to keep investing?" The answer to that question was different in each case, but overall, trustees were growing impatient with constant renewal grants that could instead have been going to newer endeavors and emerging needs. With the foundation's sunset in sight, they reasoned, all projects would have to become independent sooner or later, and those with the longest history of support ought to face that reckoning the soonest.

Some of these organizations, especially Tzohar and Hartman, had become so popular and successful that backing from other sources seemed highly likely—indeed, in Hartman's case, other donors were already lining up, and Tzohar lost little time in finding new sources. In those cases, the AVI CHAI board reasoned, the fledglings were ready to leave the nest and needed only a gentle nudge to fly on their own. In other cases, like Beit Morasha and *Eretz Acheret*, a credible business plan for long-term independence had never materialized, and trustees were increasingly overcoming their personal affection for these projects (which, in the case of *Eretz Acheret*, was formidable) and acknowledging that more years of support would not change the economic fundamentals. The Jewish Encyclopedia in Russian and the piyyut website were both providing valuable content on the internet; it seemed possible that they would find a secure home somewhere else, as both eventually did. In the meantime, AVI CHAI was willing to pay a small amount to maintain them a bit longer as they made alternate arrangements.

In the tranquil atmosphere just before the market crash, the foundation could handle all these farewells as gradual affairs. Their support was designed to taper downward for three or more years and, in several cases, the grants would come with additional help in finding new donors or shoring up some organizational weaknesses before the last foundation check was cashed. Naturally, a few of the grantees found the decision devastating, and some feelings about them remained raw even a decade later. "It made no sense," one grantee said more than eight years after getting the news. "We were growing. They knew we could do more. It was a chance for them to expand, have more impact, build something that would really make a difference—all with practically no risk. Why would they cut us off to go do something else, something that might not succeed and that wouldn't have time to build up as much experience and potential as we already had?"

Yet for all the difficult trade-offs and what one trustee called "painful, wrenching decisions," all of these were gentle goodbyes compared with the abrupt terminations that would hit other grantees less than a year later.

In the first board meeting of 2009, as trustees were reviewing their ranking of projects and preparing to vote rapid terminations on nearly one-third of the portfolio, they confronted an awkward question that Eli Silver and his staff believed needed to be raised: *Is it fair* that organizations whose terminations happened to come a few months earlier should enjoy such a leisurely separation, while other, equally valuable grantees would receive an immediate 50 percent cut, with all of their support disappearing one year after that? The "Singing Communities" (Kehillot Sharot) and the "Speaking Poetry" programs at Hebrew University had both contributed to the upsurge in popular support for piyyut—a signature achievement for which AVI CHAI bore much of the credit. Both would lose all their foundation support, with no replacement on the horizon, while some older and stronger grantees continued getting their tie-off grants for two or more years. Similarly, the pioneering education program Yahalom, which AVI CHAI had helped launch but which was ranked just a hair below the threshold for termination, would lose all its money in less than two years while other education initiatives had time for a smooth transition.

Under the severe constraints of the new economic environment, staff and some trustees asked, shouldn't the earlier close-out grants be revisited and their comparatively generous amounts be trimmed retroactively? A staff review found that a cut of one-quarter to one-third in these earlier commitments—still milder than the cuts other organizations would receive immediately—could save close to $1 million. That money might then be spent softening the blow for other grantees. Amending the prior commitments would very likely be legal, Silver and others concluded. The question was more one of ethics than of law.

The ethical question, reduced to its simplest form, was: When is a commitment not a commitment? When can a promise be revisited and revised? In this case, AVI CHAI had not only written letters to grantees promising precise amounts of support year by year, but members of the staff and board had informally assured some of these grantees that the financial meltdown would not jeopardize their grants. By what ethical standard could the foundation now turn back to these same organizations and say, "Sorry, you're getting less"?

Some board members considered the present circumstances—the global economy in shreds, the endowment deflated, nearly everyone's business assumptions rendered obsolete—precisely the moment when such a revision would be justified. "The only reason we have these longstanding commitments to these organizations and not others is because of timing," one trustee said. "These came up at a certain time, so we projected the budget for that foreseeable future. Those organizations that did not come up that particular year have been just as exigent, but they just didn't have the luck to come up at that point. So we're not *legally* obligated to them." But, the same person asked, isn't the foundation *ethically* obligated to extend equal terms to organizations of equal merit, regardless of the date on which those terms are written out? Couldn't AVI CHAI justifiably make a single statement to both sets of organizations: "The world is changed; hardship has struck; we must share that hardship equally"?

Furthermore, as another trustee pointed out, some of the conditions that the earlier, more generous grants imposed probably wouldn't be

achievable anymore. "We thought," he said of certain grantees with earlier tie-offs, "they'd be able, after all these years, to go out on their own
and succeed. That seems to be a kind of hollow statement in view of
today's realities." So if it was clear that the conditions of the grant couldn't
be met, then, this trustee argued, changing the terms would be not only
permissible but prudent.*

"Maybe I'm too steeped in Wall Street," a third trustee replied, "but
a deal is a deal. People rely on this. If you give an organization a three-
year commitment at a certain level, they plan, hire and retain people, and
pitch other potential investors that they have a philanthropist in there
for a certain amount for a certain time. If, through reliance on our commitment, organizations have put themselves into positions where they
would be damaged by our pulling back, then I think it would be highly
unethical of us to not make good on our word." It would also be self-
destructive, this same trustee added. "If we're going to be in business for
nine more years, say, if we ever again make a two-, three- or five-year
commitment to any organization, who will take us seriously? Who will
believe an AVI CHAI multiyear commitment is really a multiyear commitment?"

In the end, the latter argument overwhelmingly prevailed, and none
of the earlier grant commitments were altered. But the need for such a
discussion rattled several members of the board and staff, who resolved
that future multiyear commitments would include qualifying language
that allowed for changes under certain circumstances.

––––––––

For the staff in Israel, the weeks that followed these decisions were full
of uncomfortable meetings, in which they had to deliver the bad news,

––––––––

* As it happens, the specific organizations to which this trustee was referring did, in fact, "go
out on their own and succeed." In the improving economy of the next few years, the statement
proved not to be "hollow" at all.

one by one, to grantees who (unlike some with the earlier terminations) were caught by surprise or, at best, were ill-prepared for the consequences. Some were forced to contemplate closing; all would need to shrink or adjust course abruptly. As in North America, a middle tier of organizations would get continued support, but at a lower level. These, too, would have to make painful, mostly unplanned adjustments, and some of them would be hard-pressed to survive on reduced budgets. For example, Elul and Kolot, the earliest batei midrash to be supported by AVI CHAI, would have to cope with 34 percent and 30 percent cuts, respectively, while facing a near-certain dip in enrollment because of the harsh economy. Tzav Pius, still struggling to establish itself as an independent organization, would have to do so with 41 percent less. Revivim, the elite Hebrew University program for training Jewish studies teachers, would have to make do with a 27 percent reduction, even as its prospective students faced a straitened job market.

For all the emotional toll on staff—the prevailing description was "wrenching"—there was an air of inevitability to most of these discussions. Many of the organizations that scored in the lower two-thirds of the rankings had been the subject of doubts or ambivalence among the trustees already, even before the crash. They would not likely have coasted along on steady support for very long, even in a smooth economy.

"No one was getting the axe where the broad consensus was that this was a terrific initiative," Silver pointed out. "All of them had questions that had been hovering for some time. This was, in a sense, an accelerator for decisions that we would have made anyway, but maybe not at quite that time, or quite so drastically." Of course, the suddenness and the sharpness of the decision mattered a great deal to organizations whose primary source of income was about to vanish. It was, Silver acknowledged, "a bitter pill for a number of grantees."

The result was a reduction in AVI CHAI's Israel budget of approximately 30 percent. After starting at an annual $20 million in 2009 (based on grant decisions that had been made largely before the crash), it fell to

$16 million in 2010 and finally to just over $14 million in 2011. These totals included money for Beit AVI CHAI, the giant cultural institution that was finishing its second year of programming in 2009 and was still growing. It would soon be receiving more than 35 percent of the Israel budget. That would leave less than $10 million for all other activities, including continued support for all the grantees that had scored well in the rankings.

Plus, there would need to be room for new activity. Fried, Mem Bernstein, and the other Israeli board members had agreed from the beginning that the cuts to current grants would reflect not only the losses in the endowment, but also the need for perhaps $2 million in unallocated money that could be used for initiatives that were still on the drafting table. "We had the option," Silver recalled; "we could have cut back just enough to hit the lower budget target, where there'd be no money left, but we could preserve more projects. But I don't recall anyone saying that we should do that, that we should just be caretakers for the existing portfolio with nothing else left to do."

On the contrary, with nine years still remaining in AVI CHAI's grant-making life, and with the sparks of Israeli Jewish Renewal beginning to kindle a bigger fire, the board seemed hungry for fresh ideas and were optimistic—despite the lingering economic gloom—about the foundation's chances for making greater, more lasting contributions to Jewish life in Israel before its grantmaking ended.

Among the first new directions that staff members began promoting, even before the all bloodletting had subsided, was an intensified focus on localities—municipalities, villages, and neighborhoods where a desire for more focus on Jewish culture and identity was beginning to brew. These "local initiatives," as some program officers called them, were aimed at embedding the idea of Jewish Renewal or Israeli Judaism more deeply in the rhythms of local life. National programs like teacher training, cultural websites, or informal study programs could create intellectual space for those who were inclined toward Jewish study—to draw people away from their day to day routine and immerse themselves in academic or textual learning. But more and more, staff members were convinced that the prospects for a Jewish Renaissance in Israel lay at least as much in that very day-to-day routine, in the proximate reality of neighbors and community, where people's encounters with one another determine their ideas about belonging, sharing experiences, and taking part in common traditions.

To some members of AVI CHAI's board, some of these ideas seemed suspiciously subjective and vague—Fried called them "wooly"—so Silver and his staff knew they had a tough job of persuasion before them. But the seeds had been planted a few years earlier, first with the foundation's launch of Olamot in Upper Nazareth and then with its support for creating the community center collaborative known as Bayit. The first few years of experience with Bayit in particular had spotlighted both the potential of locally based Jewish programming and the need to support the centers of strength and creativity in a field where they were still scattered, isolated, and struggling to be understood.

The small number of people in community centers who were keen to develop Jewish programming—activities that highlight Jewish tradition, culture, and history—felt "all alone, not very well understood, and facing a lot of doubts and suspicions," according to Tzipornit Paz, who created an Israeli Jewish Culture department in the community center of Holon, an industrial city of some 200,000 people just south of Tel Aviv. In an area where the majority of families are secular or traditional, not devoutly religious, she said, "We constantly had to explain that we're not trying to change anyone. We're not trying to make anyone more religious, or less religious, or anything they don't want to be. We're offering ways of learning and experiencing something that belongs to all of us, and that we can understand and appreciate in our own way."

In the charged atmosphere of turn-of-the-century Israel—where religion was increasingly politicized, and many secular Israelis interpreted the term "Jewish" as code for "Orthodox"—trying to instill a Judaic spirit in the heart of a community's activities was bound to provoke at least some mistrust and resistance. Paz and a few colleagues at other community centers around Israel were determined to prove that community centers could embrace "a pluralistic Jewish identity" that threatened no one and offered something precious to every Jewish resident.

Bayit started in 2009 with half a dozen community centers, selected with help from the Israel Association of Community Centers, based on their demonstrated commitment to rich Jewish programming. The centers then set about assessing their own strengths and weaknesses as purveyors of Jewish heritage, guided by a diagnostic tool drawn up by a small pilot group of community center staffers working with AVI CHAI program officer Karen Weiss. When the participating centers had identified shortcomings and proposed effective ways of filling the gaps, Bayit helped them by funding a local coordinator, providing a budget for enhanced programming, and offering ongoing guidance on successful practices in Jewish community development.

The idea, as Silver described it, was to "transform community centers from service organizations—places that offer a menu of programs developed by professionals for residents in their catchment area—to genuine *community* centers, where the local community is mobilized to participate in developing a local vision and programmatic ideas." For the centers that made the best and most creative transformation, Bayit would confer a kind of "Seal of Quality," thus both establishing a bar of excellence and implicitly encouraging other community centers to rise to it.

The problem with this idea, as Weiss and Silver acknowledged from the outset, was that every participating locality would have to "mobilize its resources—human and material—to align the center's efforts with Bayit's goals." This would be a tall order for multifaceted local institutions serving many purposes for many overlapping constituencies. "The obstacles to success are substantial," Weiss acknowledged in presenting the idea to the board. "Community centers and the localities in which they operate are highly complex entities, with multiple stakeholders that

can sabotage efforts; local politics can be unstable, and even the normal
cycle of local elections can derail plans; and the process of achieving
Bayit standards is expected to be demanding and difficult, testing the
commitment of those involved."

Still, the first cadre of leaders, including Paz of the Holon Community Center, were passionate enough about the project to suggest that at
least a handful of centers could rise to the challenge. If they did what
they intended, they would be demonstrating something of uncommon
value—possibly something that would inspire other centers to climb on
board—and would be pouring fuel directly into the engine of the accelerating Israeli Judaism movement.

But the goal of Bayit was more than just bringing that movement into
community centers. It was to press forward both of the main tenets of
AVI CHAI's mission: drawing Jews toward a deeper understanding and
appreciation of their heritage, and bringing more- and less-religious Jews
into greater harmony. "AVI CHAI's mission," Silver said to trustees at a
board retreat in 2019, "to be fully realized, has to be realized within a
community." The attempt to solidify the role of Jewish programmers at
community centers—and to help them tailor study groups, cultural
events, and celebrations to local preferences and needs—was at its heart
an effort to build a capacity for unifying different kinds of Jews in a
common, continuing discovery of their heritage, in the places where they
live, work, and raise families.

In the end, Bayit did not achieve its goal of cultivating this kind of
rich Jewish programming in thirty community centers. After six years
and twenty-one centers, the project sputtered, mostly for lack of outside
funders to keep the momentum building, and AVI CHAI ended its support. The level of excellence Bayit tried to establish seems to have been
more demanding than the broad spectrum of Israel's community centers
was prepared to deliver, given all the competing demands for their attention and resources. But the idea of embedding Jewish spirit in the
cultural fabric of localities was bigger than the community center world

alone. In Upper Nazareth, for example, the community center had been just one player (although an especially enthusiastic and energetic one) in a broader municipal effort to create a unifying and inspiring Jewish atmosphere. Even before Bayit came into existence, leaders in other towns and regions, not directly affiliated with their community centers, had been proposing similar "local initiatives" that would weave together their resident cultural organizations, schools, informal learning programs, donors, and municipal governments in a common effort to create a more fully Jewish communal life.

Part of the idea for this broader kind of community mobilization came in 2005, in a spontaneous phone call from David Aviv, an employee of a tech firm who lived in Emek Hefer, an agricultural region north of Netanya. Aviv was in his thirties, with three children in an overwhelmingly secular community, and was beginning to wonder, and to worry, about how they would receive the legacy of Jewish culture and tradition that was so integral to his own inner life. "I was not religious," he told an interviewer several years later, "but still felt as a parent that I had a responsibility to pass on the richness of Jewish culture to my children."[31] A friend suggested he call Weiss, who offered a small study grant to help him gather information and draw up a proposal for a regional initiative.

After a few months of conversations with leaders in his community and in cultural centers elsewhere in Israel, Aviv came back to Weiss with a familiar lament and a novel proposition. The familiar part was his description of the status quo in Emek Hefer. Like most nonreligious communities in Israel, the area was fairly rich in educational programs for children and cultural activities for families, but none of them featured Jewish content. The region's small religious population had its own Jewish activities but kept them to itself. Aviv's novel idea was to create what came to be known as *Zayit* (Hebrew for "Olive," and an acronym for "Jewish cultural identity" in Hebrew)—a grassroots organization offering study groups for adults, holiday and life-cycle activities for families, programs for youth, and large-scale public events. Having decided to leave his tech career behind, Aviv devoted himself to forming the new organization and building its roster of programs and events.

A prime example of these was Mekorock, an annual series of rock music performances by teenagers, guided by professional artists, playing original songs made from Biblical texts. "Since teenagers are not so keen on reading the Bible," Aviv told a visiting journalist in 2014, "I had to find something that will help them connect with these texts. I wanted them to open this book and get acquainted with the ideas and stories presented there. . . . The teen musicians who joined the project had two sources of inspiration: the Bible and the artist who guided them through the writing process. Eventually they were taught how to read a biblical text and how to make it their own through the music they wrote."[32] In a few years, the festival had spread to half a dozen other regions in Israel.

Zayit's broad alliance encompassed the community center, the regional government, educators, and an assortment of other residents. Some people who became active partners were wary at first, mostly out of a fear of religious indoctrination, but grew to take ownership of the concept and to organize their own initiatives under the Zayit umbrella.

At the same time, or soon thereafter, similar sparks were catching fire in other places, including in Gan Yavne, a village near Ashdod, and in Ramat HaSharon, just north of Tel Aviv. Each of these early stirrings was unique, with its own particular alliances and mix of programs, though they had many basic elements in common. But unlike AVI CHAI endeavors of the past, these projects were rising up from below, not in response to any overarching strategic design, and often not even in response to any direct action by the foundation, but simply sprouting in the fertile soil that AVI CHAI had begun to nourish. Like the proposal from Aviv, many came in over the transom, as local instigators began to confer with one another and pass along the news that an elite foundation in Jerusalem just might be interested in supporting what they wanted to do.

"These are all bottom-up initiatives," Silver reminded the trustees in a 2019 retrospective. "As such, the nature and character of each local initiative is different. But what's common to all of them is a belief that Jewish culture should play a more profound role in local life. It provides meaning to individual residents and families and provides a sense of belonging and responsibility to the local community and the Jewish People."[33]

But as the number of these local projects multiplied, it became increasingly difficult for the staff to deal with them one by one, as separate applicants and grantees. Nor could the organizations themselves thrive for long as scattered islands of improvised programming. There needed to be some kind of unifying network through which the various initiatives could share experiences and ideas, pool resources, develop some standards and models, and seek a sustainable level of financial support for all of them by the time of AVI CHAI's sunset.

The foundation's answer to this need for a unifying framework became *Nitzanim* ("Buds" or "Beginnings"), a network of local initiatives through which foundation support, plus that of other funders, could flow to the most promising, well-run local programs. Nitzanim would help a handful of localities form steering committees like the ones in Upper Nazareth, Emek Hefer, and Gan Yavne, to begin planning programs. If the plans are strong and rich enough, with enough support from the essential local players (particularly the municipality, the schools, and the major civic organizations), AVI CHAI would provide enough money to hire a full-time director and create an organization to implement the programs and hold the local partnership together.

It was an expansive, ambitious vision, but it got less than a warm reception when it first landed on the board's agenda. The initial proposal conveyed more enthusiasm than detail; it was long on vision but short on specifics about who would do what for how much money. The lack of specificity, the staff tried to explain, was a necessary feature of a program whose virtue lay in its flexibility, where details would be worked out locally and would vary from place to place. Maybe so, trustees replied, but the idea—whose eventual cost could be expected to reach many millions of dollars—seemed half-baked and utopian, far from the kind of meticulously designed project the foundation had always insisted on.

In their initial discussion of the idea, in the autumn of 2009, the kindest words trustees offered were that it was "a wonderful dream" that would probably "do no harm." But anything that relied on the talent and dedication of local leaders—especially municipal politicians—could easily run aground when those leaders changed or were distracted. A recent attempt to foster regional programming in the Tel Aviv area had derailed because of precisely that kind of instability. The foundation, one board member pointed out, would be "relinquishing much more responsibility than ever before in our work. We will have to tell local residents that this is theirs to develop, implement, and succeed with—a very different kind of project."

Another concern was that AVI CHAI was already struggling with the challenge of shoring up existing national grantees—including learning communities, projects in schools, websites, media programming, Tzav Pius, and Beit AVI CHAI—to ensure their survival through 2020 and beyond. Wouldn't a new initiative, building entirely new organizations dispersed across many localities, soak up resources that would be needed for strengthening and expanding current projects? Worse, might it not end up duplicating those projects in miniature, creating atomized little versions of Elul or Ma'arag or Kehillot Sharot?

On the contrary, Silver replied, those national initiatives would be prime resources for the Nitzanim communities. Localities wouldn't be replicating Elul; they would be inviting Elul to establish satellite programs in places with a demonstrated hunger for them. They would be providing an opportunity for Elul and other informal learning programs AVI CHAI had supported to extend their work further across the country and to reach many more people—something the foundation had long been urging them to do. And they would be knitting these disparate projects—formal and informal education and culture—into a coherent whole, serving the same population in multiple ways. That kind of synergy was also something the board had long been seeking without much success.

Though the discussion was occasionally heated and ultimately inconclusive, on the strength of Fried's confidence and encouragement the board allowed Silver and his team to try again. "We must get this right," one supportive trustee cautioned, "because we will not have time for another round of experiments five years from now if this effort does not succeed." If the staff could answer the concerns that had just been raised and describe a program that trustees could clearly envision and understand, offering reasonably well-bounded costs and a plan for mitigating risks, the idea might yet move forward.

And so it did, after another three months of review and revision led by Weiss. A longer, more concrete proposal in February 2010 set forth a cautious start, selecting just three new localities and carefully observing and documenting what they accomplished before deciding whether to go further. Any of these that didn't meet their benchmarks for forming a broadly representative steering committee, developing a diverse range of programs, and attracting broad participation could be discontinued. Several points of reckoning, with interim evaluations, would provide an opportunity to withdraw support in case of failure or increase it if progress was better than forecast.

The price tag would be large, if everything went well and the initiative expanded all the way to ten communities. It could cost perhaps $17 million in aggregate over the next decade. (The actual outlay ended up being only half that amount.) But even that maximum would still be no more than 15 percent of the total projected expenditures in Israel, not counting Beit AVI CHAI. So plenty of money would remain available for national initiatives. Nitzanim would not interfere with efforts to strengthen and expand those other grantees; on the contrary, it would provide additional channels for them to expand their offerings and widen their

support. Finally, to avoid creating dependent organizations that would
be stranded when AVI CHAI ended its grantmaking, the budget for each
local project would have to rely heavily on municipal and other resources.
Foundation money would be primarily a startup investment; it would then
make up a declining portion of the local grantee's revenue over five years.

This time, the reaction was far more positive. "I like the organic nature of this," Ruth Wisse said, "in the sense of bringing together everything we do, AVI CHAI and the communities. It has extraordinary
ambition and potential effect." "An impressive step forward," Lief Rosenblatt added. With most of its questions answered, despite a number of
acknowledged risks and uncertainties, the board launched Nitzanim
with a $4.6 million grant.

Before the decade was out, Nitzanim was functioning in eleven communities, fueling work by hundreds of volunteers, civic leaders, and local
officials. The local groups offered a panoply of programs tied to the Hebrew calendar and the Jewish lifecycle, *Kabbalat Shabbat* ceremonies,
batei midrash, cultural events, new approaches to formal and informal
Jewish education, social action projects, and forums for dialogue among
groups with differing approaches to Judaism. To formalize the concept
and create an enduring network among the participating localities and
partners, AVI CHAI spun off Nitzanim in 2013 as an independent nonprofit with a three-year grant of just under $3 million. The grant covered
up to half the cost of local programs plus three-quarters of the budget of
the national nonprofit.

During a visit to Gan Yavne as Nitzanim was developing, Wisse attended a meeting between a group of secular Israelis and the local rabbi,
in which they together planned activities for Chanukkah and Shavuot.
She was impressed that the two sides managed to come up with a program that honored Jewish traditions in a way that would not be unsettling for less-religious attendees. She sensed that the secular participants
were hoping for more than a good celebration; they wanted to kindle a
sense of common heritage with their religious neighbors, to draw from

their shared Judaism a source of communal solidarity. But some of their more secular neighbors bristled at any attempted alliance with the synagogue, while some members of the rabbi's congregation feared that such a big-tent celebration of religious holidays would water down their sacredness and blur the distinction between observant and secular lifestyles. "The pressures on everyone were real," Wisse recalled. "It was initially very frustrating, but they were determined to do it, and despite all kinds of obstacles, ultimately they did."

A concluding program review in 2019, by Ronen Goffer, an Israeli expert in citizen engagement, found that the activities local programs had piloted were often becoming "ongoing local traditions" and were attracting large, devoted followings. The Nitzanim brand was increasingly recognized across the participating localities as the mark of a community that takes Judaism, in all its diversity, seriously. Some programs, though not all, were also beginning to enrich the teaching of Jewish subjects in their local schools.

At the same time, Goffer recognized a problem with the far-flung network of diverse programs that had worried AVI CHAI trustees from the outset. It was hard to discern a pattern in all the variety of programs, players, and activities. "This diversity is what is unique about this field and the secret of its strength," he wrote. But "it also exacts a price in terms of the pace of its development and dissemination countrywide. In order to encourage greater growth of Israeli Jewish communities, there needs to be a countrywide framework for all of the programs, one that permits them to belong to a single movement."[34]

For all the cross-consultation and networking that had occurred among communities (with constant AVI CHAI encouragement) over the nine-year build-out of Nitzanim, the initiative still lacked a defining core, a readily comprehensible description of *what this is,* apart from an attempt to inject Jewish tradition and values into all the elements of community life. Even the definition of "Jewish tradition and values" was an unsettled question in many Nitzanim sites. Perhaps predictably, some events and programs were proving to be too religious for the more secu-lar residents and too secular for the religious or traditional. From the perspective of AVI CHAI's mission—"to encourage mutual understand-ing"—such debates, and the balancing act they prompted from local organizers, were actually a positive development, if they led to more conscious efforts to recognize and bridge cultural differences. But they did not help in clarifying the initiative for anyone not immersed in it.

The lack of what Goffer called a framework was more than a theo-retical problem. Crucially, it made Nitzanim hard for potential funders to grasp. Inherent in the very name ("buds") was a sense of something embryonic, changing, not yet fully realized, and this improvisational quality was less than ideal for inspiring confidence in potential donors. Many such donors, whether well-off Israelis or funders from the Dias-pora, might have little idea of life in the Nitzanim communities, most of which were some distance away from Israel's biggest urban centers. Most philanthropists would have a hard time picturing the vibrant suc-cesses that Goffer, Weiss, Silver, and others had seen up-close.

"To this day," Weiss conceded in mid-2019, "we have not been able to frame exactly what Nitzanim is. In a way, it's leadership and com-munity and education and non-formal education and public events and culture and democracy and innovation—it's 'and, and, and, and'—and it sounds probably not clear to anyone who hasn't seen it. Come and see it, and you will grasp it in a minute."

Whether for that reason or others, the hope that Nitzanim would attract major contributions beyond AVI CHAI and the participating mu-nicipal governments was largely unfulfilled by the time the foundation's grants came to an end. Even within municipalities, the expectation of steady financial and political backing from government remained fragile, dependent as it was on the goodwill of elected officials and of other or-ganizations that also rely on municipal support for their own activities. And yet, even if funders were slow to recognize the promise of Nitzanim, communities across the country were catching on, and more of them were seeking ways to participate. As late as 2017, AVI CHAI was still receiving and funding applications from new localities to join the Nitzanim network.

———

Another burst of local initiatives came from Israel's collective communities: the kibbutzim, where land was traditionally owned by the whole community and farmed or developed in common; and the moshavim, where plots of land were allocated to individual households although many essential services are shared. Both kinds of communities, which trace their roots to early twentieth-century Zionist socialism, have undergone profound disruptions since the 1980s. In those years, the Israeli government withdrew the subsidies and price controls that had favored collective farming and fueled its distinctive business model.

The communities responded to the policy change with years of haphazard and sometimes harmful adjustment, taking on too much debt and later having to sell assets and otherwise restructure to survive. In many places, industry replaced farming, and the atmosphere of kinship based on a common lifestyle began to disappear. Meanwhile, the ideological glue that had held the collectives together and defined their purpose was dissolving.[35] Kibbutzim and moshavim remained attractive to communally minded Israelis who drew meaning from the collectivist tradition, but that meaning had ceased to be a single, common heritage. More and more, it was defined by individual participants and families, each in their own way. For many inhabitants, these communities were becoming just another way to make a living.

In search of new sources of solidarity and community, some kibbutzim and moshavim came to recognize an unexpected power in Jewish culture and tradition. If these communities were no longer purely agricultural, or collective, or socialist, they nonetheless remained thoroughly Israeli and Jewish. As more local leaders and educators started to seek an intensified Jewish identity in their moshavim and kibbutzim, their attention was drawn to nearby localities where Bayit, Nitzanim, and other local Jewish Renewal initiatives were stirring. To several of them, the model fit their communities' needs perfectly.

"All the ideology once connected to the kibbutz has begun to crumble," Carmit Goren said in a video made for AVI CHAI in 2019. "So today, we have to fill [the gap] with this: The connection to Judaism and Jewish culture is the content we have to incorporate to define the essence of a community, and we all have to rally around that." Goren, a resident and former education director at Kibbutz Tzora in central Israel, was among the early staffers of communal villages to be inspired by the progress of Nitzanim. In time, several of them got in touch with AVI CHAI to ask if a version of Nitzanim might be tailored specifically for the kibbutz movement. Counterparts in the moshav movement were making the same case—though it was harder for them, since most moshavim had no one on staff responsible for culture and informal education. Creating such a position was, for many of them, part of the vision for which they were asking AVI CHAI's help. From both the kibbutz and moshav movements, the appeal to the foundation was strengthened considerably by a promise that the participating communities would share the cost initially, then try to absorb it all by the time the foundation departed.

To Weiss, it was another sign that Jewish Renewal in Israel was growing in the fertile soil of towns and neighborhoods at least as fast as in the rarefied intellectual enclaves of Jerusalem and Tel Aviv. Perhaps, she believed, it actually had more room to grow there, where "identity" was not just a concept, but the anchor that holds people to a place, to neighbors, and to the basic habits of citizenship. It struck her as significant that, as early as 2010, with Nitzanim still in its infancy, already one-quarter of the participants in pluralistic batei midrash nationwide were studying not in the flagship urban centers but in the satellite programs hosted by the foundation's first three local initiatives—"at considerably less than the cost invested in the traditional learning community organizations," she added.

The future of all this activity, after the last of AVI CHAI's $12 million aggregate investment has been spent, remains far from clear. Much of it will shrink for lack of money. But individual initiatives, even if not whole networks, did manage to attract local funding, and some national organizations that had been nurtured by the foundation were offering programs at the local level, even if not to the extent that the staff had hoped at the outset.

Participants in these initiatives often point to a subtler, less tangible reason why their hyperlocal strain of Israeli Jewish Renewal is likely to persist. It is creating habits and expectations among community residents that are increasingly embedded in local life. It is, in a word, becoming normal. That does not mean it enjoys universal appeal across whole localities, or that residents would necessarily rise up and protest if programming were withdrawn. But if the programs, ceremonies, and events offered by local alliances are becoming standard features of the civic calendar, they may be less likely to fade altogether, even with less funding. If the more expensive ones are unable to continue, other, less costly activities will still go on. And more important than the fate of any given event or set of programs is the underlying idea for which AVI CHAI first set out on the path of local action: that Jewish identity and tradition can and should hold a fundamental place in the definition of an Israeli community, and should be expressed in a variety of ways throughout the year, at holidays, at significant moments in the life cycle, and in all the educational and cultural venues that give a locality its vibrancy.

From the perspective of AVI CHAI's mission, even if the formal structures of Nitzanim or Bayit or the kibbutz and moshav programs don't survive forever, the expectations they have tried to engender, the sense of normality, the routine assumption that Jewish heritage is somehow at the core of local life, would be enough to constitute success. As with many other foundation programs, the goal is not necessarily to create organizations, but to inspire a yearning and a will to shape a common Jewish identity, seeking ways to learn and inquire, with whatever organizations and activities happen to suit the purpose at any given place and moment.

Ehud Saley, a kibbutz resident and education official with the Jordan Valley Regional Council, summed up this kind of achievement at a panel presentation in 2019, when he described the change in thinking and talking about Judaism that he perceived among his neighbors. For many years, he said, "we had stopped asking ourselves questions and, in my opinion, we lost our way. We didn't know any more into what kind of world we wanted to raise our children." But in the past decade or so, he has felt the fog lifting.

"Now," he said, "we challenge ourselves, asking what kind of world we want our children to enter. Besides the learning and the personal experiences in programs, the most important thing is that we developed a new—let's say, an old-new—discourse, taking a look at what we are doing, asking ourselves why we do it, starting a conversation, looking out from the old traditions and asking ourselves who we are and why we are here. And then, sometimes, maybe doing things differently, doing something new. And that, I think, is the most important thing."

To engender a new discourse, to create new ideas and patterns of Jewish life, it helps to engender new leadership. Inspiring whole communities begins with inspiring the inspirers. AVI CHAI had started its search for ways of galvanizing young leaders first with its support of batei midrash like Kolot, aimed at rising young adults who were plainly on a leadership path. Then, dropping one notch down the age scale, the foundation helped widen Jewish learning opportunities for the motivated young people in pre-army mechinot, willing to spend a year after high school on further inquiry and learning. Mechinot graduates tend to go on to significant roles in society after the army and university.

The foundation's next step was to focus on others of the same pre-

army age, activist-minded high school graduates in the yearlong voluntary service program called Sh'nat Sherut, known for short by its Hebrew
initials, Shin-Shin. Like the mechinot participants, these activist young
people, more than 1,500 a year, tend to move on to successful post-army
careers, not always in leadership roles but in circles of community-
minded Israelis committed to improving society—for example, in health
care, education, law, or public service. Their desire to devote a year of
their youth to serving in disadvantaged Israeli communities, or to bringing an Israeli spirit of volunteerism to the Diaspora, made them a logical
target for AVI CHAI's vision of a thoroughly Jewish approach to service,
achievement, and community. Too many of the young people in Sh'nat
Sherut programs, the foundation ultimately concluded, were living lives
that radiated Jewish values—without ever knowing the Jewish roots of
those values or the way Jewish leaders, thinkers, and activists had shaped
the ideals by which these young people strove to live.

The idea for a new program aimed at this population arose from a few
small efforts, beginning with a project for alumni of the mechinot and
progressing to a couple of small study programs for Shin-Shin participants organized by MiMizrach Shemesh and Beit AVI CHAI. In mid-
2010, program officers Miriam Warshaviak and Weiss presented to the
board the possibility of organizing a larger, more deliberate initiative
aimed at Shin-Shinim, modeled on the earlier program for mechinot. It
was not an easy argument to make. AVI CHAI had tried in earlier years to
engage organizations serving idealistic young people but had found almost no inroads.

Unlike members of mechinot, who are already committed to a year
of study and could readily incorporate Jewish subjects into their learning,
the Sh'nat Sherut program entails full days of frontline activity, volun-
teering in schools, community organizations, youth programs, and the
like. As Avital Darmon pointed out in 2010, "More than ten years ago
we tried to work with the Sh'nat Sherut; they are so busy. They do not

take this year off to study their identity in an isolated, calm atmosphere. They volunteer into the hot spots in the name of ideology. We couldn't find the time to get them together for two hours to study."

But now Warshaviak pointed to something new and unexpected in the current atmosphere. Increasingly, Shin-Shin programs were approaching AVI CHAI or its grantees seeking—on their own initiative—ways of incorporating Jewish understanding into the work of their young volunteers. Earlier efforts to reach them, Warshaviak argued, had hit a dead end because the foundation was pushing something that, at the time, no one was asking for. Now, she believed, something in the culture was shifting. Shin-Shinim were not only asking but eager to implement something. As Silver saw it, this atmospheric change was part of the "recurrent theme of our last decade—interest bubbling up from below and seeking us out."

Even more intriguingly, Warshaviak reported, the traditionally independent, atomized world of the Shin-Shinim was beginning to coalesce into networks of common learning and mutual support. These networks might now provide a channel that AVI CHAI could work through. "Our leverage there is a network," she told the board. "We don't have to work with each individual community as we do with the mechinot. We can work with this network."

"There is something definitely going on here," Silver agreed, "a need and a drive we are tapping into." He felt the same trends in the gathering of local coalitions in Nitzanim communities and in the community centers in Bayit. "We're looking to leverage and bring added value to that kind of movement: people in Israel looking for meaning within community frameworks." To Lauren Merkin and some other American trustees, the trend evoked the same hopeful trend, a gathering force, that was driving the search for "tribes" and "movements" in North America. In both places, consultant Jack Wertheimer believed, "there is a common language" being spoken about a search for purpose and mission in life that is rooted in Judaism.

ISRAEL   141

Not every board member was convinced. Not only was the idea still too inchoate for some, but even the longer-term vision struck a few members as risky. After a quarter-century of working through national organizations and pursuing a nationwide agenda, the idea of shifting to little volunteer groups in small communities was jarring.

"This impulse to create your own community," Wisse suggested, "which is strong in young people anyway, is also a fragmentation of something central. It is troubling that nothing here is reflected in people saying, 'I want to be a member of Parliament to influence the nation.' If you want to influence the nation by going to a community in Be'er Sheva, and thousands of the best people in your country think of doing good as withdrawing into little communities, ultimately that becomes a problem." This argument wasn't an objection but a caution, she added. It's fine for a number of Shin-Shinim to organize study programs and create small networks, and it's fine for AVI CHAI to support that development—provided that the foundation's ultimate vision is bigger: something that spreads, that seeps into the broader Israeli society and influences, in widening circles, the way young people think about their social action, and later their adult lives, and ultimately about their country and the Jewish people worldwide.

Over the next few years, the foundation increased its support for the experimental Sh'nat Sherut programs at MiMizrasch Shemesh and Beit AVI CHAI, and then established and gradually expanded new programs with two established networks of Shin-Shinim. With the Jewish Agency for Israel, the foundation also created a brand-new network, called Shin-Shinui, to promote Jewish learning across many Sh'nat Sherut groups.

One of the two Shin-Shin programs supported by AVI CHAI operated through the network of kibbutzim, taking advantage of the movement's organizational infrastructure. The other was run by the youth organization HaShomer HaTza'ir, the world's oldest functioning Jewish youth movement. Like Israel's dozens of other youth movements, HaShomer HaTza'ir enlists children from elementary school onward in weekly activities that combine service, learning, and summer camping. Leaders of the organization worked with AVI CHAI to design a program for post-high school activists that would weave Jewish content into their regular Shin-Shin activities, culminating in what would become "On Judaism," a program of two-hour study sessions each week, plus five full study days during the year. The organization created a committee to formulate the program, consulting with current members and alumni and with AVI CHAI advisers, and deciding on the timing and structure of the learning sessions.

But the introduction of this new kind of activity was far from easy. HaShomer HaTza'ir has its roots in an adamantly secular and socialist form of Zionism, and for many young members, the reaction was similar to that in the most secular kibbutzim and moshavim: any suggestion that they would spend time immersing themselves in Judaism smacked of religious indoctrination. Further, as an evaluator noted toward the end of AVI CHAI's involvement, the program was "trying to offer *study* programs to young people who have just completed twelve years of school and have specifically elected to devote a year of their lives to *work*—that is, to *not studying*" (emphasis in the original).[36] Their days were taken up fighting poverty, helping disadvantaged children and families, organizing local self-help programs, and so on. Why should their limited time away from the frontlines be occupied in batei midrash studying Jewish texts and traditions?

Yet despite this difficulty—in fact, because of it—HaShomer HaTza'ir presented exactly the kind of audience that AVI CHAI's mission compelled it to reach. To "encourage mutual understanding and sensitivity" among Jews of different backgrounds and attitudes, it was essential to combat the notion that Jewishness belonged only to the devout, and that Jewish heritage was irrelevant to everyone else. The lesson that "there are many ways to be a Jew," as one program document put it, needed to be conveyed with a richer understanding of the many facets and forms of Jewish identity and the extent to which Jewish ideas and values underlie the highest motives of Israel's socially conscious young Jews. To be sure, the socialist ideology of HaShomer HaTza'ir was well to the left of that of many members of the AVI CHAI board (and would have appalled the politically conservative Zalman Bernstein). But the prospect of reversing the alienation separating this population from its Jewish birthright overrode questions of political philosophy.

For the fervent teenagers of HaShomer HaTza'ir's Shin-Shin program, these ideas took time to digest, and the new study regimen had to be introduced carefully and diplomatically. It helped that the leaders of the study sessions were themselves recent Shin-Shin alumni, thus affirming the program's bona fides as an authentic outgrowth of the organization's social mission. The result is that once it was established, the program proved to be surprisingly popular. On Judaism was piloted in 2012–13, and a preliminary, formative evaluation just three years later found that it "was reported by most participants to have significantly strengthened their Jewish identity and enhanced their views of Judaism." Most tellingly, more than 72 percent of the participants told the evaluators that they'd favor continuing the program, and one-fifth said they'd like to make it bigger. Only about one-quarter favored shrinking or ending it.[37]

"In the program's first years, the movement leadership encountered opposition from peers and teens to the new focus on Jewish study and Israeli Jewish identity," the AVI CHAI staff reported to the board in 2017.[38] "Today, engagement with the topic spurs curiosity, questions, and an understanding that this is an important subject that merits attention." Two years later, a final summative evaluation found something even more encouraging: "The sum total of activity in this field contributed to the general trend of a *change in Jewish identity discourse* in Israel, which includes *strengthening the overall bond to tradition* (especially among the secular population), and the first buds of *an identity discourse that under-*

mInes identity dichotomies (where the choice is only between religious or secular)" (emphasis in the original).[39]

This would appear to be a strategic bull's-eye for AVI CHAI, touching all the notes of mission and aspiration with which the program was formed. The seemingly deep engagement of individual participants appeared, as the trustees had hoped, to be bubbling outward toward a broader "change in Jewish identity discourse in Israel." And in time, those bright hopes may well be realized. However, it's important to note that the evaluations between 2016 and 2019 were early, qualitative, and near-term. Participants answered questions about their opinion of the program and its effect on their thinking only a short time after it ended. The warm glow of a satisfying experience—wrapped, as it was, in the heady atmosphere of a year of community service—could easily produce a more favorable response than the same participants would offer a year or four years later.

The goal, after all, had not been merely to enrich the one-year experience of Sh'nat Sherut, but to alter people's understanding and perceptions of Judaism, preferably for a lifetime. Did that happen? With AVI CHAI preparing to draw the curtain on its grantmaking, and thus on its collaboration with the Shin-Shinim, there was no more time to conduct long-term evaluations or to tinker with the program to boost its value further. "It is possible," the final evaluator wrote, "that some programs are too short in duration to produce any discernible effect on identity." Perhaps, with more research, organizers might have found value in adding more sessions or otherwise raising the "dose" of intervention. As it was, the foundation could withdraw, as it did in 2019, only with some assurance that it had opened the minds of hundreds of young Israelis to a Jewish inheritance that they might never have discovered or understood on their own. What they did with that discovery from that point on would be up to them.

Even less certain was the ultimate significance of the ShinShinui program that AVI CHAI created in partnership with the Jewish Agency.

In that model, half the study sessions focused on social issues related to the participants' volunteer activism; only the other half concentrated on the Jewish texts and values. With just half as much attention to the latter subjects as was paid in the HaShomer HaTza'ir program, it was not surprising that the reported impact of the program was smaller. Staffing and other changes to the program midway through may also have undermined its effectiveness. After three years, a majority of participants reported learning about the diversity of social values embedded in Judaism, but just one-fifth said they "developed an interest in acquiring knowledge about matters related to Judaism." The comparable number on the latter point in HaShomer HaTza'ir was 47 percent.[40] By the time of ShinShinui's final evaluation, results had deteriorated further, and AVI CHAI wound down its support for the program.

What distinguished ShinShinui was its attempt to draw participants from multiple Sh'nat Sherut organizations in a given geographic area into a single bimonthly study curriculum, thus encouraging interaction among teenagers of different backgrounds and degrees of observance. It's possible that this cultural cross-pollination would have had social benefits that outweighed the comparatively smaller dosage of actual study. But devising a program that would satisfy these different constituencies, each with its own proud worldview and way of operating, proved much too difficult. Again, with only a short running time before AVI CHAI's departure, it was too soon to know what alternative approaches might have worked, and too late to experiment further.

Still, AVI CHAI's foray into the Shin-Shin world seemed, at the end of its run, to be paying big dividends. In 2017, the Education Ministry set aside money for the first time for Sh'nat Sherut programs, much of it earmarked for education. The budget allocation was close to the level of state funding for pre-army mechinot and instantly shone a spotlight on the role of learning—and specifically of Jewish study—in the makeup of the service year. In the meantime, interest in these kinds of Jewish learning programs had been swelling among many operators of shin-shin programs, especially youth movements, which saw the study curricula as opportunities to link their ideology and values more directly to Jewish tradition. These developments were not solely to AVI CHAI's credit, certainly, but its years of support and advocacy of Jewish education in the post-high school year surely helped to till and fertilize the ground.

Other experiments in what AVI CHAI classified as "inspiring Jewish change agents" reached both up and down the age ladder from the Shin-Shin participants. The goal, as program officer Efrat Shapira Rosenberg put it in 2015, was to "create an educational continuum—beginning with elementary school-age children in youth movements, through pre-army mechinot and Sh'nat Sherut, and continuing with communities of young adults—that will help nurture a generation of young people who are committed to social activism to engage in constructing a meaningful and relevant Jewish identity for themselves." Aiming at a younger population was a program tailored for youth movements, beginning with HaShomer HaTza'ir's younger cohorts. That organization had grown so satisfied with its experience in the Sh'nat Sherut program that it sought AVI CHAI support in extending the opportunities for Jewish learning to its youth movement as well. Programs for children and early teens also included the Scouts, Israel's largest youth movement, and B'nei HaMoshavim, the youth program of the moshav movement.

Reaching toward older participants, the foundation briefly supported a program, together with the New York Federation, for what it broadly described as Young Adult Communities: residential clusters made up mostly of recent graduates of mechinot, Sh'nat Sherut programs, or youth movements, all of whom want to continue living in an environment suffused with Jewish culture and social activism of one kind or another. Their evident desire for a way to study together and deepen their Jewish learning seemed all but tailor-made for AVI CHAI, but after three years and $225,000 in grants, matched by the New York Federation, the project never really jelled. The communities were too different from one another, and the concept behind them may still have been too new for a clear, coherent program to emerge. Still, Rosenberg, among others, believed that the experiment had been worth the price. At a minimum, she believed, it helped nudge forward a search for structures in these idealistic communities that might help sustain them, or at least might help sustain the appetite for Jewish learning and self-discovery that had led them to AVI CHAI's doorstep.

_____

The bedrock of all these projects for young people—the reason they came to AVI CHAI's attention and the reason the board chose to support them— was what seemed to be an emerging trend in Israeli society, what Silver had summed up as "something definitely going on here." Despite a lingering wariness among some very secular Israelis, the idea of a *Jewish* heritage both ancient and thoroughly modern, an identity forged in thousands of years of history and yet perfectly suited to present-day social action, was plainly influencing the life choices of more and more young people. If this proved to be more than a fad, if it made its way deep enough into the patterns of Israeli life, it would be an immense step forward toward a youthful, idealistic, but lasting version of Israeli Jewish Renewal. For a foundation with AVI CHAI's mission, it would be hard to justify *not* pursuing this trend, at least to discover how far it might lead.

Still, the foundation happened upon many of these projects at a time when the trend (if that's what it ultimately proves to be) was still in its infancy. As a result, several of the initiatives AVI CHAI supported remained, at the end of its time in the field, still pieces of a fragile and uncharted landscape. The same might be said of Nitzanim and the other projects for Jewish life in smaller communities. The sense of "something going on here," while palpable, was only starting to register on Israel's cultural seismometers. What aspects of it were strong and possibly enduring, and which were ephemeral or inconsequential? In the few years it had available for this work, AVI CHAI was essentially navigating through a fog, with no way to know the answers to these questions and only the impressions of knowledgeable people on which to base its strategy.

For a perpetual foundation, of course, this would be not a problem but an opportunity. It could embark on a period of small-scale experimentation and discovery, take time to build on whatever seemed to be strengthening, adjust course if promising ideas foundered, and continue to observe and learn as the field matures. A foundation in the final years before sunset has no such luxury, and its experiments, of necessity, often end in ambivalence. So, they did, in many instances, in AVI CHAI's work with localities and with young activists.

In one project for young people, however, the foundation had enjoyed substantial running room and ample time to experiment, pilot, observe, and expand. AVI CHAI had begun supporting pluralistic pre-army mechinot in 1998, which afforded it a twenty-year run, with gradually widening ambitions and accomplishments. After the first ten years of foundation investment in mechinot, the Knesset formally recognized them in a new law that funded their growth. AVI CHAI's final push in support of the mechinot, starting in 2015, capped its gradual accumulation of experience and allies. Even as it was winding down its financial support for individual mechinot—all of which would be sustained on government funding—the foundation invested in professional development seminars for their senior staff and, more substantially, in the movement's umbrella group known as the Mechinot Council.

Foundation support allowed the council to build expertise and credibility, set a strategic course, and begin offering an array of services and networking opportunities for its members that would help cement them into a mature, durable branch of youth activity in Israel. Alongside its financial support, AVI CHAI offered the kind of guidance and advocacy that helped fortify the council's reputation and self-discipline. It was a significant act of institution building, even by the standards of a foundation that had spent much of its history building institutions. But it was possible only because of the years of gradually expanding activity that proceeded it—grant by grant, mechina by mechina. Those years of cumulative support had built a field so popular, both with young people and with the Israeli government, that by 2017 there were at least five applicants for every available slot, and the Ministry of Defense was carefully expanding the number of army deferments it was granting so that more young people could participate.

In December 2019, at the end of AVI CHAI's $11 million stream of support for the pre-army program, the head of the Mechinot Council, Dani Zamir, could write with confidence that the foundation's support had "helped us research and learn and address what needs improvement, and to build a world of contemporary, exciting, and vital Jewish social renewal and creativity. They helped us to raise questions, disagree and argue, and to be better, wiser, and more precise." Zamir, a pioneer of the movement as founder of one of the first secular mechinot, viewed the legacy of AVI CHAI in his field in much the same way as Mem Bernstein frequently did—it was not so much the organizations and programs, but the lives they enriched, and, by extension, the many more lives that the mechinot alumni would touch in the future.

Research in 2013, commissioned by the foundation, bore out this view of the impact of studying in pre-military programs. Researchers from the Hizun Institute, with guidance from AVI CHAI's director of evaluation, Liora Pascal, examined the later lives of young people who had participated in foundation-sponsored mechinot, and specifically their later pursuit of Jewish study or cultural programs. Compared with a sample of young people from the general population with similar characteristics (such as age, tendency toward voluntarism, and service in command positions in the military), the mechina graduates were nearly twice as likely as other comparable young people to be enrolled in some form of Jewish learning one or more years after their army service. The effects of the pre-army year appeared to have a lasting effect on young people's lives, and that effect included an appetite for Jewish knowledge and continued discovery of Jewish heritage.[41]

"The graduates," Zamir concluded, "are dispersed across Israeli society, embarking on various paths, working and leading, innovating and creating, and dealing with the meaning and purpose of Israeli society and the Jewish People."[42]

_____

Over the course of more than twenty years of grantmaking in formal education—projects to train teachers, develop curricula, create online teaching tools, elevate the teaching of Jewish subjects, and transform whole schools into centers of Jewish learning and discovery—the one consistent theme of AVI CHAI's experience had been a failure to forge lasting partnerships with Israel's Ministry of Education. Time after time, the foundation would conduct research on educational gaps and opportunities for improvement, share its findings with the ministry, launch pilot projects meant to test and demonstrate new ways of doing things, and even, on occasion, draw senior ministry officials into formal discussions about how the government might adopt and expand the demonstration. And time after time, some tantalizing sign of interest from the ministry would flare for a moment and then vanish, leaving the foundation with a library full of costly research and demonstration projects, a few proud (but not necessarily sustainable) beacons of excellence in the field, and not much else.

And so it happened again, between 2010 and 2014. AVI CHAI, in its final decade of philanthropy in Israel, had set out to scan the landscape one last time to find areas where it might still make an enduring difference in the quality of Jewish education. It carried out a systemwide survey of needs in the field and launched a series of discussions with education officials about how the foundation and government could work together to meet the needs. The immediate response was promising. AVI

CHAI and ministry representatives worked up a three-part proposal that would have encouraged elementary school teachers to get master's degrees in Jewish education, expanded teacher certification in Jewish subjects, and established a research center on the teaching of Jewish culture.

Pascal, who commissioned and directed the research for AVI CHAI (and who was herself a former employee of the Education Ministry), later summed up the sadly predictable outcome: "Despite the Ministry's initial enthusiasm, we were unable to secure a clear commitment from the Ministry for any of these directions."[43] Exasperated, Silver and the board were ready to give up. "How many times are we going to push the same rock up this hill?" he remembered asking himself. But Pascal had a different idea. Rather than trying to crack the adamantine bureaucracy of the national government, why not forge a partnership with a local school district instead?

She happened to have a district in mind. The head of the Tel Aviv Regional School District, Haya Shita'i, had worked with AVI CHAI before, as part of a project to promote Hebrew culture in Tel Aviv. That project made a bit of progress over a few years but ended up stalling for lack of broader municipal support. Shita'i had also supervised the successful implementation in Modi'in of the Hartman Institute's curriculum and teacher training program, an initiative AVI CHAI had supported from its inception. In 2014, just as the foundation's attempted collaboration with the Ministry of Education was falling apart, Shita'i was working with a group of schools to launch innovative projects for teaching Israeli Jewish culture—exactly the kind of effort AVI CHAI was hoping to promote. Pascal sensed an opportunity here.

The two women ended up creating what they called an "incubator project," in which schools would be invited to propose improvements in their teaching of Jewish subjects, and AVI CHAI and the regional district would fund the cost of implementation. Proposals could come from a single school or from several; they could be at the elementary or secondary level. They could focus on individual topics like Jewish thought or

Zionism, or could cover multiple subjects. It would be another bottom
up project, like Nitzanim, which might be expected to make foundation
trustees nervous. But in this case, as Pascal pointed out in a memo to the
board, the initiatives would be specific and fully planned before they
were funded, and the end goal—superior teaching of Jewish subjects—
lay squarely at the heart of AVI CHAI's mission. Most important, the incubator would be evaluated to determine which projects deserved to
continue and which did not.

The bottom-up approach to education reform was hardly radical. The
government was already granting schools more and more autonomy over
their curricula, so trying to impose a uniform program on all of them
would probably have failed. (A similar insight lay behind AVI CHAI's
Morasha and Ma'arag initiatives, which also relied on schools designing
their own approach to an overarching goal.) Giving schools the opportunity to design their own solutions would mean, first, that each one
would own and value the project it was undertaking, and second, that
the project would meet what Pascal called "the needs and values of its
community of parents, students, and teachers." The projects would also,
of course, have to meet standards of quality defined by the school district
and AVI CHAI.

Furthermore, the bottom-up model had already been shown to work
well in another context. In the mid-1990s the Ministry of Education had
launched an innovation-incubator program called "Tomorrow '98" to
upgrade the teaching of science and technology. Not only did it turn out
to be widely popular with both teachers and students, but a rigorous
evaluation showed that it made a significant difference in the level of
teaching and learning in those subjects. Pascal knew this history inti-
mately; she had conducted the evaluation when she was a senior researcher at the Education Ministry. She saw no reason why something
that worked so well in science wouldn't work just as well for Jewish
studies. The board bought her argument and approved the project.

The first cohort of twenty-seven schools to win grants started planning their new initiatives in late 2015 and most had them up and running in early 2016. The program, named *Otzarot* ("Treasures"), went on to fund a second cohort of twenty-one schools, bringing the total in two years to 12 percent of the schools in the district. In each case, AVI CHAI's money was spent on planning and initial implementation. Schools got a smaller grant in year two to finish implementing, and then carried on with the new activities as part of their normal operations, with no further grant. Program officer Aliza Corb, who oversaw the project for AVI CHAI, and a team of evaluators gave the first two years' work high marks, and interest in it was expanding all across the school district. The board approved a second grant for a final two years, thus extending its support for Otzarot all the way to the foundation's sunset.

If that had been the end of the story, it would have been good enough. With an enthusiastic director and without the complex bureaucracy and constantly shifting politics of the national government, the Tel Aviv Regional District was able to mobilize quickly and implement Otzarot with fidelity and vigor. And it began producing tangible results almost immediately. Pascal and Silver had premised the whole effort on a belief that a program in a single municipality would create something of sustainable value. Creating a high-quality program in just one large district—especially a district with a high percentage of secular families, who represented an above-average risk of losing touch with Jewish culture altogether—would have had lasting effects on Israeli education all by itself, even if it didn't spread to other places.

But it was, in fact, about to spread to other places. As Silver remembered it, "I was at one of these meetings where we were reviewing progress" on the first cohort of Otzamot schools, "and Yuval Seri was there from the Ministry of Education. I had never met him before. He was a Hartman graduate and had recently been appointed head of the ministry's Department for Jewish–Israeli Culture. At some point, he threw out the idea that he's got some money for experiential education that he's looking for what he could do with it that would be really effective, and maybe he could take that money and apply it to this, and take the idea and use it for other districts. And my reaction was, 'Sure, right.' We had heard the same kinds of thoughts so many times, and nothing came of it. So I thought, 'Wonderful, let's see.' But I figured nothing would happen."

Something happened—and quickly. "We took Otzarot, and now we're doing it in the whole country," Seri told the AVI CHAI trustees two years later, in 2019. "Every school can now propose something new in Jewish studies, and if we find it acceptable, we give them twenty-five thousand shekels to do it." The amount was significant; it was more than one-third higher than the grant the foundation had been providing. And given that a basic curriculum in Jewish studies is now compulsory in all Israeli elementary and middle schools, the chance for a principal to innovate, to tailor the school's work on this subject to the particular characteristics of its students and community, is a way of ensuring that schools genuinely embrace the teaching of Jewish culture, rather than merely comply with requirements. "It's amazing to see," Seri continued. "In most of the schools, it's now something they need. Principals want the schools to be like a community, and you can deal with Jewish subjects all the time—it's your holidays and your ceremonies, it's in your classes. Everything is an opportunity to teach about Judaism."

"That," said Darmon upon hearing Seri's presentation, "is the power of the State."

It is also the culmination, for AVI CHAI, of what may well be the most enduring dream in Western philanthropy: to invent something, demonstrate it, and see it adopted by an appreciative government. The dream usually fails, as it did for AVI CHAI for much of its history. In many cases, government agencies are too overwhelmed to appreciate unplanned and unmandated new ideas. Many public bureaucracies, proud of their knowledge of their field, are reluctant to embrace innovations from outsiders, unless those can clearly further the agencies' own priorities. And in any case, with budgets tapped to their limits, even the most apprecia-

ISRAEL — 155

tive agency may have too little money to try anything substantially new. But this time, Silver said, "it was kind of a collision of fortunate circumstances." Seri had available money in his budget, he was fairly new to the position, and he wanted to do something significant. "He saw what we were doing, he was impressed, and he saw an opportunity." Within forty-eight months, the opportunity was a national program.

How long that program will last is still an open question. Seri is relatively young and could well move on. The political tumult in Israel that launched a series of inconclusive elections in 2019 and a fragile government coalition in 2020 could end up shifting government priorities yet again. Enthusiasms sometimes fade on their own as time wears on. Any number of factors could make Otzarot a temporary phenomenon.

But it's important to remember that the purpose of Otzarot is not to launch an ongoing stream of foundation grants. The purpose is to embed a self-sustaining activity in a school's normal operation. Even if the national version of Otzarot continues for just a few years, it will have had an effect on a substantial percentage of Israeli schools, and that effect may well linger. Each initiative springs, after all, from the schools' own diagnoses of their needs in Jewish studies and from their own creativity in designing solutions.

The gathering phenomenon becoming known as Israeli Jewish Renewal (later renamed *Yahadut Yisraelit*, or Israeli Judaism), which underlay the great majority of the foundation's work in Israel, was not an AVI CHAI creation. Instead, as Fried put it toward the end of the foundation's grant-making life, "we were pushing on an open door." A desire for contemporary forms of Jewish consciousness and identity was already in the Israeli atmosphere by the time the foundation started thinking strategically about the issue in the late 1990s. But at that stage, it was at most an undercurrent—pursued mainly in universities and other high-culture circles, debated in cafes, galleries, and lecture halls, among people prone to think in depth about abstractions like identity, culture, and heritage. Or, in other ways, it may have been discernible in a smattering of small cultural or community organizations forming study groups or sharing Kabbalat Shabbat or some poetry or music. These were important and meaningful to their participants, but almost totally obscure to everyone else.

What brought Jewish Renewal to the surface in Israel, what made it a visible current bearing along many kinds of activity in a growing stream, was the proliferation of batei midrash, community events, cultural activities, websites, and eventually mass-market entertainments like films, television programs, festivals, and big concerts. And these, to a considerable extent, were planted, nurtured, and multiplied by AVI CHAI.

Yet even if the currents of Israeli Jewish Renewal were discernible everywhere in the early twenty-first century, the phenomenon was still far more broad than deep. The study groups, cultural venues, and community programs that sprouted in the first twenty years of AVI CHAI investment were mostly fragile institutions, living grant-to-grant or struggling along on participants' fees and contributions, and prospering mainly from the dedication of small, but growing, squadrons of true believers. The field encompassed many scores of organizations, and yet it enjoyed hardly any consistent support from government and only the occasional, relatively small-scale backing of philanthropies. As AVI CHAI was preparing to depart, the prospect that Israeli Jewish Renewal could soon revert to being a niche rather than a movement, preserved mainly by the voluntary efforts of enthusiasts, was palpable.

In mid-2012, Silver and the Israel program staff drew up a proposal to shore up the field's public stature and to bring the disparate elements of Jewish Renewal to the attention of a wider audience—including, most of all, the Knesset. The idea was a classic philanthropic advocacy program: bring together a board of well-connected eminences and influencers, staffed by entrepreneurial types with skills in strategic communications, marketing, and policy development, and build a public relations campaign arguing that Jewish Renewal and the organizations that support it deserve to be national priorities on a par with other civic and cultural organizations the government routinely funds. The goals would be to raise public awareness, attract government support, appeal to philanthropy, and beef up the management—especially fundraising, financial management, and communications—of the organizations in the field.

Trustees' reactions to the idea were decidedly mixed. Some, like Fried and Mem, argued that an advocacy effort like this was the best way—maybe the only way—to leave the field stable and healthy after AVI CHAI closed its grant window. "We're going out of business in seven years or so," Fried told his colleagues on the board. "The government supports most activities in Israel—sports, culture, religion. We've been in the Jewish Renewal business for most of the years we've been operating in Israel, and yet that area gets *zero* from the government. Before we're not here any longer, we should try to do something to ensure continuity. This is an effort to give Jewish Renewal in Israel the capacity to continue after we're gone."

While acknowledging the risks of failure, Mem made her own appeal. "I think it's a greater risk for us *not* to try this," she said, adding that "the chances of our finding individual funders that will pick up where we leave off is a pipe dream" if the government can't first be persuaded to do its part.

Yet others regarded the idea as little more than a stab in the dark. "I still think this is extremely intangible and difficult to judge," Alan Feld said. "If this were presented to me by someone else asking me for philanthropic capital, I would decline." Rosenblatt concurred. The proposal, as he saw it, was simply to create an as-yet-unknown organization to pursue some as-yet-unspecified legislation in hopes of raising an uncertain amount of money. "It does leave us in this queasy no-man's-land of hoping it will succeed but not having a way to calibrate whether to approve this and for how much. I'm in favor of the concept, but I feel I just don't quite know what I'm voting for."

Silver countered that his team, after extensive research with experts on advocacy projects in Israel, had laid out some rough target achievements by which the project's value could be judged over the next few years. Though he described these as "educated guesses"—nothing is scientifically predictable in the give-and-take of politics and PR—he considered it reasonable that the new organization would secure $2 million in new government funding for the field within three years and also achieve changes in funding rules that could bring more favorable treatment and money down the line. If that goal were reached and foundation support for the new organization continued beyond 2015, higher funding targets would apply to later years.

In the end, the board accepted the vision and its risks—"No one thinks this is a lay-down hand," Fried acknowledged—and agreed to invest $900,000 a year for the next three years to see what might be achieved.

The new organization, named *Shearim* ("Gates" in Hebrew), quickly made three critical strides that helped reassure the more hesitant trustees. First, Dani Danieli, the hard-charging AVI CHAI veteran, agreed to become staff director, stepping aside from the directorship of Beit AVI CHAI after five highly successful years. Not only was the board's confidence in Danieli ironclad, but organizations in the field also recognized him as a trustworthy partner who would represent them vigorously and with savvy. Second, two outside funders, the Posen Foundation and the New York Federation, agreed to join AVI CHAI in funding the new venture. Although their commitments were much smaller than AVI CHAI's, they instantly bestowed an independent credibility on Shearim as a voice of funders and practitioners alike, not just a mouthpiece for a single foundation.

Third, Fried, Mem, and Silver managed to recruit a gilt-edged board that included a former member of the Knesset, an influential attorney deeply connected to Israel's power structure, and the head of the national umbrella group for batei midrash. The chair would be Sallai Meridor, former chair of the Jewish Agency. Other government insiders were also expressing interest in joining. "Our ability so far to recruit quality Board members," Silver wrote in early 2014, "reflects both the broadening appeal of Jewish Renewal in Israel and the realization that advocacy represents an essential tool in the field's arsenal."

Sadly, Shearim's stars seemed crossed almost from the beginning. Just as the board and staff felt they were making headway with Israel's thirty-second government, in which both the finance minister and the education minister were responding positively to Shearim's overtures, that government ended and new elections brought a change in ministers. As the next government was being formed, initial negotiations for a set-aside for Israeli Jewish Renewal seemed to be making headway, but then the new ministers showed less openness than their predecessors had. When that government in turn fell two years later, Meridor began to despair.

AVI CHAI's initial grant for Shearim was based on an expectation of some results—at least a small government appropriation—within three years. That may not have been a realistic target, but it was critically important to several board members who felt that without it, the whole venture would be too vague to endorse. Realistic or not, Meridor now felt it was out of reach. "I said to myself, 'We've now spent other people's money for a year and a half. We tried two different governments.' And the likelihood of changing the dynamics with this outgoing government were limited. So, starting all over from the beginning, with now just a year and a half left and new ministers coming in, was there really a good chance that we were going to succeed?"

And then there was the problem of staff leadership. Despite all his assets as director of Shearim, Danieli left the job for personal reasons after only a few months. His successor, Lior Weintraub, a protégé of

Meridor's, stayed longer but also left after just over a year. So here, too, Shearim would have to start over, essentially from scratch, after more than half of its trial period was already gone. With neither a promising channel into the government nor a staff director to guide the ship, it was not clear what more could be done. The organization had tried working through the prime minister and his close aides, through cabinet ministers, even through individual Knesset members, but so far, no doors had opened more than a crack. Meridor, who had experience running a venture capital fund, sadly concluded that "you don't stick to a startup just because you started it."

At AVI CHAI, Mem, Fried, and Silver were reluctantly coming to the same conclusion. Skeptics on the board had been won over mainly by the promise that Shearim would have to meet concrete milestones if its grant was to continue. Other funders had signed on with that same understanding. It might be possible to revise the milestones now and try again, acknowledging that hostile forces outside of Shearim's control had slowed its progress. But to do that, it would be necessary to have a gifted director committed to staying in the job, a board confident of its ability to score some victories, and a concrete plan showing how the future would not resemble the past. Lacking those essentials, Shearim and AVI CHAI both concluded that the end had come.

"It was the great failure of our last decade," Silver concluded. "This was one of the most important things we could have done to provide for the future of this field and all we had invested in it. And it just didn't happen. The results of that are going to be felt for a long time."

Yet even if the creation of an advocacy organization hadn't borne fruit, the underlying problem still remained to be solved: how to bolster the finances, organizational strength, and staying power of the Israeli Jewish Renewal organizations and programs before their AVI CHAI support vanished. At the time the first proposal for Shearim was under discussion, the staff had also written a companion proposal to support a membership organization for Jewish Renewal groups, consisting of and controlled by the groups themselves. In the staff's original vision, this would be different from Shearim largely because it would be a forum for organizations to meet and network with one another, set standards, and meet common challenges. It would focus on strengthening its member organizations and would give them a megaphone through which to speak with one voice. Members would pay annual dues and elect a board from among their ranks.

As it happened, such an organization already existed, though in vestigial form. Panim, the original umbrella group for about three dozen batei midrash, had received AVI CHAI support for a time but lost out in the 2009 round of cuts. That loss of funding, combined with internal stresses and fractures, had sent the organization into a tailspin that nearly finished it off. By 2014, however, it was showing signs of new life, with renewed support from its members. In this unexpected show of resiliency, Silver and his staff saw an opportunity to fully revive Panim, broaden its membership base, and equip it to play a bigger role in securing the future of Jewish Renewal in Israel.

In the staff's original plan, however, the responsibility for seeking government and philanthropic support for the field was supposed to have been left to Shearim, not Panim. The reason was that, in the view of AVI CHAI's consultants and advocacy experts, membership organizations tend to fail as policy advocates, because the members naturally set their own organizational interests above those of the field as a whole. While trying to advocate collectively, they often end up pushing their own, separate agendas instead. Advocacy for a broader cause, as opposed to an organization, requires a 30,000-foot perspective that individual groups rarely possess.

Still, after a year or so of renewed AVI CHAI support, Panim was looking stronger, better managed, and more cohesive than before. It was still a membership organization, with all the caveats and internal rivalries that entailed, but it appeared to be a good one, with signs of increasing discipline, a good leadership team, and a near doubling of its membership in just two years. The Posen Foundation and UJA-Federation of New York had agreed to join AVI CHAI in funding Panim, as they had for Shearim. It did not have the staffing or the panel of high-octane political figures that Shearim had had, so it could not be expected to take on the same grand scale of advocacy and fundraising. But it could, and did, make some efforts to pursue additional government and philanthropic support.

By 2016, Panim had taken control of the Midreshet website, the online library for informal learning programs that AVI CHAI had launched with the Center for Educational Technology in 2007. Expanding on the site's original catalog of educational source sheets on Jewish–Israeli identity and culture, Panim started adding new material on Jewish ceremonies. It was holding roundtables and seminars on topics of interest to parts of its membership base. It was gathering data to create a more complete, compelling picture of the field for possible funders, including the government. And it had created fundraising programs for its members, including new online appeals on the expanding Panim website. At this point, AVI CHAI made a three-year grant to carry the progress forward—but, as with Shearim, each year's payment was conditioned on a number of performance milestones that set escalating targets, including fundraising.

On this last front, Panim made only slightly more progress than Shearim had. By 2018, it had won a four million-shekel commitment (a little over $1 million at the time) from the Kulanu party, whose leader, Moshe Kahlon, was minister of finance. Still, it was far from the infusion of public dollars that the foundation had been hoping for when the advocacy effort was approved four years earlier. Nor was the new money in any sense a major change in the economic environment for the field. In fact, Panim's own budget remained precarious, just three years before its last check from AVI CHAI was due. To its credit, the organization had assembled a well-diversified combination of funding sources, including member dues and other foundations. But AVI CHAI still represented some 20 percent of its budget, and that gap would prove challenging to fill.

With major government resources still nowhere on the horizon, and AVI CHAI's worries about the sustainability of the field mostly unrelieved, the foundation would have to appeal to new donors in the hope that substantial new money could be raised in the next few years. The matching program Pseifas was the main vehicle for this, although staff and board members also were continuing to appeal to possible donors one-on-one and were beginning to report some limited success.

After that, the foundation's last remaining strategy was to find ways of helping individual organizations shore up their fundraising, management, and governance. The theory was that many excellent grantees had devoted whatever money they had to raising or maintaining the quality of their programs at the expense of their internal administrative functions and external relations. Their fundraising was weak, and many organizations lacked the ability to report on their finances, their accomplishments, and their growth potential in ways that would entice new funders.

In fairness, for most of its history, AVI CHAI had not exactly been bountiful in providing for those organizational necessities. It had set tight limits on the operational costs it viewed as "overhead," and its grants were often conditioned on year-by-year performance measures, which gave grantees little room for longer-term planning. As a result, the foundation had inadvertently contributed to the common Israeli practice of mounting major programs on the backs of fragile, understaffed organizations that were highly dependent on one or two funders. But in 2012, recognizing the enormous survival risks that even its best grantees would soon be facing, the board decided it was not too late to change course and try to bolster the core operations ("build capacity," in foundation parlance) of its most vulnerable grantees in the remaining seven or eight years.

The staff began by canvassing the major organizations in its portfolio and separating them into two camps. One group of eight was almost totally dependent on AVI CHAI and would face a near-certain crisis when the foundation left the scene. A second, larger group had just a few specific weaknesses (especially in fundraising and accountability) that might, if promptly remedied, provide enough strength to carry them past AVI CHAI's departure. The first group got a complete menu of management assistance, starting with an organizational assessment and progressing to as much as one hundred hours of consulting a year for three years, provided by specialists in all the areas where they were found weak, all paid by AVI CHAI. The second group got more specific kinds of consulting, up to thirty hours a year, in areas like financial management, fundraising, and board development.

Not long after starting this stream of technical support, the foundation added a new and more radical element to its capacity-building agenda. It began paying for organizations to hire additional staff, mostly for fundraising. For a foundation that had long looked askance at grantees' desire for additional staff, the prospect of actually encouraging them to hire fundraising professionals, and then paying the full cost, was remarkable—especially in Israel, where funders almost never did such a thing. To limit the danger that these positions would become just another way that grantees would become dependent on AVI CHAI money, the foundation subsidized the new salaries on a declining scale, starting at $50,000 the first year and gradually declining to $25,000 by year three.

All these steps had been recommended by consultant Joel Fleishman, a veteran of U.S. philanthropy who was accustomed to foundations mounting ambitious organizational-development programs. But in America, such programs are a well-rooted part of the philanthropic terrain. Foundations have long experience implementing them, and the field is rich with consultants who understand the management culture of thinly funded, mission-driven nonprofits. In that environment, the best capacity-building programs usually satisfy needs that the grantees have already identified, or that they come to recognize quickly with a little self-scrutiny and guidance. Foundations can then support remedial steps the grantees genuinely want to take and are prepared to carry out fully. None of that was true in Israel. AVI CHAI was breaking new ground here and, with one or two exceptions, most of its grantees were unready for it and unsure how to use it effectively. The timetable was short—barely more than three years—so the learning curve would have to be steep.

The result was a scatterplot of individual successes—several organizations used the strategic and management consulting effectively and came out with solid business plans, better systems of accountability, and a clearer sense of direction—but the fundraising support was a near-total disappointment. "In most cases," Fleishman wrote in a review of the Israel program in 2018, "the new employees were unable to raise even enough new money to cover their own salaries. When organizations tried replacing their original fundraisers with new ones, the results were largely unchanged. The disappointment has led many at AVI CHAI to doubt that this approach has much potential, and it has largely been abandoned." Overall, even beyond the specific failure at fundraising, hopes for a widespread improvement in organizational strength and effectiveness were largely unfulfilled.

A longer project with more gradual steps and more modest interim goals might have worked better. But as in many other areas, AVI CHAI no longer had the luxury of time. It had been reasonable to assume that, with a major funder about to depart the scene in just a few years, grantees would have leapt at the chance to gird themselves, organizationally and financially, for a more challenging future. But because the whole idea was so alien to the Israeli nonprofit scene, and because there were few examples to show grantees what the consultants and fundraisers might be able to do for them, they were slow to embrace the added help or make the most of it. More time might have solved that. But time was running out.

———

Most of the foundation's support for Israeli Judaism in these years amounted to a kind of philanthropic acupuncture: strategic interventions aimed at precisely defined targets, like a teacher training program in one place, an informal study program in another, specific improvements in a few carefully chosen schools or communities. But a few projects aimed much more broadly: at changing the overall cultural climate in favor of a deeper embrace of Jewish identity. By far the broadest of these was the film and television project, begun haltingly and with much frustration in 1992, but then revived and pursued more vigorously from 2002 onward.

In the single year 2009, even amid the general economic gloom and the difficult trimming of the grant rolls, AVI CHAI produced sixty-three hours of prime-time programming, including dramas and documentaries, films, and TV series, with some of them broadcast several times. The following year, after absorbing a 25 percent budget cut in the foundation's general downscaling, the media project still turned out six more productions, totaling twenty-eight hours of content. Ten more followed in 2011, and by 2012, with more than 250 hours of programming already in circulation, the pace of production leveled off at eight to nine new shows or films a year. Ratings were strong, especially for dramatic series, and the flow of quality proposals far outstripped the program's ability to fund them all. As commercial broadcasters increasingly chased low-budget, mass-appeal programs, AVI CHAI was becoming the prime address for higher-quality dramas and documentaries focused on Jewish identity.

But none of these marks of progress could have prepared the foundation for the spectacular success of *Shtisel*, a family drama set in the

Haredi enclaves of Geula and Mea She'arim in central Jerusalem. The series follows the day-to-day lives of Shulem Shtisel—played by the eminent Israeli actor Dov Glickman, with an exquisite blend of wit and pathos—and his sons and daughter and their complicated loves and careers. From the perspective of AVI CHAI's mission, the program was significant in its portrayal of Haredi life as something that others, outside the devoutly religious world, could understand and sympathize with. But as a matter of pure production quality, the program was groundbreaking: elegant, visually riveting, elegiacally written, with a strong cast of some of Israel's finest acting talent, and generally polished beyond anything typical of an Israeli TV drama up to that point.

Originally released in June 2013, it immediately won four Ophirs, the Israeli Emmys, for Best Drama and for Best Actor (Glickman), Best Directing (Alon Zingman), and Best Script in a Drama Series. The second season added four more: Best Actor in a Drama Series (Glickman again), Best Actress in a Drama Series (Neta Riskin as his daughter, Giti), Best Directing and Best Original Music. A few years later, Netflix acquired both seasons, subtitled in multiple languages, and they became an international phenomenon. Plans for a third season were announced in 2018.

And yet, when the proposal first arrived at AVI CHAI, it got a nearly instantaneous rejection. "They sent me a synopsis of the first season, I read it, and I hated it," Suri Drucker, the foundation's lead staffer for media, said in a reminiscence in 2019. The filmmakers Yehonatan Indursky and Ori Elon "were young, and it was their first drama series. They had loaded it up with every kind of dysfunction you could imagine. I guess they wanted to show real life, but they pulled out all the stops, and there was nothing that was positive. There was nothing in there that was redeeming. There was nothing that would make me want to love these characters." Still, knowing that a lot can change between synopsis and script, and out of faith in the young writers' talent, instead of merely saying no, Drucker wrote seventeen pages of notes, commenting on nearly every aspect of the synopsis. Then she all but slammed the door, figuratively speaking, and told them, "I will never go near this project."

The producer, Dikla Barkai, kept coming back anyway. After a couple of her further overtures were rebuffed, the filmmakers finished shooting the first season and then asked Drucker one last time at least to take a look. They didn't need much financing at that point, but they wanted the AVI CHAI stamp of excellence. It was all still very rough, but Barkai assured Drucker that she would see something altogether different from what she'd seen before. That was true. From the simplicity of the story-lines to the deft writing to the complex humanity of the characters and artful direction, the segment she saw was unrecognizable from the original proposal, and it was stunning. "I was floored," she remembered. "I was in tears. And I said, 'This is genius. I am in—big time.'" She presented the project to the foundation's media committee—Mem Bernstein, Avital Darmon, Meir Buzaglo, and Eli Silver—who had a similar reaction. AVI CHAI joined as a funder, injecting critical support for the postproduction phase of Season 1 and overall collaboration and support for Season 2. Its logo now concludes every episode.

Renee Ghert-Zand, a Jerusalem-based critic for *The Forward*, described the rapturous nationwide audience response it received:

In Israel, *Shtisel* wasn't just on cable—it was everywhere. Huge billboards featuring the show's bearded and side-locked characters popped up in secular Tel Aviv, a city where it's more usual to see images of bikini-clad supermodel Bar Refaeli looming over the freeway. Articles, reviews and blog posts about Shtisel appeared in major publications. Memes based on the show filled social media feeds. It even got to the point where tossing around the Yiddish expressions regularly uttered by the show's characters was the way to prove you were hip.

For AVI CHAI's purposes, Ghert-Zand's comments on the diversity of *Shtisel*'s audience showed how perfectly it fit the foundation's mission in Israel: "*Shtisel* became a huge, popular success in its second season among viewers of all backgrounds, including some ultra-Orthodox Jews without televisions who admitted to watching it via streaming video on the Internet. . . . Praise has been heaped on the artfully produced *Shtisel* for drawing the interest of secular Jews toward Haredim and the way they live."[44]

To be sure, *Shtisel* would have been produced with or without AVI CHAI. As in all its media projects, the foundation provided only a fraction of the budget—its general practice was to contribute 20 percent for dramas and sometimes a bit more for documentaries. Although it was not the driving force, financially or creatively, behind the shows it supported, the foundation was deeply involved in content and character development, often beginning in the earliest stages of a program's concept. With *Shtisel*, its timely contribution, and some further suggestions from Drucker, richly improved the first season's postproduction.

Much of the visual elegance of the show, the combined feeling of intimacy and swift dramatic pace that makes it distinctive, was the fruit of these late stages. What critic Ghert-Zand described as "an accomplished feature-film feel to the small-screen production" was in no small part the result of the meticulous editing the foundation's investment helped to make possible. In the following season, Drucker's participation in story and script development was more typical, running from start to finish (although, she acknowledged, "the team is so talented and intelligent there wasn't much to be improved on"). By the time the show was set to produce a third season, AVI CHAI's share of the budget had grown, and producers said the foundation's continued participation was crucial to making Season 3.

Apart from its quality and market success, another aspect of *Shtisel* demonstrates how AVI CHAI's approach to film and television evolved over the years. Unlike the foundation's earlier successes *Meorav Yerush almi* and *Merchak Negi'aa*, *Shtisel* doesn't depict a diverse Jewish world. It takes place almost exclusively in the Haredi community, and its characters rarely interact with people of other backgrounds. In the foundation's early years in media, Danieli, as the lead staff person, had insisted that programs bearing the foundation's logo must encompass Judaism in all its varieties, and characters of different backgrounds had to grapple with questions of common identity and coexistence. That approach led to some excellent programs, but it severely limited the number of high-quality scripts the foundation would receive. The roster of writers and producers interested in satisfying such a demand wasn't large.

Over time, and particularly during Drucker's tenure, the foundation's view of how its mission applied to creative projects shifted. Rather than demanding that films always show some encounter between characters of different persuasions, she said, "I feel that the real encounter is between the screen and the viewer. So it doesn't bother me if we're seeing the inside life of one particular community. In fact, that's a very good way of becoming deeply intimate with a particular character and a particular way of life. Watching the program, I'm having a dialog with that character at home."

Nor is it necessary, or even necessarily useful, to depict understanding and reconciliation in every instance, Drucker believed. Sometimes, baring a raw conflict and allowing viewers to understand the conflict in its own terms can be a way to inspire thought and understanding in the audience, even when understanding does not take place on the screen. "Some people will find something beautiful; some people will find it ugly," she said. "For me, that's OK. The important thing is to *find* it, and to have it speak to you in its own language. And if that provokes a struggle, so be it."

Even so, some significant projects still did focus on cross-cultural encounters and met with critical and popular success. For example, in a development studio that AVI CHAI created for leading screenwriters and filmmakers—where artists fleshed out story ideas based on Jewish themes, studied and discussed textual sources, and incorporated them into their scripts—the distinguished director Avi Nesher developed the feature film *The Other Story*. The plot revolves around a young woman from a secular family and her fiancé, a hard-partying pop star, who have lately become devoutly religious—a choice that alarms her parents. A subplot involves a divorce and custody battle between a Jewish husband and a wife who has rejected Judaism. Many of the details of the characters' differing approaches to Jewish life and tradition were honed in the AVI CHAI studio.

The title's double meaning hints at all the "others" in the plot—people who are seen, outside their own communities, as alien and frightening. Nell Minow, author of the popular "Movie Mom" column in the United States, wrote that "Nesher skillfully balances a lot of characters and storylines, each illustrating a different kind of Israeli and a different connection to Jewish life, culture, and practice, but he never lets any of them become symbolic rather than real."[45] In short, it was a quintessentially AVI CHAI film: portraying both the full rainbow of Jewish society and the rewards of holding that diverse society together with understanding and compassion.

In 2014, AVI CHAI and its frequent partner, the Gesher Multicultural Film Fund, joined forces to create a freestanding partnership called the Film and Media Collaborative. The partnership was designed to survive the foundation's sunset and to preserve the AVI CHAI brand, which was widely recognized in Israel's media as a mark of artistic quality, conscientious Jewish content, and deeper, more intelligent scripts. The film fund provided about one-third of the partnership's initial budget—about $400,000, with AVI CHAI providing the remaining $800,000. Gesher joined foundation representatives on the governing Media Committee and established a project office, headed by Drucker, in its headquarters.

By the end of its second year, the collaborative had nearly thirty projects in some stage of development and ten finished pieces entered in various international festivals the previous year.

The partnership with Gesher Multicultural Film Fund was set to run through 2026, though as this is written, its lifespan seems sure to be longer than that. In 2017, Mem approached the Maimonides Fund—a frequent and close collaborator on a number of initiatives—with a proposal to join the project and carry it beyond the last of the AVI CHAI investment.

Mem's appeal was itself a media production. She made her case in a sleekly designed video brochure, containing a professionally produced sales pitch on a seven-inch-diagonal video screen wrapped in a full-color printed case. The video started automatically when the cover was opened. After a stark, white-on-black opening screen ("A People is defined by the stories it tells"), Mem appeared to deliver her onscreen proposition, intercut with snippets of hit AVI CHAI productions and quick graphics on audience share, distribution, awards won, the project's financial model, marketing strategies, and other details. She elaborated on how the film and media project promotes "Jewish engagement in a spirit of understanding, tolerance, and diversity—on a mass scale."

The message was perfectly tailored to fit Maimonides' goal, prominent on its website, of "sharing Jewish stories and ideas to generate a greater openness and engagement with Jews, Israel, and Jewish content." Nevertheless, the video brochure was designed and presented not as a proposal to one foundation, but as an appeal to Jewish donors in general ("We call upon philanthropists who share our passion for Jewish culture . . . ," the text on the cover began). The production showed every sign of being the centerpiece of a broad-based campaign. But Mem hoped it would serve its whole purpose in one meeting, by enticing the Maimonides Fund to back the project. She was right.

When the fund's anonymous donors saw the video, they were captivated, Mem recalled. But they first wanted to know, "Who else are you showing this to?" For now, she answered, they were the only ones; the project was theirs if they wanted it. The deal was effectively closed on the spot. It was a rare example of a project that had been created and branded solely by AVI CHAI and then embraced, intact and all but unconditionally, by another funder.

———

Inviting Israelis to encounter Judaism in new ways and apply it to their lives has been at the heart of AVI CHAI's programming from the beginning and in almost every aspect of its work. In its late years, the foundation's effort to bring that vision to the broad public, to infuse the whole Israeli culture with it, extended not only to the film and media project, the cultural cornucopia of Beit AVI CHAI, and the broadcasting power of the internet, but deep into the most intimate place in Jewish life: the Sabbath table.

An initiative that came to be known as Shabbat Unplugged began as a daring effort to leap headlong into the maelstrom of Israel's religious politics and to rescue a treasure of Jewish life from factional manipulation. Buzaglo, in proposing the measure, argued that observance of Shabbat—a quintessentially Jewish rite of weekly serenity, reflection, and family time—had become captive in the cultural struggles between the two poles of Israeli society: the devout and the strictly secular. Although these two groups make up a minority of the Israeli public, their anxieties and mutual distrust tend to inflame political debate and taint every facet of Judaism in the public sphere. And yet the great majority of Jews recognize, Buzaglo believed, that Shabbat is not solely a religious treasure of Judaism, but also a cultural and emotional one. It is an opportunity to refresh and recharge the mind and soul in ways that are steeped in Jewish tradition and peoplehood.

AVI CHAI, Buzaglo told the board in 2016, uniquely has the reputation and resources—not to mention a mandate rooted in its mission—to alleviate the tension. But first, as the board's initial discussion of the topic made clear, it would be nececeary to pin down a goal. It was easy to rule out the extremes. The foundation would not attempt to push religious observance on the unwilling, and it would not seek to neuter the Sabbath by sponsoring irrelevant distractions. But between those two, what exactly would the foundation be promoting? Would it, as one trustee feared, be trying to change the weekly habits of large numbers of people, altering the way families interacted and spent their leisure time? Would any foundation have the resources to make that kind of sweeping societal change?

In a preliminary proposal, Ruth Kabbesa-Abramzon, a Buzaglo protégé who had just completed a doctoral dissertation on the link between culture and governance, set out to answer some of these questions. She suggested a program aimed at stimulating and expanding activities that would make the essence of Shabbat available to people of virtually any religious persuasion, from the most observant to the least, even to atheists. The idea would be to create a network of organizations already offering activities on Shabbat and help make those activities more visible, more widespread, and more popular. It would also involve working with organizations to create altogether new activities—to "expand the options for celebrating the day and finding meaning in its commemoration."[46] It was a big, bold, but slightly blurry concept that was designed to become more and more concrete as the network, the activities, and the marketing expanded.

It would also be AVI CHAI's final entirely new initiative, launched just three years before the foundation's grantmaking came to a halt. And yet in many ways it harked directly back to Zalman Bernstein's original vision for Israel: helping Jews of varying backgrounds and degrees of religious observance find common ground in the richness of their Jewish customs and heritage. It bore echoes of the original grand vision of harmony that created Tzav Pius, and of the great hopes for spreading Jewish literacy through pluralistic batei midrash. But unlike those early Bernstein initiatives, which had decades to make their mark, this last one would have to find its legs within thirty-six months, and then soldier on without AVI CHAI to stand behind it.

At Buzaglo's urging, Kabbesa-Abramzon agreed to become the full-time director of the new initiative and quickly began assembling a roster of programs that came to number around three dozen by the end of the second year. They took place in thirty cities and towns all around Israel, sponsored by roughly fifty organizations. Some programs were new, developed in a kind of innovation lab that the program called its "House of Creation." To design these new offerings, provider organizations would work with Kabbesa-Abramzon and her staff to come up with ways of appealing to people who might not have made a regular observance of Shabbat before or who might not have a ready opportunity to celebrate it with others. Other initiatives were not new, but grew out of expanded versions of existing activities, made bigger or more extensive with grants drawn from an initial allotment of $1.5 million from AVI CHAI.

Activities sponsored under the banner of Shabbat Unplugged included various approaches to Kabbalat Shabbat, some musical programs in open-air or café settings, activities for families with children, and other cultural programs on Sabbath themes. Some involved activity that would not be permitted during Shabbat, so those programs took place at other times, usually early afternoon on Fridays. The foundation had instructed, from the outset, that its money could not be used for any activity during Sabbath hours that would be forbidden under traditional Jewish law.

Still, the programs made minimal demands on participants, except that they join in respectfully and with tolerance for others. Those who were more observant needed to be prepared for the presence of others who might be less so. The point of these activities was not necessarily to be religious events—some were, some weren't—but to be unifying experiences for Jews to celebrate a common heritage and a treasured tradition. There were programs sponsored by environmental groups, ethnic organizations, schools, community centers, rural collectives, hiking clubs.

Keeping the programs respectful toward tradition yet welcoming and diverse demanded a delicate balancing act, but most organizers made it work. Collectively, they exceeded their participation goals almost immediately. In all, Shabbat Unplugged programs in the first year attracted 7,600 participants, more than 25 percent above the original estimates. A year later, the number was just under 17,000; a year after that it was close to 40,000 attendees. After a point, even some for-profit businesses were asking whether they, too, could join the network and sponsor Shabbat Unplugged activities. In a country of 9 million people, the numbers obviously weren't huge, but that was not the point. The goal was to create ways of celebrating and observing that are unifying, not divisive, and that could become, over time, parts of the Sabbath routine for many families and communities.

Alongside the programs came an ad campaign in print, online, and on radio (television was considered too high-profile, and some at AVI CHAI feared that TV spots might provoke a backlash). The campaign's message, drawn from extensive opinion research on Israeli attitudes toward technology, was that Shabbat was a time to unplug from the unrelenting stresses and demands of the virtual world and enjoy the deeper pleasures of face-to-face interaction, reflection, rest, and family. The ads were careful not to condemn technology, nor to present Shabbat as a time when technology was forbidden. Instead, the message was: take the opportunity Shabbat offers to savor the people and places around you. The message evidently struck a chord. More than 85 percent of respondents to an audience survey reported strong positive feelings about the ads. It was much too soon to say whether any of this changed people's behavior, but the survey response suggested that it resonated at some level. Even if people found it hard to set their devices aside for a day, they seemed to be saying they wished they could, and they saw a value in doing so. To Kabbesa-Abramzon, that was a start.

"We see ourselves as creators of a new language about Shabbat," she said in 2019, well into the program's third year. The choice of Shabbat

Unplugged as the organization's name was based on a desire to cast the Sabbath as a weekly time of liberation both from technology and, for the less religious, from a narrow conception of Sabbath observance that had associated it only with prohibitions and restraints. "We chose the notion of 'Unplugged' because it is worldwide," Kabbesa-Abramzon explained. "The desire for family time, personal time, community time, quiet time—it's universal. It's healthy for the wellbeing of individuals and of society. And, of course, it's also completely Jewish."

The problem with running a program of grant-funded activities, both startup and expansion, was predictable enough. The money from AVI CHAI would soon be gone, and Kabbesa-Abramzon would therefore have to choose between making Shabbat Unplugged a temporary project, three or four years and out, or scrambling to find new resources. Choosing the latter course, she pointed out, would mean changing the basic structure of the program. It could no longer be based mainly on seeding Shabbat activities with grants, because "if donors want to give money for activities, they can give it to organizations directly to sponsor activities. They don't need to give it to me."

Still, she saw a path forward—admittedly narrow and uphill—in which Shabbat Unplugged would pursue partnerships with municipalities to organize local networks of Shabbat activities. Her reasoning was that dealing with nonprofit organizations one by one is labor-intensive, retail work, but "if you can change the municipality or the local government, the impact you can have is tremendous." (This was, to a considerable extent, the same insight that had led Pascal to promote Otzamot.) The idea soon won a grant from the New York Federation to support an initial, pilot stage, which suggested that the initiative might have legs. Kabbesa-Abramzon also envisioned creating programs and products with the Shabbat Unplugged brand that could earn revenue to defer the cost of basic operations. These might include after-school programs, weekend retreats for families, and other experiences and games that could attract paying customers.

As this is being written, the new direction is still unfolding, and it is far too soon to know where it will lead or how successful it will be. Creating a "new language" about something so fundamental and (at the moment) so contentious as Shabbat would surely take many years of sustained effort. Launching it with just a three-year runway was at best a long shot. "The project is trying to turn Shabbat from a negative into a virtue," Rosenblatt noted when the board approved the initial $1.5 million grant to launch Shabbat Unplugged. "The key will be to create habits that cultivate the virtue." Habits—especially the habits of a whole society—take a very long time to form. So Kabbesa-Abramzon's decision to try to give Shabbat Unplugged a longer life makes sense, and may even be the only way for the initiative to have anything close to its intended effect. But that effort will have to forge ahead, hastily and under pressure, without her prime backer to stand behind it.

"We see, after every campaign or marketing effort we are doing, that a lot of people like the message," Kabbesa-Abramzon said toward the end of her third year on the job. "And these things make them think about the message, and they want to change the way they behave. And some of them are even saying that they changed something. But, of course, it works for a week or two. If you really want to change people's lives, if you want to change society, you have to be in people's head every week, and constantly give them ideas about what to do, and strengthen them in what they're doing."

———

The goal of Shabbat Unplugged, like that of most other AVI CHAI projects in Israel, was aimed equally at the twin purposes set out in the foundation's mission statement: to draw Jews closer to one another, and closer to their heritage and traditions. But the essential challenge confronting Shabbat Unplugged—that many secular Israelis were wary of those same traditions and of the people who observed them—also hovered over other parts of the program.

Swimming against the hard currents of religious politicization and secular anxiety in Israel, AVI CHAI had to promote a Jewishness that was neither religious nor anti-religious, that fit comfortably, unthreateningly into a secular consciousness without being itself secular and without diluting or dumbing down the treasures of Judaism that it sought to promote. It had to be true to the spirit of the Ba'al T'Shuva who created the institution, inspired by his own religious awakening, but it could not push piety on the unwilling.

Even the mission statement itself had to bend to the pressure of these conflicting demands. As originally written in English, the statement made the religious inspiration behind AVI CHAI's formation all but unmistakable. The foundation, it said, would "encourage Jews toward greater commitment to Jewish observance" and to the "practice of Jewish traditions, customs, and laws." In North America, where cultivating "religious purposefulness" was a capstone of AVI CHAI's philanthropy, that language suited the program and its environment perfectly. In Israel, however, it had not been translated into Hebrew for the foundation's first twenty-four years and was rarely quoted. Only in 1998, when AVI CHAI was preparing the first annual report to be published in Hebrew, did the question of how these terms would be received in Israel come to the fore.

The solution, with Bernstein's blessing, was to create a Hebrew version of the mission that was subtly different in tone from the literal English. Beginning with the first published translation, the relevant passage in Hebrew became: "to nurture an *affinity* for tradition *amongst all parts of the Jewish people*, and to encourage understanding and appreciation of the Jewish heritage, *its culture*, its laws, its customs, and *its values*" (emphasis added).

"Rather than 'encourage greater commitment,' we went with 'nurture an affinity,'" Silver elaborated years later. "We added culture and we added values, and we wrapped those around the laws and customs. 'Encourage' can sound like pressure, and that was not what we were about. We were trying to say that what we want for you is to become knowledgeable about and have a loving relationship with this heritage. Exactly what you do with it, we're not going to dictate." This was a great deal more than just some deft wordsmithing—it was an explicit reckoning with the role the foundation would play in Israel, the balance it would constantly labor to maintain, and the challenges that it would (and would not) embrace in trying to nourish the nation's Jewish heart and soul.

The addition of "culture" and "values" set the tone for much of the film and media work, for the community-building enterprises of Tzav Pius and Nitzanim, for the secular Jewish spirit of the kibbutz and moshav programs, and—most vividly and most enduringly—for the cultural cornucopia of Beit AVI CHAI. Even the more expressly religious canon of piyyutim became, in AVI CHAI's widening promotion of the art form, a cultural expression that large numbers of less-religious Israelis found engrossing. That, by itself, hints at a warming of secular attitudes toward Judaism's religious heritage, which, if true, bodes well for a further rapprochement between more- and less-observant Israelis over time.

In a broad retrospective reflection in 2019, the prominent Israeli journalist Yair Sheleg traced the origin of this warming of attitudes to AVI CHAI's seminal early support for pluralistic batei midrash like Elul, Alma, and Kolot. The opening of this traditionally religious form of study to a wider range of Jewish subjects—including, but not limited to, religious texts—and the invitation to secular and religious Jews to learn together eventually led, in Sheleg's opinion, to a "positive brand" for Judaism among Israel's more secular elites. The batei midrash "opened the door to the whole process of Jewish Renewal." From there, through other initiatives and wider channels, the message slowly spread: "There is a revolution," as Sheleg put it; "there is a renaissance toward Judaism," visible even in the most secular corners of the news media, the academy, and popular culture.

Sitting with Sheleg on the same panel in 2019, other researchers drew similar lines of causation between AVI CHAI initiatives and the warming landscape of Israeli Judaism. Decades of work enriching and diversifying Jewish studies in state schools, for example, "strengthened and expanded a multifaceted view of Judaism," according to Nurit Chamo, an education scholar at the Levinsky College of Education in Tel Aviv. In the judgment of Ronen Goffer, the expert in participatory democracy who evaluated AVI CHAI's programs at the communal level, those programs have set in motion "a trend of local communities that aspire to conduct their lives according to Israeli Jewish values and to create a sense of local pride and renewed belonging to Judaism as a tradition and a culture that belongs to everyone." Regev Ben-David, a researcher and lecturer specializing in Jewish identities and peoplehood, credited the foundation's gap-year programs—both the pluralistic mechinot and the Sh'nat Sherut experience—with establishing "a standard by which many of those who opt for this voluntary gap year deal significantly with Jewish–Israeli content." "That is an immense achievement," he concluded, "because this is where the future of Israeli society springs from."

To be sure, all the experts on the panel raised cautions and caveats—most of them related to a mountain of still-unfinished work, the uncertainties of still-evolving trends and movements, the vagaries of politics and public moods, and most of all, the scarcity of financial support, both from philanthropy and from government, to sustain and bring to fruition the cultural currents that AVI CHAI had helped to animate. Still, it was a strikingly upbeat and coherent verdict from a team of observers piecing together scores of disparate programs on multiple themes.

Although the foundation's program in Israel lacked the strategic focus and theory of change that characterized its work in North America, the results did, it seems, home in on a single, definable achievement: planting seeds of a renewed Jewish identity in Israel, expansive enough to embrace all the ethnic, cultural, intellectual, and religious approaches to Judaism that make up the country's social mosaic, but rich and solid enough to have meaning and appeal for a growing number of Israelis. It had, in the terms of its Hebrew mission statement, "nurtured an affinity for tradition amongst all parts of the Jewish people." Or, as Silver more informally put it, the foundation had helped a significant, still growing number of Israelis who had drifted from Judaism "become knowledgeable about and have a loving relationship with this heritage."

How many more people this trend can reach, and how long it may last, remain to be seen. But the achievement, as AVI CHAI drew its grant-making to a close in Israel, was widely recognized. "It's a small country," Weiss had said near the end of the program's life, "and here, in this place, we created—not we alone, and we didn't finish, the game is not over yet—but there is a clear potential of an ecosystem forming here, which can now be fertilized and can grow."

XVI

THE FORMER SOVIET UNION

Opening Gateways

The market crash of 2008 struck Jewish philanthropy in the former Soviet Union (FSU)—and many of the projects AVI CHAI was supporting there—with particular force. Not only did the crisis take the wind out of the economy generally, jeopardizing business models for the schools, universities, and cultural programs that were at the heart of AVI CHAI's FSU program, but it deflated the fortunes of some key foundation funding partners. Two prominent philanthropists in particular emerged from the crash economically battered and unable to continue supporting critical AVI CHAI grantees at anything like their prior levels.

The first, Stanley Chais, had been a prime funder of Booknik, the Jewish literary website; of the series of Jewish nonfiction books in Russian; of the cultural and literary programs known as Eshkol; of advanced Judaic scholarship programs at universities; and of the umbrella group for university-level Jewish studies known as Sefer. Chais's family foundation was devastated by the 2008 collapse of Bernard Madoff's Ponzi scheme, in which it had invested. Second, the diamond and real estate entrepreneur Lev Leviev suffered severe losses when the global real estate market imploded, and his businesses went through years of restructuring. His foundation, Or Avner, had helped fund Sefer and had been a prime funder of many Jewish day schools, camps, and youth programs supported by AVI CHAI. Or Avner survived, but with reduced budgets for several years.

These losses were especially painful for the FSU program and its executive director, David Rozenson, because the program had been premised, from the start, on recruiting significant contributions from other funders. Unlike most AVI CHAI projects elsewhere, efforts in the FSU were never dependent solely on foundation money. Rozenson and trustee George Rohr had made a determined effort to cultivate wealthy Russians like Leviev and international donors like Chais as a way of softening the blow of AVI CHAI's eventual departure. These two donors in particular were more than just financial partners with AVI CHAI; Chais, for example, had formed a close personal and intellectual bond with Rozenson and conferred regularly with him about program opportunities and possible directions. Now, with two major allies on their heels, AVI CHAI's expectations about the future of Sefer, Booknik, and especially Or Avner's programs for day schools and summer camps would all have to be rethought.

"As wonderful as it is to have donors have that strength and commitment," Arthur Fried lamented at a 2009 board meeting, "it's tough when a storm blows them over." The best way to protect the program from future surprises of this kind, he suggested, is to continue broadening the base of funding partners, avoiding too much dependence on "what happens to the giants."

The foundation upped its support for some projects that had been drawing sustenance from the wounded donors, most notably an emergency grant of $800,000 in mid-2009 to keep the Or Avner network of camps and youth programs alive through the summer while they sought new donations. However, AVI CHAI's international belt-tightening in 2009 would ultimately have meant further damage to the financial health of several of its projects in Russia and Ukraine. The FSU program, being much smaller than those in North America and Israel, was meant to take just a 20 percent cut, compared with 25 to 30 percent in the other two regions. Still, piled onto the hard loss of support from Chais, Leviev, and others—and given the need for a large emergency grant for the camping program—even that level of reduction would have jeopardized some important initiatives, still in their formative years, that were bedrock elements of the program.

After a couple of years of reduced spending at the $4 million annual target, outlays soon floated back up to their earlier $5 million level. But the overall amount of money allocated to the FSU through the end of AVI CHAI's grantmaking did not change. Faced with that constraint, the program chose to maintain its higher level of annual spending, burn through its available resources more quickly, and end three or four years before the rest of the foundation. In Rozenson's view, it would still be possible to solidify key projects in that amount of time, provided they were given extensive help in planning for the end of AVI CHAI support and in finding new contributors.

Fortunately, one source of new money appeared quickly, in the form of the Genesis Philanthropy Group, an international charity formed by five Jewish Russian businessmen to promote a sense of peoplehood among Russian-speaking Jews. The group planned to spend $2.5 million in the former Soviet Union in 2010, and its interests overlapped extensively with those of AVI CHAI. Genesis soon became a funding partner of considerable value, covering multiple areas of foundation interest, including book publishing, cultural events, and Hebrew language teaching.

Still, the program and its grantees would not have as much time to recover from the economic constriction of 2008 as did its counterparts in Israel and North America. Work in the FSU came to a close in 2016, more than three years before the rest of the foundation's grantmaking. From the beginning, its purpose had been to seed the fields of Jewish education, culture, and youth programs with enriched content and new ways of reaching unaffiliated Jewish populations. The growth of philanthropy in Russia, including among very wealthy Russian Jews like those who had created Genesis, suggested that the seeds thus planted would have reasonably fertile ground in which to grow, once their potential was demonstrated.

But the time was short, the landscape huge, and the habits of philanthropy not yet fully formed in the FSU. The labor of forming partnerships with other funders, building and preserving their enthusiasm, and helping grantees to secure a future beyond AVI CHAI would prove arduous and, in some instances, less than fully satisfying.

In one area, however, success came early and with unmistakable results. The establishment of a full-fledged Department of Jewish Studies at Moscow State University marked a milestone in post-Soviet Jewish history, not only because of the university's prestige, but even more because its faculty and alumni were disproportionately represented among the nation's leaders in culture and academia. The likelihood that a greater number of influential people would now at least be exposed to Jewish scholarship at a high level, and might thus be more inclined to think of Jewish education and culture as something important, even precious, was by itself a remarkable philanthropic achievement. Even assuming that the number of people directly involved in the new department would be small—roughly one hundred students were enrolled in the 2008–09 academic year, out of a total student body of more than 35,000—its presence on campus, its ability to host programs and lectures, the increased funding that would flow to it, and the aura of legitimacy and importance it bestowed on its subject all contributed to an important change in the way Jewish scholarship would be perceived among elite Russians.

Accordingly, as the foundation was tightening its FSU budget in 2009, support for Moscow State was one area of activity that could be wound down without anguish. Although, under more ideal circumstances, some trustees would have preferred to continue supporting the department at full strength for another year or two, as it fleshed out its program and pursued additional funders, Rozenson felt confident that AVI CHAI could safely declare victory and withdraw. The department's budget from the university was growing, he reported; its facilities and faculty had expanded significantly, and other donors, including Genesis, were signing on. "I think we've done everything we could" to put the program on steady footing, he said. A final grant of $500,000 would cover scholarships for one more cohort of students, through 2014, after which nearly a decade of support would come to an end.

The next milestone in university-level Jewish studies would soon be met at St. Petersburg State University, the nation's oldest and second-largest. The university's Center for Jewish Studies, part of the faculty of philosophy, had begun accepting new students annually starting in the 2008–09 academic year, and had recently added a Judaica collection to the main university library. It was then on track to win its independence, and in 2011 it became the free-standing Department of Jewish Culture and Research. That move led to increased faculty and higher enrollments, more scholarships, and better facilities and equipment. After years of AVI CHAI support, a first-time grant from Genesis, and additional funding from others soon followed. By the end of the 2011–12 academic year, AVI CHAI's share of the department's funding was falling, and fully half its budget was coming from either the university or the government.

As Rozenson pointed out to the trustees in early 2012, the combined presence of these two departments at the country's preeminent universities virtually guaranteed that Judaic scholarship would gain stature elsewhere. Meanwhile, for young scholars not enrolled full time in Jewish studies, but whose interests or research touched on Jewish themes, the seminars, publications, and summer academies offered by the Sefer network presented a growing forum for learning and networking. A 2011 evaluation of Sefer, commissioned by AVI CHAI, described the program as "the only organization to offer consistent opportunities for students of Judaica in the former Soviet Union to gather together."

The evaluator, Harvard student (and later *New Yorker* journalist) Talia Lavin, wrote that Sefer "provides an invaluable service that must continue to be supported." While noting with concern the group's bare-bones staffing and shoestring budget—a problem that persisted well beyond AVI CHAI's tenure in Russia—the evaluation concluded that "the wide net Sefer casts, and its effort to pursue programming in many different locations in the FSU foster an environment of true intellectual adventurousness across regions, borders, ethnicities, religions, and communities."[47]

Having observed five different Sefer programs, Lavin described the alchemy of weighty discussions and sometimes hard partying that made them unique. They were a blend of scholarly forum, research expedition, and what AVI CHAI's North American staff had called the makings of a "tribe"—gatherings of leaders and thinkers bound together by both professional affinity and personal fellowship. For example, one Sefer field school that Lavin visited took place two hours outside Volgograd in cement huts without plumbing, where students interviewed the few remaining members of a crypto-Jewish sect called the Subbotniki, or Shabbatniks. Participants later presented their research and observations at Sefer's winter conference, and their papers were archived at the Russian State University for the Humanities. At another Sefer event, an ethnographic field school in Beltsi, Moldova, the mission was to explore Jewish customs and traditions in prewar Bessarabia. But the informal interactions with locals added a rich personal experience on top of the research—including, for example, an interview with a local Romany woman about Jewish–gypsy relations (she told their fortunes as a parting gift), and a Shabbat dinner where, as the night went on, guests belted out tunes ranging from "Yiddish and gypsy love ballads to American blues."[48]

The point is not merely that Sefer's catalogue of programs was unusual, multifaceted, and sometimes eccentric, but that it was aimed exactly where AVI CHAI increasingly wanted its focus to be: at the intersection of mind and spirit, mingling serious study and a more emotional or experiential form of discovery and understanding. Sefer's version of "tribe building" created an intellectual and social space for advanced Jewish learning outside the formal academy, among people who might not pursue Jewish studies degrees or careers in Jewish education, but who would still have spent quality time soaking up an atmosphere of Jewish history and culture, and have memories and friendships in which all that they learned could be anchored. It was in that way similar to AVI CHAI's Day School Leadership Training Institute in North America or to the Journey to Jewish Heritage or MASA programs it sponsored in Israel. Except that, in the former Soviet Union, Sefer was the *only* experience of its kind available anywhere.

At the time of Lavin's evaluation, new donors were starting to take note, including the New York Federation and Genesis. The amounts they contributed were at first comparatively small and still awarded only year by year, making it hard for Sefer to develop longer-term plans. The organization "has always teetered on the brink of financial crisis," Rozenson observed in 2012, and his expectations about Sefer's survival post-AVI CHAI remained ambivalent.[49] But donations grew over time, and by the time the foundation's program in the FSU closed in 2016, all of its contributions for advanced Jewish scholarship, both to Sefer and the universities, had been fully replaced by local donors.

———

The goal of elevating Judaism among the pantheon of important cultural topics in Russia extended beyond the universities, to include the libraries and bookshops where book-hungry Russians sought information and entertainment. By 2010, the book publishing series that AVI CHAI had launched five years earlier had produced seventy-one titles in high-quality Russian translations — forty nine fiction, sixteen nonfiction, and six children's books. Sales were brisk (nine of the fiction titles had sold out their first runs of 5,000 to 10,000 copies) and critics and literary publications were taking note.

"The series is continuously covered in the Russian press," Rozenson reported in early 2010, "with numerous book reviews, editors' picks as 'books of the week,' and several cover stories."[50] Later that year, a specially designed catalogue went out to all government schools, libraries, and youth programs, offering new Jewish books grouped by categories, along with teaching notes. A reader survey in 2008 found that, among adults, the books were reaching precisely the intended audience: well-educated young professionals, almost one-third of whom had no involvement with communal Jewish life, and close to half of whom got their primary contact with cultural Judaism through AVI CHAI's literary festivals and events.[51]

In 2011, with close to 350,000 books sold, a new series on Israeli and Jewish history joined the roster, with two-thirds of it funded by the Russian businessman and philanthropist David Aminov. The first title in the series, a three-volume history of Israel, sold quickly and was named one of the "Top Books of the Year" by the Moscow International Book Fair—an unprecedented honor for a Jewish book in Russia. In 2012, another new series appeared, offering classics of Yiddish literature—but this time, the funding came entirely from local donors, not from AVI CHAI.

This was crucial. The main goal of the publication project had not been simply to put more Jewish books in circulation, desirable as that was. The bigger purpose had been to test, prove, and ignite an ongoing market for Jewish literature in Russia—a market that would sustain itself after the foundation was gone, whether purely through sales revenue or with local philanthropic backing or both. By the middle of 2012, all the available evidence suggested the strategy was working. Not only were more Jewish donors like Aminov adopting book projects, but publishers were beginning to make money on more and more titles even without philanthropic sponsors.

Between 2012 and 2013, of the twenty new books being issued in the fiction series, half were being published with income from sales and from local sponsors as well as from AVI CHAI. And of the remaining ten titles, seven were purely commercial ventures, with no foundation support at all. Children's books were a similar story. Of the twenty new books for children released in that period, fourteen were being underwritten by local donors, and three of the seven new nonfiction titles would be the result of local philanthropy.[52]

By the time the foundation closed its doors in the former Soviet Union three years later, the pace of new publications and new donors had slowed, but production remained steady at around five new titles a year, even in the absence of AVI CHAI money. Profits from earlier publications were supporting new ones, and while the profit margins were not large, they were proving to be reliable.[53] In 2020, four years after the foundation's last ruble had been spent, Rozenson could report with pride that new books were still in production, and funders who had had their first taste of literary philanthropy at AVI CHAI's side were now firmly committed to keeping the book programs alive.

The Jewish "edutainment" program known as Eshkol had been operating with widening success for five years by the time AVI CHAI began trimming its grant rolls in 2009. The four or five monthly events in literary cafés around Moscow and, later, St. Petersburg were drawing up to 9,500 patrons a year and becoming increasingly well known as a hot destination for sophisticated Jewish culture. Despite a relatively high overhead cost, Eshkol was popular with trustees and so survived the round of budget-tightening. It was, by all evidence, reaching exactly the target audience that Avital Darmon had imagined figuratively as "students of physics"—

smart, accomplished, inquisitive, embedded in elite scholarly or professional social circles, perhaps curious about their heritage, but not (yet)
steeped in Jewish life.

Still, to some trustees, Eshkol was barely scratching the surface of
AVI CHAI's mission. Although the programs brought some of the best in
contemporary Jewish literature, art, film, and music to elite Russian audiences—some events were co-sponsored by respected cultural institutions and some by the Israeli embassy—they didn't go very far toward
encouraging a "greater commitment to Jewish observance and lifestyle,"
as the mission statement prescribed. Wisse in particular wondered
whether the foundation could follow up Eshkol's "toe in the water" approach with something a little weightier, more immersive. For those
whose interest in Jewish culture and learning had been piqued by the
pleasures of Eshkol, shouldn't there be some enticement to deeper learning? And shouldn't that next step delve, at least a bit, into classic Jewish
texts, alongside the lighter, more accessible contemporary fare?

Rozenson shared Wisse's interest in taking Eshkol a step farther, and
he had a pretty good idea of who could do it. Some years earlier he had
met Simon Parizhsky and Alex Budnitsky, young educators who dreamed
of creating a program of Jewish study for unaffiliated Jews in Moscow.
Parizhsky, a Russian doctoral candidate at the Institute for Oriental
Studies in St. Petersburg, had years of experience running batei midrash
and other Jewish learning programs, including some under the Sefer
umbrella. He had studied in Israel and spoke Hebrew fluently. The
Ukrainian-born Budnitsky was likewise a veteran of informal Jewish
study programs. He was working in the United States at the time, but
he visited Moscow frequently and had consulted for a number of organizations reaching out to Russian Jews.

Their idea, fleshed out in a concept paper they developed with a small
foundation grant, was to create a middle ground somewhere between the
fun of Eshkol's one-night events and the more prolonged and demanding
style of study offered, for example, through Sefer. The format needed to

be social, to create a feeling of both enjoyment and community, while offering a substantive introduction to Jewish texts and history. The goal was not simply to help individuals learn, but to wrap them in a kind of Jewish intellectual camaraderie, to cultivate a feeling of belonging as well as learning. The program needed to incorporate contemporary culture as well, to keep the classic matter from being too off-putting for people making a maiden voyage into this kind of study. Most of all, it would offer a higher level of exposure for people who might have been enjoying Eshkol, reading Booknik, perhaps even perusing some of the Jewish titles in the AVI CHAI book series—but who didn't yet consider themselves part of anything expressly Jewish. If the other programs were meant to be gateway experiences, then this would be a salon into which the gateways led.

Rozenson and Rohr, the board's Russia expert, thought this sounded exactly right, but they wanted a field test. So Parizhsky and Budnitsky in 2007 organized a trial run: a program pairing sixteenth-century Jewish texts with pieces of contemporary literature touching on the same themes. It was held in a coffeehouse atmosphere—no hint of either classroom or synagogue. A barista served coffee as it had been brewed in the 1500s, and musicians performed Jewish music on sixteenth-century instruments. The organizers publicized the event modestly, mostly through the Booknik and Eshkol websites, hoping for enough of a turnout to determine whether people found the evening valuable and might recommend it to their friends. "We hoped maybe fifty or sixty people would come," Rozenson reported a few months later. "Then about one hundred eighty people showed up. It was a little overwhelming."[54]

Rozenson and Rohr were delighted, and over the next two months, two more trial events followed. Both were oversubscribed, lively, and rich in content. Interviews and written evaluations from participants furnished glowing reviews. The program was named Eshkolot—the Hebrew expression *ish eshkolot* describes a master of many branches of knowledge, and the name also provided continuity with the Eshkol brand. The board formally launched it with a three-year trial run starting in late 2008. "The first year will be experimental," Rozenson told the trustees, "trying to define the group and testing different approaches. The second year might be just a reaction to what happened in the first. It is only in the third year that we could put together a complete picture of what's happened and lay out a long-term plan."

By the end of the third season of Eshkolot, after two rounds of participant surveys and focus groups, the program had settled into a three-tier format. It hosted some large-scale "edutainment" programs, often in partnership with Eshkol and Booknik, to keep the gateway open and to ensure that Eshkolot would not be associated solely with challenging study. Mini-seminars, lasting for at least three sessions, made up a middle layer of participant commitment, covering topics like Jewish music, poetry, and theater, with texts both ancient and modern. An Eshkolot Study Group, with at least four study sessions, constituted the top tier, with participants reading and discussing Jewish texts in their entirety. (In 2011, for example, two groups studied books of the Bible—one the Book of Esther, the other the Song of Songs.) The lighter programs drew audiences of between 120 and 600 people. The more intensive groups averaged forty to seventy participants, mostly university-age students and young professionals. In all, roughly 5,200 people took part in the second season, when all three tracks were up and running.

Professionally recorded video and live-streaming of Eshkolot's programs and events became more and more common as years went by, with multiplying numbers of online viewers from beyond Moscow. Trendy venues, including a converted chocolate factory in central Moscow teeming with clubs and galleries, added to the project's aura of style and élan. Over time, to keep the audience size up, some content became less demanding and more participatory, like a class on Hebrew calligraphy or one on Hasidic music, but the idea of sustained participation and ongoing learning remained at the center of the initiative.

As demand for the programs grew—including from some groups

outside of Moscow—Eshkolot added a fourth track in 2012: movable Festivals of Jewish Texts and Ideas. The events took place over four to five days in retreat centers near Moscow and other large cities. Each one covered a few related Jewish topics in depth, guided by local and international Russian-speaking educators. Evenings offered networking and edutainment-style programs, activities related to Shabbat, and time for reflection and socializing. By 2016, when AVI CHAI finished its work in the FSU, Eshkolot was easily one of the most popular and influential programs in its portfolio. Eshkolot's database of participants exceeded 12,000 names; average participation in even its more demanding study group sessions had more than doubled in seven years, now reaching 150 people per session.

Eshkolot drew support from the Genesis Philanthropy Group to continue post-AVI CHAI, but not in an amount equal to what the foundation had been providing. Nonetheless, its support has been steady over the years, suggesting a solid relationship between the funders and the program.

In 2013, Rozenson stepped aside as director of the FSU program, returning to Israel to direct Beit AVI CHAI. He passed the baton to his program coordinator, Svetlana Busygina, who oversaw Eshkolot's transition from AVI CHAI's sponsorship to that of Genesis. As AVI CHAI was preparing to exit the stage in the former Soviet Union, Busygina was able to assure the trustees in a final report that "while perhaps [Eshkolot's] budget beyond 2016 will not be as high, it will continue to provide Jewish content for unaffiliated Jewish audiences."[55]

In 2009, the American media measurement and analytics company Comscore declared Russia the home of "the world's most engaged social networking audience."[56] Although the number of Russians online was still much smaller than the ranks of Americans or Chinese, their use of social networking platforms like Facebook and its Russian counterpart,

VKontakte, was much more intense. In May 2009, for example, the average Russian web user spent an average of 6.6 hours per month in social
networks, visiting some 1,300 pages—far above the American averages
of 4.2 hours and 477 pages. For a foundation like AVI CHAI, focused on
matters of identity, peoplehood, and communal attachment, finding
avenues into the virtual communities where more and more social relationships were being forged seemed imperative.

The foundation had already judged the internet to be a critical tool
for reaching the far-flung landscape of post-Soviet Jewry. Its investment
in Booknik.ru was its first major attempt to make Jewish literature available across all of the region's eleven time zones, and grants for Eshkol
and Eshkolot were helping them create websites on which more and
more of their programs were becoming available. But those were more
for learning than for networking. They were repositories of loftier and
lengthier content than is typical in the swift, bite-size communication
of the social networks. To engage young Jews interested in spending time
online with people of similar backgrounds and interests, AVI CHAI would
need something more conducive to interaction and exchange than to
quiet contemplation.

In late 2009, the Russian author and social entrepreneur Sergey
Kuznetsov, who had created Booknik under AVI CHAI auspices, offered
a solution: a project to establish online communities centered on Jewish
themes in all of the most popular Russian-language social networks. This
was Kuznetsov's professional home turf; besides founding Booknik, he
had created SKCG, one of Russia's largest companies for online networking, with clients that included Nike, Intel, and Molotok, Russia's
equivalent of eBay. Creating attractive communities that lured customers, held their attention, and elicited their ongoing participation was his
specialty.

In this case, he proposed creating Jewish news groups, under Booknik's
umbrella, that would then be subdivided into various interest areas like
Jewish holidays, cultural and literary events, Israeli/Jewish heroes and

personalities, food, family, and travel. These would be designed to draw readers into conversations, point them to real-world activities they could join, and provide inviting, digestible information, especially videos, that viewers could learn from and share. Some of this material would be taken from other AVI CHAI-supported sources like Eshkol and Booknik. Each group would have a moderator responsible for developing and promoting content and keeping the group on topic, but the content would ultimately be determined as much by the interests and contributions of the users, whose peer-to-peer interactions would be the main point of the project. Kuznetsov projected reaching some 400,000 occasional visitors in the first year, plus 100,000 more who are dedicated, registered community members, and at least 5,000 who regularly submitted content of their own. These numbers, he believed, would multiply thereafter.

Here once again was a project—like the LRP Collaborative in North America, or Nitzanim in Israel—whose energy was meant to rise from the ground up, and whose ultimate direction would be shaped by the participants, largely beyond the foundation's control. This was, until very recently, alien territory for AVI CHAI, whose emphasis on strategy, planning, meticulous implementation, and sharply defined objectives fit awkwardly in the spontaneous, helter-skelter world of community organizing and social networking. In early discussions of the project, at least one trustee feared that the users' free-form conversations would ultimately drift away from the foundation's core purposes and that users might not "pay attention to what you want them to pay attention to."

Kuznetsov and AVI CHAI's technology officer, Eli Kannai, countered that moderators could set a tone and keep the groups on course to prevent serious deviations from their purpose. But moderators could not, of course, regulate what readers found interesting or dictate how much they conversed with one another. In the end, swallowing some unease but tantalized by the prospect of reaching a wide audience at an important emotional level, the board gave Kuznetsov $425,000 for two years to start the venture and see where it led.

Under Booknik's auspices, however, the project didn't become quite the free-wheeling, wide-open kind of community that Kuznetsov's original proposal hinted at (and that some AVI CHAI trustees feared). Instead, it added a new kind of content to the Booknik milieu—mostly videos, photos, brief items on Jewish history, some just-for-fun quizzes—plus a means of advertising Booknik's other content as well as that of other AVI CHAI programs. Followers were welcome to comment, and did so, but the comments were few and usually mild. A year after its launch, the number of registered members of the network was less than half the original forecast, and the extent of interaction and bottom-up community formation was at best modest.

All the same, the social networking project filled a valuable slot in a growing roster of Booknik offerings, and it added a more playful, less formal way of engaging with the site and discovering its content. Meanwhile, Booknik was hosting an expanded library of videos touching on various themes like the Jewish calendar, cinema, cuisine, history—and, of course, literature. The videos were hugely popular and drove traffic sharply higher, nearly doubling the total number of visits in their first year. A new online-reading section offered some e-books on Jewish themes—a major breakthrough, given how difficult the electronic rights had been to negotiate—and the Torah was likewise made available in PDF format. A few years later a new, fully searchable Russian translation of the Bible was added. A grant from Genesis, matched by AVI CHAI, helped Booknik deliver several online courses from the Open University of Israel. Partnerships with Jewishideasdaily.com (later Mosaicmagazine.com) and the Jewish Review of Books created links to those English-language sites, with Russian translations of some of their articles provided by Booknik.

As the site's traffic continued to climb, an incident in 2010 provided an unexpected insight. A controversial new book on the Bible, disputing the idea that Jews constitute a nation, had sparked a flurry of visits to Booknik by people looking for a response. Caught off guard by the sudden demand, the site had nothing ready to offer in Russian. "It took us a while to translate" something usable, Rozenson explained later, but the incident also gave him and the Booknik staff a jolt. The site needed to be better prepared for cultural adversity. It needed to be stocked with positive information about Judaism and the Jewish people and have a trove of historical resources readily available in Russian. Wisse took the idea a step further. She noted that flare-ups of anti-Jewish propaganda were nothing new, although their incidence seemed to be rising. Now would be the time, she suggested, to have a regular feature and a dedicated editor "to deal preemptively with these types of problems and publications, posting material by those who have written about these issues in a positive way."

It took a while, but by the beginning of 2012 a new blog and video series called "Positively Jewish" was ready to launch. (The name, Rozenson assured the board, "sounds better in Russian.") Edited by Linor Goralik, a noted writer and blogger in Russia who had also written a popular column in Israel, the section offered online discussions, suggested readings, and interactive features presented in an "engaging, funny, and didactic but entertaining manner." A separate page featured similar material for children and their families. The foundation set aside up to $275,000 to get it started. [57]

Much more than the effort at social networking, this was the kind of online project that suited AVI CHAI's style as well as its mission. It equipped readers with thoughtful, well-curated information that defended and strengthened the Jewish people, and it was much more likely to lead people to "pay attention to what you want them to pay attention to." It would also be yet another avenue by which visitors might come to explore Booknik's expanding world of literature, culture, and history.

Yet for all AVI CHAI's cumulative investment in Booknik, the encyclopedic richness of its content, and the healthy expansion of its audience over the course of a decade, it was the one project in the FSU portfolio that never caught on with other funders. The reason is something of a mystery. Some donors in Russia eagerly supported projects to promote Jewish literacy and literature—including some projects created by AVI CHAI—and several devoted money to Jewish studies in schools and universities. But not to Booknik. Some Jewish funders sought ways to reach the Jewish population far from the big cities—a challenge arguably best answered by the internet and the global appeal of literature. Yet Booknik did not capture their imaginations.

By 2016, Booknik was drawing 700,000 visitors a month; it had become the former Soviet Union's preeminent internet address for Jewish thought, culture, and current events. Fried had described it as "vastly more popular than anything else the foundation supports." True, its accumulation of new features and pages over the years had added considerably to its cost. But some trimming and downscaling could have brought those costs within any reasonable requirements. Nonetheless, as AVI CHAI was winding down in the FSU in 2016, Busygina sadly reported to the board that a sponsor had still not been found. "We have knocked on many doors," she wrote, "and while interest was displayed, thus far there have not been any active buyers."[58] Parallel efforts to help Booknik raise earned income through advertising and subscription fees were likewise only partially successful. They were not enough to carry the site into the future without a major backer.

One possible explanation for the lack of donor enthusiasm for Booknik had less to do with the site than with the tenor of the times. Readers trusted and respected Booknik, Busygina said, both for the quality of its content and for its neutrality and balance in matters of politics, religion, and ideology. It was, in her words, "comprehensive, authoritative, and objective."[59] But if those qualities are virtues in the eyes of readers, they may have seemed much less attractive to funders, many of whom had strong views and beliefs of their own and wanted to see those views promoted online. Some prospective backers suggested that they might be willing to take Booknik in a more ideological or polemical direction, but they had no interest in just a wide-open, neutral cultural forum. Both

AVI CHAI and the Booknik staff were convinced that such a change would have been the death of Booknik in all but name.

Another problem for Booknik may have been that it was a virtual temple of culture but not a physical one. Donors at the time tended to be attracted, as Rozenson later put it, to "projects that could be named for them. Booknik was not a building they could name or a book they could dedicate." Besides, he added, the idea of a sophisticated online media venture simply didn't seem charitable to many donors. "Their interest could not be ignited the same way as it would in providing support toward Jewish books, schools, university programs, et cetera."

In a 2017 interview, Busygina reported that Booknik was still alive but little more than a shadow. "It exists," she said. "Online materials are available, so you may find it. There is not so much money now, and little input in advertisements."[60] Traffic was way down; the staff had dispersed. Sergey Kuznetsov, mostly as a labor of love, contributed new pieces every so often, so loyal readers would still have cause to drop in now and then. Perhaps, Busygina imagined, a funder might one day see the remnants of the site and remember what a contribution it had made. Then, perhaps, it might be resurrected or recreated in some form. In any case, that remained a lingering hope.

———

AVI CHAI's most basic contribution to Jewish education in the former Soviet Union was in its support for day schools, which had been its first initiative when it started in the region in 2002. It had set out to strengthen the Jewish atmosphere of some twenty day schools with both better formal Jewish studies and richer experiential learning through various extracurricular and family programs, including Shabbatonim, weekend retreats centered on celebrations of Shabbat. It had also contributed to general academic excellence at five distinguished day schools, although that was always a much smaller line of work, at about $150,000 a year, less than one-eighth of the total day school budget. Even at that scale, the program helped bring about a significant rise in the schools' reputations, the prizes they won in interschool academic competitions, and the number of their graduates admitted to top universities.

Nonetheless, the foundation's primary focus remained on what it called "Judaic enhancement" in thirty schools, an effort that also drew significant support from Israel's Ministry of Education and the Jewish Agency. One important facet of this effort was the promotion of the Hebrew language and Jewish studies curriculum TaL AM, which was in use in nearly thirty schools in the FSU by the 2011–12 academic year. A related initiative, beginning in 2010, brought a group of outstanding high school students from around the FSU to one of six cities, where they took part in four- to five-day seminars preparing them to lead Shabbatonim and other communal youth activities back home. Originally called the "Jewish Day School Incubator," this project consisted of classes on Jewish traditions and heritage, plus practical training sessions on how to organize and lead programs. Afterward, the young people stayed in contact online and via videoconferencing, to reinforce their sense of fellowship and common purpose.

What made the incubator project significant, apart from the stature of the young people and the quality of their training, was that the participating schools covered the whole denominational spectrum of Jewish education in the FSU, from the Orthodox schools affiliated with Chabad to the tech-oriented community schools in the ORT network. This was groundbreaking. Until the AVI CHAI initiative opened, every network of day schools had run its own youth programs, many of which essentially duplicated one another. "The incubator project," Rozenson wrote in 2012, "may very well represent the first pluralistic educational initiative in the FSU."[61] It was later renamed JAM (for Jewish Agency Madrichim), and within a couple of years, it had developed a such a reputation that schools as far afield as Vilnius, Baku, and Bishkek had joined. Local donors joined AVI CHAI and the Education Ministry in underwriting the program.

But the foundation's efforts to improve Jewish learning rested on an underlying structure of day school education in the FSU that was perennially fragile, and that was facing even greater risks after the market crash. Not only had the schools lost some critical homegrown philanthropic support, but some foreign donors had been forced to cut back and Israeli sources were warning that they would likewise be unable to keep up their level of grantmaking in the FSU much longer. Overall, the schools' heavy reliance on Western and Israeli donors was a crisis waiting to happen, and if it did, all the effort at Judaic enhancement would be washed away in the flood. The problem was not a lack of local Jewish philanthropists, but their preference, as Rozenson put it, for "projects outside of Jewish day schools: social welfare, museums, universities, synagogue activity, literature, informal Jewish activities, and others that they or their relatives take part in and with which they can identify."[62] In short, if donors were not themselves day school graduates—and hardly any were—they were unlikely to grasp either the opportunity or the need.

The challenge, therefore, was similar in some ways to those that AVI CHAI faced in North America and Israel: trying to draw Jewish philanthropists and Jewish education closer together in ways that would help educators appeal to donors and help donors understand and value the role of education in the preservation and enrichment of Jewish life. So the foundation borrowed a page from its strategy in those other two regions and created a matching-grants program.

In the autumn of 2012, AVI CHAI organized simultaneous announcements in roughly fifty cities across the region, in which educators, rabbis, and representatives of communal organizations invited donors to take advantage of a ruble-for-ruble match for new contributions to day schools. As in Israel and North America, the donations had to be first-time or substantially increased to qualify for a match—at least $2,000 from a new donor or at least $2,000 more than a donor's largest prior day school donation. The contributions could be for any aspect of day school education—

scholarships, support for specific subjects, faculty salaries or other administrative expenses, anything. The main requirement was that the money had to go directly to a school, and it had to be paid, not merely pledged.

Encouragingly, two major local supporters of Jewish education, Leviev (whose fortunes had stabilized for a while after the crash years) and the real estate and energy magnate Mikhael Mirilashvili, agreed to join with AVI CHAI in creating the pool of matching funds. With $350,000 a year from AVI CHAI, the pool thus came to $700,000, which would produce a total $1.4 million infusion for day schools each year if enough money was raised to qualify for the match. Within a couple of months of the announcements, qualifying offers were flowing in. The program lasted three years, and although the amounts raised never came close to the $700,000 annual target, they did produce roughly $200,000 a year in new donations, a not inconsiderable sum in the cash-starved world of post-Soviet day schools. Most important, the new money helped assure that all the schools weathered the decade's difficult economics. None of them closed.

The ultimate goal, of course, was more than financial. The fund was meant not just to prompt a temporary spike in money for Jewish education, but to lure the donors into a more prolonged relationship with schools, once they saw the results of their contributions and became better acquainted with the educators. That plan worked to some degree, although building enthusiasm among new donors usually takes time, and AVI CHAI's time in the former Soviet Union was drawing short. The matching programs in North America and Israel had run for fifteen and ten years, respectively. In the FSU, the foundation would continue to operate for just one more year after its three-year matching program was finished. At that point, it would be up to the local champions and the schools to continue cultivating sponsors and spotlighting the value of the education day schools provide.

Rozenson had agreed to establish AVI CHAI's program in the former Soviet Union and run it for two years. Twelve years later, he prepared at last to return to Israel. There, he would take over the leadership of Beit AVI CHAI and resume the Israeli life that he and his wife had planned for their children, three of whom had been born in Moscow. It was, he said, a "bittersweet" transition that meant "letting go of overseeing successful projects in the FSU, many of which AVI CHAI initiated, and which took many happy but difficult days and nights first to identify top-rate local leadership and then, together with them, to work continuously to strengthen, widen, and refine" all that had been accomplished.

Although the program still had another four years to run, Rozenson already believed, in late 2012, that the foundation had met with "growing success in identifying significant financial partners" to lead and expand the field of Jewish philanthropy in the FSU. In passing the reins to Busygina, he felt confident that

> the Trustees' support for programs in the FSU, including a number of unique and successful initiatives that we literally birthed from conception, have strengthened and enhanced Jewish and Israeli education and activity in the FSU, attracting new audiences of those previously unaffiliated to Jewish and Israeli life and study, opening new doors, and engaging those in ways that would never have existed had AVI CHAI not made that clearly risk-filled decision, over a decade ago, of expanding its philanthropic reach to the former Soviet Union.[63]

In her concluding remarks to the board four years later, Busygina concurred that, with the disappointing exception of Booknik, the foundation's most important programs had indeed established themselves well enough to survive, at least in some form, beyond its departure. Because the foundation had not pursued any major line of work in the FSU without enlisting at least one other funder, there would be almost no orphaned grantees left behind.

Still, after just sixteen years of effort, it would not be realistic to expect a clear, enduring legacy to have rooted itself firmly in the post-Soviet soil. Much of the story of AVI CHAI's work in the FSU, including any judgment about where it succeeded and where not, would depend on the outcome of years, maybe decades, of further effort by the local philanthropists it left behind.

"We continue to do all that we can to ensure that supported organizations have funding available to continue their work," Busygina assured the trustees in her final months on the job. "This will not be possible for all programs, a fact that is of course painful; but we face the future knowing that the legacy of AVI CHAI in the FSU will be the Jews who became involved in Jewish life and study, at least in part, due to our work."[64]

That outcome was far from assured when AVI CHAI's foray into the former Soviet Union began. "It's essential to remember how precarious this project was when we decided to go there," Wisse pointed out. "We were breaking new ground. The atmosphere in Russia was always uncertain. We were there on thin ice, and most of us, other than George [Rohr], were much less familiar with the territory than we were in North America or Israel. The region had had only recently escaped from Communism, and the new system was untried, still evolving, constantly changing. So it's remarkable how robustly the foundation went into this given those circumstances—the *chutzpah* of it is striking. And then to see all that was accomplished there, it's impressive, really, far better than one had any right to expect."

XVII

LAST WORDS

For at least a decade, AVI CHAI had come to be known in American philanthropic circles as a "time-limited" philanthropy—a charity designed to distribute all its assets in a fixed period of time and then disappear. And the foundation did, in most of its public statements, encourage that perception, or at least didn't rebut it. It even commissioned a series of nearly annual reports by Joel Fleishman of Duke University on "The Progress of Its Decision to Spend Down." Among foundations and the people who follow them, the phrase "spend down" normally means gradually liquidating the endowment and going out of business. But in this case, that wasn't actually the plan. When all other business concluded, the foundation would retain one last responsibility: the ongoing funding of the Beit AVI CHAI cultural center in Jerusalem. For this, the board would continue to meet, and a sizeable residue of foundation money would remain as a permanent source of annual income for the center.

Still, although the institution technically lives on, to the people and organizations that made up the rest of AVI CHAI's philanthropy in Israel,

North America, and the former Soviet Union, nearly everything they had known of the foundation ended on December 31, 2019, when, as its website declares, "AVI CHAI concluded its general grantmaking." It did spend down, therefore—even if not all the way. And it did bring the great bulk of its philanthropy to an orderly close, just as it vowed to do. What continues after that, although it will bear the same name and be led by the same governing members and board, will be a completely different kind of institution.

Reaching that punctual, orderly conclusion took years of planning and preparation. In North America, Susan Kardos, senior director of strategy, led a two-year-long planning effort to ensure that grants were wound down effectively, staff responsibilities were mapped out to the end, and the lessons and records of AVI CHAI's thirty-five years were preserved and made available to anyone who might benefit from them. In Israel, where the staff was smaller, the planning didn't take the form of a distinct project, but was integrated into normal, ongoing program management. Even so, it covered all the same areas and demanded an increasing amount of attention from 2018 and, especially, throughout 2019.

A few planning challenges that normally confront foundations that spend down wouldn't apply to AVI CHAI. Deciding how to manage the institution's financial assets so that they glide smoothly to zero, for example, wouldn't be necessary, given that AVI CHAI's endowment was not meant to reach zero. Some assets could remain invested without worrying that every dollar would soon have to become liquid, or that market volatility might undermine final grant commitments. Also, the legal and administrative obligations involved in dissolving a tax-exempt charity wouldn't be needed here; the charity was continuing. But in most other respects, the prospect of an ending meant orchestrating nearly every aspect of foundation management so that they all concluded, without surprises or drama, at roughly the same time.

For example, a critical concern of nearly every time-limited foundation is how to keep employees on the job for as long as they're needed, even though they know their days are numbered and other opportunities beckon. The solution most often comes in the form of some kind of retention incentive—a benefit that can be earned only by staying for as long as one is needed. In AVI CHAI's case, the incentive was a supplemental pension, originally available only to employees who remained on the job until the last day. Jokingly referred to as "golden handcuffs," the pension offer actually appears to have played only a small role in keeping the staff in place. As Yossi Prager wrote in mid-2018, many people considered AVI CHAI "as much family as workplace" and were in no hurry to leave. Other time-limited foundations have had similar experiences with retention incentives. People tend to work for foundations out of dedication to a cause at least as much as for the salary, and they therefore prefer to hold onto these jobs as long as possible.

The exception, of course, is when an employee with only months left on the payroll receives an unusually attractive job offer—especially one that serves the same cause—and the offer must be seized quickly or will be lost. The employee is then faced with a wrenching choice between the retention bonus and a desirable new job, while the foundation plays the not exactly altruistic role of blocking a career opportunity for a valued staff member. The early departure scenario did arise for a couple of North American staff members in mid-2019, but by that point it had already become clear that the foundation wasn't going to need every hand on deck until the very last day. As early as the autumn of 2017, Mem Bernstein and the board had decided to unlock the golden handcuffs and allow people to take opportunities if they arose without sacrificing their pension. As Prager had predicted, the change in policy made only a small difference. Very few people left early, and although he regretted losing a few close colleagues sooner than expected, a little workload redistribution kept the moves from being disruptive. In Israel, the consequences were even smaller. One employee briefly took an outside position a few months before the end, but soon changed her mind and returned to AVI

CHAI until the last day.

Yet even if the extra pension benefits proved to be mostly unnecessary for retaining staff, Arthur Fried and Mem still considered them money well spent. "Philanthropy starts with a bank account," Fried said. "But to turn that money, which by itself does nothing, into real philanthropy, you need talent and people, commitment, compassion, and understanding. It's the people who make it possible, and it's the people, not the money, that are your richest philanthropic asset." The supplementary pension, he explained, was initially administered as a retention incentive, but it was ultimately paid, with gratitude, as a reward for "dedication, diligence, and loyalty."

The most visible aspect of endgame planning—setting the timing, amount, and purposes of the final grants—had been built into AVI CHAI's grantmaking regimen for six years or more, as grantees were urged (and in many cases helped) to recruit new funders and prepare for what would be, in most cases, a gradual diminution of foundation support. A few of the newest initiatives, like Prizmah in North America and Nitzanim in Israel, were allowed to coast on higher levels of support for a longer time, to give them the best possible runway for their post-AVI CHAI future. Some others, whose efforts seemed unlikely to survive intact after the foundation departed, got steady grants all the way to the end, so that as many people as possible would benefit in the time remaining. But most saw their grants shrinking year by year, as the remaining time grew short, so that they wouldn't easily overlook the signal that a day of reckoning was close at hand.

"Recently, the staff have charted what remains to be done by AVI CHAI in the next 18 months for each program," Prager reported in mid-2018. "Having this information already collected helps us plan ahead, ensures that our grantees experience AVI CHAI's sunset in an orderly way, and prepares us for the early departure of any staff."[65] But that eighteen-month drill was just the last in a long stream of strategic thinking about how to line up resources for a productive finish. Well before that late-stage reckoning with grantees' needs and staff's responsibilities, the terms of grants and the offers of organizational help had been calibrated to provide the best possible odds of survival for each grantee. By 2019, when the foundation was taking its final bows, the plans had largely played out as intended. The results, of course, were not all as hoped. But the measures the trustees and staff had laid out over several years were implemented faithfully, with at least annual reports to the board—and often more frequent ones—on the progress of each area of work as it made its way toward the finish line.

The most distinctive aspect of AVI CHAI's end-time planning was its burst of effort in the realm of "knowledge leadership." The idea of spreading messages, online and in person, about the foundation's core principles—LRP in North America, Jewish Renewal or *Yahadut Yisraelit* in Israel—had been an escalating priority throughout its last decade. But the effort intensified noticeably in the final year, when North American staff members released a surge of blog posts, articles, and conference presentations, and staff in Israel prepared for a series of final conferences, panels, and published evaluations. It was, in Eli Silver's words, "a year of reflection, summation, self-assessment, saying goodbye, and imparting a vision for the future to our colleagues and successors."

The goal of securing solid funding for AVI CHAI projects before the grantmaking ended was proving, by 2019, to be only partially achievable, and some big arid patches remained on the programmatic landscape. So the culminating effort—as much an act of faith as an exercise of strategy—was to try to articulate, as clearly as possible, why the foundation believed in its initiatives, why they deserved the backing of other philanthropies, and how funders could make a significant mark by helping them realize their full potential. Then, as Fried had written in 2006, "it is our desire that the work not end—rather, that it be continued by others, who perhaps will be animated by what we have started, and by the standards we have tried to set."[66]

In North America, the vast terrain and wide distribution of Jewish populations and communal organizations made it hard to appeal to the whole universe of other funders in person—though private meetings and presentations to groups like the Jewish Funders Network did present opportunities for face-to-face communication. Much more was possible online, however, and the New York-based staff accordingly made more and more use of blog posts at eJewishPhilanthropy.com, whose audience included nearly every funder who might be drawn to AVI CHAI's projects.

The pace of this blogging, and the expansiveness of the issues it tackled, rose markedly in 2018, as the messages became more exhortatory and valedictory. In a post in late 2018, for example, Leah Meir offered a Chanukah reflection on what AVI CHAI had learned about the needs of Jewish educators and how philanthropy should meet those needs to ensure the future of Jewish schools. Earlier that year, Michael Berger had posted an essay on how to equip day school leaders with skills and knowledge that will remain with them through their careers. In January 2019, Deena Fuchs reflected at length on AVI CHAI's sense of obligation to pass on the lessons it had learned with candor, clarity, and humility. Dozens of these summative messages poured forth in the eighteen months before the grantmaking ended.

In Israel, small gatherings and big donor conferences are more common and feasible. (Wherever they live, Israelis are no more than four hours from Jerusalem by car.) Consequently, the Jerusalem-based staff was much better able to meet funders one-on-one, even multiple times. Those meetings became more common as the end approached. Then, in the last months of 2018, the staff started preparing for a more organized and large-scale farewell to Israel's nonprofits and philanthropists— delivering what Silver described as AVI CHAI's "closing argument to the field."

The preparations started with a small but crucial audience: the foundation's own board. For months, the Israel staff prepared for a final presentation at a trustees' retreat scheduled for June 2019, where Silver and his colleagues would try to pull together a complete picture of AVI CHAI's

hopes and achievements over the last thirty-five years. To assemble a
clear, coherent agenda, they consulted, researched, and collected wisdom
from dozens of people who had led the foundation's projects over the
years and toiled in its various fields of activity. Research director Liora
Pascal commissioned "reflective reviews" by Israeli experts on four broad
areas of foundation effort: informal education, schools, "young Jewish
change agents," and Israeli Jewish communities. Each of these was built
on encyclopedic consultation with people ranging from activists at the
front lines to observers in academia to public officials and funders.

Pascal, Silver, and chief technology officer Eli Kannai gathered data
for a statistical picture of the foundation's work, while staff and consultants created video vignettes to present the human and emotional side.
The resulting presentations, screenings, and panels spanned two days
and formed the staff's formal concluding statement on what the program
had done and what it all meant. (A similar set of presentations had taken
place in New York two years earlier, summarizing the North America
program. But because the program still had two more years to run, that
summary was necessarily unfinished, and thus didn't carry the same fi-
nality.)

Next came a much larger event three months later, when the Israel
staff assembled some 200 people at Beit AVI CHAI for a review of the
foundation's history in Israel and for a series of discussions about its
meaning and consequences. The audience included grantees, researchers,
government policymakers, philanthropists and their advisers, and foundation employees past and present. Unlike the more intimate presentation to trustees, this was "a big production," Silver said, "professionally
managed by an outside producer, with its own logo and brand." For six
hours, in small groups and plenary sessions, foundation staffers shared
insights and listened to reactions from the field, in what was likely the
largest and most detailed forum on a philanthropic program ever held in
Israel.

The last formal event was a much smaller and shorter presentation to the Forum of Foundations in Israel, where the discussion focused on what Silver called "the gritty details of executing a philanthropic program, and what we'd learned"—essentially an insiders' analysis for an audience of practitioners. Overall, the three events, along with their component videos and research papers, created an in-person version of the message the North America staff was delivering bit by bit online: a summation of what the foundation had tried to do, what it had learned, and what it hoped other philanthropies would do to keep the momentum alive.

From that point, there was little left to do by way of reflections and goodbyes, except for the formalities of packing up, emptying offices, and wishing one another well. New York employees had gathered for a session of mutual tributes and appreciations in June, before the first of their colleagues departed for other jobs, and they then reconvened for a celebratory lunch in the last week of 2019. Israel staff held their final party in a club space at Beit AVI CHAI on December 30. The next day, on schedule, everyone who had not already departed, or who were not moving to other jobs in the same buildings, gathered up their remaining belongings and left for the last time. The orderly conclusion that Fried had promised nearly twenty years earlier, in his first annual Chairman's Message, had come to pass.

———

Thereafter, when the offices were empty, the conferences were over, and the blog posts and social media pages had receded or disappeared, what would be left would be the record that Zalman Bernstein himself had wanted: a thorough documentation of what his trustees had done and how they had done it—both to clarify forever his original intent and to inform the Jewish philanthropists who would come after him. But establishing an archive for "the most thoroughly documented foundation in history," as Bernstein had put it, would be a bigger-than-usual challenge, given the sheer volume of the written record. The files consisted of many hundreds of thousands of pages, not counting audio and video recordings, photographs, and other non-textual artifacts, and much of it had sat in boxes and on computer disks for years, uncatalogued and unreviewed.

Further, some of the written documents—for example, verbatim transcripts of every board meeting—contained sensitive material, like carelessly worded or garbled statements or harsh judgments that would surely have been phrased more carefully had the speakers or writers expected their remarks to be publicly available. In a 2019 blog post, Prager admitted that in reading through the transcripts, he came across a few "boorish comments" and some statements that later proved to be simply wrong. But he found nothing unprofessional or ad hominem—a fact that led him to think the trustees might agree to make the documents public. Documents from outsiders posed thornier problems, he wrote, "such as a grantee report detailing reasons for terminating a senior staff member." Those would have to be scoured more carefully—and there were a lot of them.

In thinking about creating an AVI CHAI archive, staff and trustees had to weigh not only the usual questions that arise with the storage of any foundation's papers—what material is fit for preservation, what part of it would actually be interesting or useful, and to whom—but also how to honor Bernstein's outsized desire for a voluminous record of his foundation's activities. On one hand, it seemed reasonable to assume that Bernstein would not have wanted to squander resources on maintaining documents that no one would read. And one key reason for creating such a meticulous record—Bernstein's fear that future trustees might deviate from his intended goals and methods—was now moot, given that the foundation had only one grantee left, and that was one he had specified himself. Still, the founder had given another reason for wanting a complete archive, and that reason was still valid. Having dedicated a fortune to the well-being of the Jewish people, he believed he owed the Jewish people a fair and complete accounting.

'The guiding principle, then, would be that the archive would be fair and complete but not exhaustive. Emails, for example, would be excluded. The rapid-fire pace of email writing encourages a kind of verbal sloppiness that could, Prager wrote, "embarrass or damage the reputation of foundation Trustees or staff, grantee organizations and their people, or other organizations and individuals." Besides, emails are usually written with the expectation that they will soon be deleted or, at a minimum, not opened to public scrutiny. Similarly, documents expressly marked as confidential would be kept private.

Nonetheless, it was clear that not every embarrassing or ill-chosen word could be shielded from history, nor would a thoroughly sanitized account be truly fair and complete. So, on the advice of a rabbi and historian whom Prager had consulted, the foundation chose to make the vast majority of its papers available through two respected archiving institutions, the American Jewish Historical Society and the National Library of Israel. Prager, Silver, and their respective staffs would work with archivists on a general review, eliminating documents whose disclosure would plainly do more harm than good, on the understanding, as Prager wrote, that "the problematic material is rare, and the overwhelming majority of the archive would prove useful to the public." The staff work was extensive and sometimes burdensome, but it served what appeared to be the best interpretation of the founder's wishes. Some documents would be restricted for a time—though decisions about which documents would be held, and for how long, were still being made as the foundation closed its doors.

AVI CHAI had put off thinking about its archive in any detail until very close to the end of its life. Most of the critical decisions were made in the final twelve to twenty-four months, under pressure, at a time when all sorts of other final responsibilities also had to be discharged. It would plainly have been better to start sooner—a lesson many time-limited foundations have also learned the hard way. Still, as the material was being handed over to the archivists at the end of 2019, Prager felt confident that the difficult push to create a comprehensive record had been worthwhile—a final gift of knowledge and experience, and a gesture of submission to the judgments of history.

"Jews are a people steeped in memory," he wrote. "We consider the past part of our lived experience, and when planning for the future, we think not only of the next ten years but the next 4,000 years. At AVI CHAI, we hope that the lessons of Jewish history, including from our archive, will inform the future."[67]

While still in the prime of life and at the pinnacle of his career, Zalman C. Bernstein had a life-altering encounter with his heritage and undertook a journey of return to Jewish faith, study, and tradition. It lasted the rest of his days. He devoted a sizable share of his fortune to inviting others to make a similar journey and to stand in peace and solidarity with their fellow Jews everywhere. He endowed his foundation with a mission both sweeping and profoundly intimate, a call addressed at once to "the full spectrum of the Jewish people" and to the quiet core of each Jewish life, a target population that Marvin Schick described as "one person and one soul, one by one by one." The mission Bernstein created for AVI CHAI was not necessarily to create programs or institutions, books, schools, or films, or even movements or tribes. It was to kindle understanding and devotion.

When he died, he left that mission in the hands of people he trusted, and he constrained them with only two final mandates: follow the mission, and create Beit AVI CHAI. After trying, for more than a decade, to marshal every moral and legal defense he could against the danger that his foundation might someday drift from its original purpose, and after fifteen years of directing virtually every move the institution made—and many of the moves its grantees made, whether they sought this direction or not—in the end, he laid upon his executors nothing more binding than his vision, his blessing, and his trust.

As Fried described it, they accepted that trust as a duty not to ask at every turn, "What would Zalman have done?" but to pursue his ideals of knowledge, reverence, and respect for Jews and Judaism by the best means that research could identify and that the available talent could deliver. In the view of Fried and Mem Bernstein and their colleagues on the board, it was a living mission, changing with time and opportunity, pointed toward a destination so distant that they would never fully reach it, but drawing from a core of principle and hope on which they would rely until the resources were gone and the vision could be entrusted to others.

At that point, it would seem fair to ask how much of its work could be reckoned a success. The answer, of course, would have to depend partly on how "success" is defined, and on the evidence one would use to measure it. One common definition, frequently used when foundations try to gauge their impact, has to do with the creation of enduring organizations and programs. Did AVI CHAI establish significant new lines of activity that would not otherwise have existed, that materially advance its mission, and that will continue advancing it long after the foundation stopped funding them?

Plenty of important organizations and program models now exist only, or primarily, because AVI CHAI backed their creation and nurtured them through formative years, until other forms of support could be mustered. Some of these, like iTaLAM in North America or the mechinot in Israel, seem all but certain to survive long after their foundation support is just a memory. Others, such as the American program Prizmah or the Israeli projects clustered in Nitzanim or KIAH, are still young and their budgets still fragile. All of them, whether they endure for many years or fade sooner, are accomplishments in which the foundation has taken pride, bolstered by mostly favorable evaluations, and sometimes resounding ones.

But to some eyes, endurance isn't the only, or even the best, criterion of success. To the extent that these programs enriched Jewish minds and

hearts in ways that resonate with AVI CHAI's mission—drawing Jews into
a deeper understanding of their heritage and into closer kinship with one
another—Mem and others argued that they succeeded, regardless of
their ultimate lifespan. "The legacy," as she has said, "is the people." In
her view, even if all the organizations and program models were to evap-
orate tomorrow, the people whose lives they touched would still be out
in the world, influencing their communities and families. School children and college students would be entering adulthood more knowledgeable about Judaism and better equipped to enjoy a satisfyingly Jewish life.
The message of Jewish identity and heritage would have been broadcast
and amplified and would remain in the atmosphere, influencing thought
and creativity in ways both subtle and overt.

In his series chronicling AVI CHAI's spend-down, Fleishman took a
similarly upbeat view of the foundation's contributions to Jewish life—it
"succeeded in strengthening Jewishness in countless measurable initiatives," he wrote in 2019. But he measured true "success," which he considered a higher standard, in a different way. By Fleishman's reckoning,
making a meaningful contribution in its own lifetime is not sufficient to
allow a time-limited foundation to claim victory. Instead,

> for an organization that has seeded multiple fields with unprece-
> dented amounts of money, creating scores of new institutions and
> programs in three regions with large Jewish populations, I believe
> it is essential to examine which of those activities are likely to con-
> tinue. One reason is that most or all of those activities were plainly
> launched with the hope of long life and lasting influence. But an-
> other reason is at least as important: One way to know whether
> these activities are as valuable as they seem is to ask whether other
> donors and philanthropies, with similar missions or kindred aspira-
> tions, value them enough to help prolong and enrich their efforts.
> Whatever other definition of success one might espouse, a program
> that has developed the means to persevere, that has attracted sus-

taining support from other funders, and that has disciplined itself
to soldier on beyond the nurture of its original and most generous
funder—that program is unquestionably a success. Foundations
that choose a limited life and plan to exit their fields of activity
should, and probably must, confront this admittedly stern standard
of judgment, as at least one reckoning of their success.[68]

On one hand, Fleishman is right that many, perhaps most, of AVI
CHAI's projects were undertaken in the express hope that lasting institutions would carry them into the future. To define success, after the fact,
without reference to that original intention would be to move the finish
line after the race has been run. In cases where foundation-sponsored
institutions or programs did not survive, or survived only in vestigial
form, it would seem necessary to acknowledge a result that, however
good, fell short of the initial intent. For projects like *BabagaNewz*, Mi-
vchar, and Booknik.ru, which achieved something of very high quality
yet didn't survive as intended, it is reasonable to conclude that the effort
was worthwhile, the results were at least largely positive, many people
benefited in ways that will probably ripple into the future—but full success was elusive.

In truth, AVI CHAI has not been reluctant to acknowledge failures of
this kind, and has been reasonably public in its disappointment with the
outcome of several projects over the years, including the three just mentioned. Yet even with that acknowledgment, its belief that the survival
of its grantees is not the prime or only standard of achievement is also
an honest and reasonable one, as many time-limited foundations are
discovering in their own final years. Startup enterprises fail far more
often than they succeed—a 2012 Harvard study of businesses backed by
venture capital put the failure rate at 75 percent.[69] Nonprofit startups are
at least as fragile as for-profit ones—more so, probably, because their fate
depends not only on their own performance, but on the availability and

enthusiasm of charitable donors, whose interests can be unpredictable and mercurial.

So, although the goal of creating lasting programs and organizations is a natural and often bold one, it is highly unlikely to be achieved every time, or even most of the time. If, as Fleishman argues, philanthropy should aspire to the creation of enduring solutions to long-term problems, and needs to own up to its failures when those solutions die young, it nonetheless deserves credit for honest attempts that succeed for a time, make a positive contribution, and in the best case, produce a communal benefit greater than their cost.

In North America, in at least the case of the Jewish New Teacher Project, iTaLAM, the principals' training program at Harvard, and several camping programs, the higher standard of likely survival and continued achievement seems to have been met, at least as far as could be reckoned at the time the foundation closed its program. In Israel, Tzohar, the teacher training programs at Hartman and the Hebrew University, the groundbreaking film and media project, the online Bible program Mikranet, and the piyyut website, among others, clearly pass the test. In the former Soviet Union, the new Jewish studies departments at Moscow and St. Petersburg state universities are all but certain to be permanent; Eshkol and Eshkolot continue to have solid backing and an extensive catalog of programs; and Jewish content at day schools and camps continues to be richer than when AVI CHAI arrived. Alongside these enduring programs and institutions, of course, are a number of others whose fates are uncertain at the time this is written. But some of them, too, may prove to be lasting presences on the landscape.

In all, though AVI CHAI can't claim 100 percent success by the "enduring institutions" criterion, it can boast a stable of solid, ongoing programs housed in reasonably secure organizations. Although, as Mem Bernstein has said, the ultimate legacy is human, not institutional; although, as Arthur Fried has said, Beit AVI CHAI is the foundation's supreme legacy;

nonetheless, there are many other legacies as well, each with a different story, a different calculus of costs and benefits, a different scale and reach, and maybe a different ultimate life span. All of them will bear the flame of AVI CHAI's mission well after the foundation's grantmaking is forgotten.

In the final installment in his series of reports, Fleishman wrote that AVI CHAI had "set out to pursue an eternal mission in a fixed period of time—not expecting to conquer all the challenges its mission statement elaborated, but to press forward, creating resources, elevating good ideas, and nurturing talent, to help ensure a richer and more secure future for the Jewish people."

"The real results of AVI CHAI's philanthropy," he concluded, "inherent in the teachers and principals, community and camp leaders, alumni of batei midrash and mechinot, and thousands of other influential learners who have studied with the Foundation's curricula, read its publications, attended its events, seen its films and TV programs, and found—on their own and with expert help—a path toward a deeper, more knowledgeable, and more fulfilled Jewish life."

———

Yet for all the talk of conclusions and final reckonings, in the end, the death of AVI CHAI, like that of Mark Twain, was exaggerated.* From at least 2006, Fried had periodically written that the foundation would conserve a substantial portion of its assets—initially, at least $130 million, and later much more—to provide for the permanent operation of Beit AVI CHAI. Of course, that plan could have been construed (and often was) as meaning that the foundation would, sometime around 2020, make a substantial gift to Beit AVI CHAI in the form of an endowment,

———

* In 1897, while he was traveling abroad, the American novelist was rumored to have died. When a reporter sought to verify the story, Twain wrote back that "the report of my death was an exaggeration."

and then the grantmaking institution would disappear. Instead, the three governing members ultimately chose to keep the AVI CHAI Foundation alive indefinitely, administering a fund sufficient to supply the cultural center with annual grants for its administrative costs and ongoing programs.

In late 2018, the board added a new provision, Article VIII, to the foundation's bylaws, providing that *nearly* all of AVI CHAI's former activities would end "on or about January 6, 2020, . . . which is the 21st anniversary of the passing of Zalman Chaim Bernstein." The institution would thenceforth "focus on supporting the programs and activities of Beit AVI CHAI in Jerusalem." The article goes on to spell out the cultural center's mission in full, including that it is to be "dedicated to the creation, development, and expression of Jewish thought and ideas," and that it seek "to engage a wide and diverse Jewish population."

The rest of the mission statement for Beit AVI CHAI, as elaborated in Article VIII, closely tracks the language of the original foundation mission, including "encouraging mutual understanding and sensitivity among Jews of different religious backgrounds and levels of commitment" and nurturing "an affinity toward Jewish tradition." But the connection between foundation and cultural center would consist of more than just overlapping missions. The two boards, though legally separate entities, would be made up of the same people who had governed the foundation for decades. They would meet twice a year, first to consider an annual grant proposal from Beit AVI CHAI, and later to review the progress of its programming and operations. In other words, the AVI CHAI Foundation would live on, but with only one grantee and only one responsibility: to ensure the grantee's continuous fidelity to its mission.

To be sure, that grantee had always held a special stature in AVI CHAI's world—the sole project specifically mandated by its founder, and one whose every detail was personally overseen by his executors. "Our late friend, benefactor, and colleague, Zalman C. Bernstein, gave but one restricted grant to our Foundation," Fried wrote in AVI CHAI's 2006 Annual

Report, "and it required us to build in Jerusalem 'a conference center and office complex in order to further our mission in a world-class environment.'"[70] "This building," Fried said at the grand opening of Beit AVI CHAI that same year, "will be our legacy."[71]

The building did become, almost instantly, a pulsing embodiment of everything the AVI CHAI Foundation had stood for in Israel. Beit AVI CHAI hosted programs that drew directly from the batei midrash that the foundation had incubated and sustained; from the cultural programs of song and poetry; the traditional observances of holidays and Shabbat; the Jewish-themed activities for communities, families, and children; the films and media programs; and the publications and commentary on Jewish writing from classic texts to modern literature. Bernstein had not been specific about the kinds of activity he wanted housed in his center, but the banquet of programs on offer at Beit AVI CHAI seemed almost perfectly arrayed to mirror the varied enthusiasms the late donor had brought to his philanthropy.

For Fried, it was those programs, not the stone majesty on King George Street, that were the foundation's real legacy. As the rest of the foundation's grantmaking came to a close, he and Mem resolved that bringing those programs to a wider audience would be the next priority for the board and for Beit AVI CHAI. The dream of *M'Beit avi chai*—expanding outward *from* the confines of the headquarters building and beyond Jerusalem—had been a subject of early planning at the time David Rozenson assumed control of the center in 2013. But those plans were shelved at that point, to give the new director and the institution more time to solidify the Jerusalem programs and continue building its catalogue of online offerings before taking on the considerable strategic and logistical challenges of satellite programming. The internet, meanwhile, would provide its own kind of outward expansion, as online programs, videos, and audio recordings radiated outward to audiences everywhere.

Beit AVI CHAI's digital capacity grew steadily under Rozenson's watch, and then it accelerated unexpectedly, when the coronavirus pandemic forced Israel (and much of the world) into a public health lockdown beginning in the spring of 2020. Compelled to produce online programming that would not merely supplement live events but temporarily substitute for them, the center began promoting a raft of virtual programs with email blasts announcing lectures, celebrations, and live performances, all available via the website and on Facebook, with some interactive events via the web-conferencing app Zoom. In May 2020, for example, programs included lectures, exhibits, and a musical performance to mark Yom Yerushalayim ("A Jerusalem celebration not only for Jerusalemites!" the announcement proclaimed to an international mailing list), along with a presentation by Russia's chief rabbi on Jewish life under Vladimir Putin, plus the online continuation of a speaker series on *Pirkei Avot*. At the end of the month, another email announced a full roster of online classes and speakers, making up what would normally have been Beit AVI CHAI's hugely popular tradition of all-night learning at Shavuot. This time, the all-night phenomenon would be virtual—but also, by virtue of the internet, it would now be global.

Plans for live programming beyond Jerusalem took a back seat as the pandemic persisted. But the process of building a global brand and bringing Beit AVI CHAI to remote audiences, thanks to the multiplicity of new online offerings, was by then well underway. "Does M'Beit AVI CHAI have to be physical?" Mem wondered as the coronavirus lockdown was marking its fourth month. "Do you have to have a physical presence to reach people with high-quality cultural programming? The pandemic has made the whole idea of producing live events out of the question for the time being, and we don't know when that's going to change. But in the meantime, something else is happening, and we're learning a lot from it."

Whether the future of Beit AVI CHAI's expansion occurs in more dispersed physical programming or in more ambitious online broadcasting, or in some combination, remains unresolved as this is written. But either way, although the building on King George Street stands as the foundation's most visible legacy, it is merely the anchor of a panoply of activity intended to grow much larger, more widespread, and more multifaceted as time goes on.

The second sentence of AVI CHAI's founding mission statement asserts that, although its twin bases would be the United States and Israel, the foundation eventually "intends to function in all regions with major Jewish populations." In its thirty-five-year run of international grantmaking, the institution never managed to fulfill that ambitious promise. Now, through the outward push of M'Beit AVI CHAI, the ultimate expansion may at last be within reach.

Beyond Jerusalem, beyond Israel's remotest communities, beyond North American day schools and camps, beyond Moscow's schools and clubs and universities, beyond all the limits of time and geography that had disciplined the foundation's efforts since its founding, the encyclopedic, unending mission of Beit AVI CHAI now opens a vast new frontier. It carries Zalman Bernstein's dream of expanding Jewish learning, understanding, discovery, and solidarity to distant locales and future generations. With the foundation's regional grants programs now consigned to history, fulfilling that all-encompassing global dream lingers as the final duty of the group of trustees to whom Bernstein had bequeathed his fortune, his trust, and his devotion to ensuring a rich, enduring Jewish future.

ACKNOWLEDGMENTS

This history is the fruit of more than six years spent reviewing the archives and conferring with the Board and staff of the AVI CHAI Foundation, as well as with its grantees, advisers, philanthropic partners, and former employees. The generosity of everyone involved—people who endured, in many cases, prolonged hours of interviews and multiple, intrusive requests for documents and fact-checking—is the only reason these volumes can hope to bear fair witness to the important and difficult work they did on the foundation's behalf.

Every trustee was forthcoming and thoughtful in answering questions and guiding my research. But three in particular deserve special thanks. Arthur Fried (z"l) and Mem Bernstein, who were the soul of the foundation's leadership for most of its history, devoted dozens of hours to satisfying every request for information and perspective, and helped me focus on the most significant and interesting elements of the foundation's philanthropy. Ruth Wisse, a formidable scholar and elegant writer, also spent many days reviewing my drafts and suggesting avenues of inquiry and ways of telling the story that would not have occurred to me without her help. Trustees Meir Buzaglo, Avital Darmon, Alan Feld, Lauren Merkin, George Rohr, and Lief Rosenblatt, as well as former trustee David Tadmor, offered incisive reflections and insight. Although Henry Taub (z"l), one of the earliest trustees, passed away before this book was written, I was able to observe and learn from his astute, businesslike approach to philanthropy and witness his profound effect on AVI CHAI's development.

The entire staff of the foundation likewise shared with me their expertise, judgment, and passion. Foundation CFO Azriel Novick supplied volumes of data and historical context that grounded every aspect of the story and that sometimes revealed trends and patterns that had escaped most observers' notice. Even at their busiest times, AVI CHAI's executive directors—Yossi Prager, Eli Silver, and David Rozenson—repeatedly cleared hours in their schedule to help me interpret documents, chase down information, and understand the thinking behind their work, both as it was happening and in hindsight. They were unfailingly frank in describing their successes and disappointments, trusting that I would treat the former with critical scrutiny and the latter with understanding. I hope I have rewarded that trust.

The story of AVI CHAI's first decade could not have been told without the patience and diligence of its first executive director, Avraham Y. HaCohen, who worked more closely with Zalman Bernstein in those early years of his philanthropy than anyone other than Arthur Fried. Not only did Avraham consent to a grueling set of interviews that claimed, in aggregate, several weeks of his time, but he kindly reviewed early drafts, helped me unearth long-buried facts and sources, and questioned any interpretation that he considered (usually rightly) too facile, too credulous, or unduly harsh.

The people on whom I relied the most, and on whom I was the greatest burden, were Nechama Leibowitz, executive assistant to Yossi Prager in New York, and Maasha Inbar, coordinator of information and publications in Jerusalem. Both helped me arrange (and rearrange) years of interviews, travel, and documentary research and coped with a barrage of logistical challenges—always with kindness, grace, and wit. They deserve more of my gratitude than I could possibly fit in these pages.

—Tony Proscio

NOTES

1. David Rozenson, Miriam K. Warshaviak, and Marvin Schick, "AVI CHAI and Jewish Life in the Former Soviet Union," report to the AVI CHAI Board, in the June 2002 Board Book, pp. 20–21

2. George Rohr, David Rozenson, Miriam K. Warshaviak, and Marvin Schick, "Pilot Programs in Summer Camping: Executive Summary," Jan. 15, 2004, in the February 2004 AVI CHAI Board Book, p. 1

3. David Rozenson, "Publication of Jewish Illustrated Children's Books in Russian: Executive Summary," AVI CHAI October Board Book, Oct. 5, 2003, p. 1

4. David Rozenson, "Ongoing Programs on Jewish/Israeli Literature and Culture in Popular Intellectual Venues in Moscow: Proposal for Programming, December 2004–July 2005," in the November 2004 AVI CHAI Board Book, p. 1

5. David Rozenson, "Eshkol: Jewish Programs in Popular Literary Clubs in Moscow: Executive Summary," May 28, 2008, in the June 2008 AVI CHAI Board Book

6. David Rozenson, "Jewish-Israeli Literature and Culture Website in the Russian Language: Executive Summary," January 29, 2006, in the February AVI CHAI Board Book, p. 2

7. Quotes and information in this and the previous paragraph are from George Rohr, David Rozenson, Miriam K. Warshaviak, and Marvin Schick, "Tzietz: The Center for Jewish Studies at the Moscow State University: Executive Summary," May 10, 2004, in the June 2004 AVI CHAI Board Book, p. 1

8. George Rohr, David Rozenson, Miriam K. Warshaviak, "Tzietz: The Center for Jewish Studies at the Moscow State University: Executive Summary," Jan. 31, 2005, in the February 2005 AVI CHAI Board Book, p. 1

9. Joel L. Fleishman, "First Annual Report to the AVI CHAI Foundation on the Progress of its Decision to Spend Down," Center for Strategic Philanthropy and Civil Society, Duke University, April 4, 2010, p. 13

10. Arthur W. Fried, letter to the Board of Trustees, AVI CHAI Foundation, Nov. 21, 2008, as quoted in Fleishman, *op. cit.*

11. Moti Bassok, "Tax Revenues Beat Forecasts by NIS 5 Billion in 2009," *Haaretz*, Jan. 14, 2010, accessed at https://www.haaretz.com/1.5085592

12. Nathan Dietz, Brice McKeever, Ellen Steele, and C. Eugene Steuerle, "Foundation Grantmaking Over the Economic Cycle," Tax Policy and Charities Brief, the Urban Institute, March 2015, p. 6, accessed at https://www.urban.org/sites/default/files /publication/43691/2000139-Foundation-Grantmaking-over-the-Economic-Cycle.pdf

13. Joel L. Fleishman, "New Uncertainties—and Opportunities—as the End Approaches: Year Six Report on the Concluding Years of the AVI CHAI Foundation," Center for Strategic Philanthropy and Civil Society, Duke University, April, 2015, pp. 3–4

14. Neil Carlson and Theodora Lurie, "Giving While Living: The Beldon Fund Spend-Out Story," The Beldon Fund, March 2009

15. Fleishman, "First Annual Report," p. 4

16. Gara LaMarche, "The End of Atlantic as We Know It: Time to Start Thinking and Planning," memorandum to the Board of Directors, The Atlantic Philanthropies, June 2008, p. 1

17. Yossi Prager, "Framing Memo," memorandum to the AVI CHAI Board of Trustees, June 1, 2009, p. 1

18. Fleishman, "First Annual Report," pp. 3–4

19. "History of Charter Schools," Public Charter Schools Insider, at https://www.incharters .org/history.php

20. Sarah Kass, "Spending Down in the 21st Century," blog post at eJewishPhilanthropy .com, June 12, 2011, at https://ejewishphilanthropy.com/spending-down-in-the-21st -century/

21. Rachel Abrahams, Eli Kannai, Gali Aizenman, and Sarah Kass, "Blended/Online Learning and Educational Technology Experiments," memorandum to the AVI CHAI Board of Trustees, Sept. 15, 2016, p. 13

22. Tom Vander Ark, "Personalized Learning in 2016: What's Working, What's Missing," *Education Week*, at http://blogs.edweek.org/edweek/on_innovation/2016/09/personalized _learning_in_2016_whats_working_whats_missing.html

23. Jason Bedrick, "The Policy Paths to the Jewish Schools of the Future," *Mosaic*, Aug. 17, 2020, at https://mosaicmagazine.com/response/politics-current-affairs/2020/08/the -policy-paths-to-the-jewish-schools-of-the-future/

24. Information in this and the next 14 paragraphs is drawn partly from "A Case Study of a Foundation as Social Enterprise Investor: The Creation of iTaLAM," The AVI CHAI Foundation, March 2019, particularly pp. 4–6

25. Steve Brown, Susan Kardos, Michael Berger, and Deena Fuchs, "Day School Leadership," memo to the AVI CHAI Board of Trustees, May 1, 2013, pp. 3–4

26. Michael Berger, Susan Kardos, and Deena Fuchs, "Day School Leadership," memo to the AVI CHAI Board of Trustees, August 20, 2015, p. 10

27. Joel Einleger, Leiah Meir, Gali Aizenman, "Overnight Summer Camping," update memo to the AVI CHAI Board of Trustees, Aug. 26, 2013, p. 3

28. Yossi Prager, "Pardes Educators Program—One Cohort Renewal," memo to the AVI CHAI Board, Sept. 2, 2010, p. 1

29. Deena Fuchs, "Giving Away Knowledge, Free of Charge," eJewishPhilanthropy, Jan. 17, 2019, at https://ejewishphilanthropy.com/giving-away-knowledge-free-of-charge/

30. Deena Fuchs, in an interview by Joel Fleishman, July 2019, from an unpublished transcript

31. Quoted in "Zait Program Shapes Jewish Life in Israel," blog post, UJA-Federation New York, Jan. 5, 2010, accessed March 13, 2019, at the Federation's website. The post has since been deleted.

32. Sima Borkovski, "Israeli project combines the Bible with rock 'n' roll," *Canadian Jewish News*, Oct. 30, 2014, p. 7

33. Eli Silver, opening remarks at a session on "Nurturing Israeli Jewish Communities," part of a Board of Trustees retreat at Carmel Forest Spa, Israel, June 4, 2019

34. Ronen Goffer, "Local Israeli Jewish Communities: A Reflective Review of ACI Funding," summary report to the AVI CHAI Board of Trustees, May 2019, p. 5

35. Gadi Rosenthal and Hadas Eiges, "Agricultural Cooperatives in Israel," FAO Regional Office for Europe and Central Asia, Food and Agriculture Organization of the United Nations, 2013, pp. 24–37

36. Mark Waysman and Avital Schlanger, "Programs for Sh'nat Sherut Volunteers: 2017 Evaluation," executive summary of an evaluation prepared for the AVI CHAI Foundation, November 2017, p. 15

37. Mark Waysman, "Evaluation of the AVI CHAI Shnat Sherut Programs—Stage 3: Outcomes," executive summary of a report to the AVI CHAI Foundation, December 2016, pp. 7 and 13

38. Efrat Shapiro Rosenberg, "Inspiring Jewish Social Change Agents," report to the AVI CHAI Board of Trustees, January 2017, p. 9

39. Regev Ben-David, "Young Jewish Change Agents: A Reflective Review of ACI Funding," executive summary of a report to the AVI CHAI Foundation, May 2019, p. 3

40. Waysman, *op. cit.*, p. 7

41. Motti Asoulin and Eli Kleinberger, "Participation by Graduates of Premilitary Academies and the General Population in Jewish-Israeli Culture Study Programs," Hizun Institute, 2014, especially pp. 1 and 4

42. Dani Zamir, Facebook post, Dec. 20, 2019

43. Liora Pascal, "The Tel Aviv Regional School District Incubator Project," memo to the AVI CHAI Board of Trustees, Sept. 2015, p. 2

44. Renee Ghert-Zand, "Why I Can't Stop Watching *Shtisel*," *The Forward*, March 4, 2016, at https://forward.com/culture/334808/why-i-cant-stop-watching-shtisel/

45. Nell Minow, "Reviews: 'The Other Story,'" June 28, 2019, at RoberEbert.com: https ://www.rogerebert.com/reviews/the-other-story-2019

46. Ruth Kabbessa-Abramzon, "Proposal to Promote the Values of Shabbat in Israel," proposal to the AVI CHAI Foundation, May 2016, p. 1

47. Talia Lavin, "Evaluation of Sefer Student FSU Summer Programs," report to the AVI CHAI Foundation, 2011, pp. 14–15

48. *Ibid.*, p. 10

49. David Rozenson, "Future of AVI CHAI in the FSU," memo to the AVI CHAI Board, Oct. 10, 2012, p. 19

50. David Rozenson, "Progress Report on the Supported Book Series on Jewish Themes in the Russian Language," memo to the AVI CHAI Board, April 12, 2010, p. 1

51. *Ibid.*, p. 2

52. David Rozenson, "Executive Summary: Reaching Unaffiliated Jewish Audiences in the FSU," proposal to the AVI CHAI Board, Jan. 18, 2012, p. 8

53. Svetlana Busygina, "AVI CHAI in the FSU", unsigned memo to the AVI CHAI Board, June 21, 2016, p. 1

54. David Rozenson, "A New Initiative to Reach Unaffiliated Young Jews in Moscow," memo to the AVI CHAI Board, Feb. 12, 2008, p. 3. Quotation is from transcript of the

board meeting on March 5, 2008, p. 13

55. Busygina, "AVI CHAI in the FSU", p. 2

56. Ayaan Mohamud, "Russia Has World's Most Engaged Social Networking Audience," press release, July 2, 2009, Comscore Inc., at https://www.comscore.com/Insights/Press -Releases/2009/7/Russia-has-World-s-Most-Engaged-Social-Networking-Audience ?cs_edgescape_cc=US, cited in Sergey Kuznetsov, "The Creation of Jewish Social Net- working Opportunities in the Russian Language," proposal to the AVI CHAI Founda- tion, September 2009, p. 1

57. David Rozenson, "Executive Summary: Reaching Unaffiliated Jewish Audiences in the FSU," proposal to the AVI CHAI Board, Jan. 18, 2012, p. 3

58. Busygina, "AVI CHAI in the FSU," p. 3

59. Quoted in Joel L. Fleishman, "The Saving Remnant is Shining Bright, Its Fire Now Spreading Renewing Light: Year Seven Report on the Concluding Years of the AVI CHAI Foundation," Duke University, May 2018, p. 21

60. Quoted in the unpublished first draft of Fleishman, "The Saving Remnant," p. 8

61. David Rozenson, "Executive Summary: Day Schools, Youth Initiatives and TaL AM in the FSU," proposal to the AVI CHAI Board, Jan. 24, 2012, p. 2

62. *Ibid.*, p. 3

63. Rozenson, "Future of AVI CHAI in the FSU," pp. 1–2

64. Busygina, "AVI CHAI in the FSU," p. 3

65. Yossi Prager, "AVI CHAI Spend-Down Planning, North America," memo to the AVI CHAI Board, May 9, 2018, p. 1

66. Arthur W. Fried, "Chairman's Message," in "2005 Annual Report of the AVI CHAI Foundation," p. 6

67. This and all quotes in the previous six paragraphs are from Yossi Prager, "On Archiving," blog post at eJewishPhilanthropy.com, Nov. 25, 2019, at https://ejewishphilanthropy .com/on-archiving/

68. Joel L. Fleishman, "Against Strong Headwinds, the AVI CHAI Foundation's Bold Vision and Relentless Persistence Succeeded in Strengthening Jewishness in Countless Mea- surable Initiatives: Final Report on the Concluding Years of the AVI CHAI Foundation," Duke University, Dec. 2019, pp. 1–2

69. Deborah Gage, "The Venture Capital Secret: 3 out of 4 Start-Ups Fail," *Wall Street Journal,* Sept. 20, 2012, at https://www.wsj.com/articles/SB10000872396390443720 204578004980476429190

70. Arthur W. Fried, "Chairman's Message," in "2006 Annual Report of the AVI CHAI Foundation," p. 5

71. Quoted in Rozenson, "Future of AVI CHAI in the FSU," p. 1

INDEX